The Invisible Presence

Virginia Woolf and her mother
Courtesy Henry W. and Albert A. Berg Collection, New York Public
Library, Astor, Lenox and Tilden Foundations

THE
INVISIBLE
PRESENCE

Virginia Woolf and the

Mother-Daughter Relationship

ELLEN BAYUK ROSENMAN

Louisiana State University Press

Baton Rouge and London

Copyright © 1986 by Louisiana State University Press
All rights reserved
Manufactured in the United States of America

Designer: Albert Crochet
Typeface: Linotron Weiss
Typesetter: G&S Typesetters, Inc.
Printer: Thomson-Shore, Inc.
Binder: John H. Dekker & Sons, Inc.

Library of Congress Cataloging-in-Publication Data

Rosenman, Ellen Bayuk.
The invisible presence.

Bibliography: p.
Includes index.
1. Woolf, Virginia, 1882–1941—Criticism and interpretation.
2. Mothers in literature.   3. Mothers and daughters in
literature.   4. Feminism and literature.   5. Women
in literature.   I. Title.
PR6045.072Z8673   1986   823'.912   85-23683
ISBN 0-8071-1290-9

Excerpts from the following works of Virginia Woolf are reprinted by
permission of Harcourt Brace Jovanovich, Inc.: *Moments of Being, A Room
of One's Own, To the Lighthouse, The Waves, The Voyage Out, Night and Day, Mrs.
Dalloway, The Years, The Diary of Virginia Woolf,* Vol. III, and *Between the Acts;*
copyright 1920 by George H. Doran Company; copyright 1925, 1927,
1929, 1931, 1937, 1941 by Harcourt Brace Jovanovich, Inc.; copyright
© 1976, 1980 by Quentin Bell and Angelica Garnett; renewed 1948,
1953, 1955, 1957, 1959, 1965, 1969 by Leonard Woolf.

Permission to quote from other works by Virginia Woolf has kindly been
granted by Quentin Bell; the Henry W. and Albert A. Berg Collection,
New York Public Library, Astor, Lenox and Tilden Foundations; The
Hogarth Press; and The Estate of Virginia Woolf.

Publication of this book has been assisted by a grant from the
Andrew W. Mellon Foundation.

Contents

Preface and Acknowledgments   vii

Abbreviations   xiii

Part I   THE MOTHER-DAUGHTER RELATIONSHIP

1   The Empty Center   3

2   The Body of Our Mother   20

3   The Maternal Legacy   45

Part II   THE WOMAN ARTIST

4   *Mrs. Dalloway*   75

5   *To the Lighthouse*   93

6   *Between the Acts*   114

7   Female Literary History   134

Bibliography   169

Index   177

Preface and Acknowledgments

THIS INQUIRY explores the intersection of gender, psychology, and art in the career of Virginia Woolf. It seeks an intimacy with the author as well as her works, a knowledge of the heritage and experiences which formed her as a woman and as a writer—two identities which, in Woolf's case, are inextricably intertwined. Refusing to be either masculinized or marginalized, Woolf continually attempted to represent and evaluate women's lives apart from patriarchal prejudices in a brand of feminism which seems contemporary today. Woolf's feminist commitment expressed itself in political activity, in an interest in other women writers, past and present, and in a literary preoccupation with female characters and domestic activities. Yet for Woolf, female identity extends beyond these concerns, although it certainly includes them, beyond the realm of deliberate choice and self-conscious awareness. "[A] woman's writing is always feminine; it cannot help being feminine," Woolf insists ("Women Novelists," *Contemporary Writers*, 26), implying an almost irresistible tropism toward characteristic modes of experience and expression. I have followed this lead in considering Woolf's own femininity as more than a political stance or an interest in a particular subject matter; as more than a wardrobe of clothing, a repertoire of gestures, or a code of behavior; rather, I take it to be a state of consciousness, a fundamental way of perceiving reality.

Because attempts to reify gender have often been used as weapons against women, the question of what constitutes femininity is a dangerous one, charged with unpleasant overtones of the "biology is destiny" theme. But a recognition of gender's pervasive influence need not ground itself in biological determinism; one can view gender as culturally constructed rather than a given of human nature, as susceptible to change and re-evaluation so that what is trivial, negative, or even invisible under one set of assumptions becomes valuable and essential under others. Without assigning absolute, unchanging roles to men and women, one can assert that "masculine" and "feminine" are meaningful categories of experience and interpretation, for Woolf and consequently for the critic. They illuminate Woolf's self-image and experience as a writer as well as the content of her writing.

Apart from political dangers, reifying gender also gives rise to analytical problems. What creates and composes these categories? Woolf throws down this particular gauntlet a moment after her initial assertion of the woman writer's inevitable femininity, saying, "The only difficulty lies in defining what we mean by feminine." "Defining what we mean by feminine" is a large part of my task here, and I have turned to the mother-daughter relationship as the source and center of female identity. Woolf's "obsession" with her own mother—that highly charged word is her own (*MB*, 80)—suggests how compelling the relationship was for her. If she was "fathered by an intellectual and his library," as Avrom Fleishman says, she was also mothered by an apparently perfect embodiment of Victorian womanhood, a great beauty, an accomplished hostess, a self-sacrificing and adored mother of eight.[1] At once inspiring and daunting, Julia Stephen left a permanent imprint on her daughter, a legacy of values and conflicts which shaped Woolf as a woman and as an artist.

I feel fortunate to be writing now, for new approaches in psychoanalytic and feminist theory have been invaluable to me. Happily, the mother-daughter relationship is no longer "the lost tradition," to borrow the title of a collection of critical essays about mothers and daughters in literature which appeared several years ago.[2] If the Oedipal struggle offers a powerful model for male experience, both psychological and aesthetic, the pre-Oedipal attachment increasingly seems central to female experience, through the groundbreaking work of psychoanalytic theorists such as Nancy Chodorow and literary and cultural architects of the new feminism(s), both French and American. Addressing the conditions and internal logic of femininity, these approaches stress the ways in which the mother continues to create her

1. Avrom Fleishman, *Virginia Woolf: A Critical Reading* (Baltimore, 1975), x.
2. E. M. Broner and Cathy N. Davidson (eds.), *The Lost Tradition: Mothers and Daughters in Literature* (New York, 1980).

daughter long after she actually gives birth. Not only gender identity, but a more general sense of self in relation to other people and the outside world originate in this attachment. It is a source of both coherence and conflict, of stability and threat as, paradoxically, the daughter must define herself both with and against the mother to achieve selfhood. I consider the mother-daughter relationship the central problem of female experience. It is, like all serious problems, deeply engaging and often rewarding, offering possibilities for self-affirmation commensurate with its intense challenges; but, fundamentally, it is a locus of tension rather than the pastoral haven suggested by cultural myths of motherhood. Its intensity and the issues of selfhood entangled in it lend this relationship its power and its ambivalence; idealizing the bond not only falsifies it but diminishes its complexity. My study is concerned with what might be called the fruits of this ambivalence: the ways in which psychological conflicts press outward, seeking expression, compensation, and resolution.

Julia Stephen's archetypal maternity seems to have magnified rather than reduced the complexities of this problematic relationship. In one of her earliest and most intense episodes of madness, Woolf was discovered talking to her mother—who had been dead for years—remonstrating vehemently and gesticulating wildly, as if she had summoned Julia from the grave to settle some ancient, bitter score. The incident reveals the two faces of Woolf's maternal obsession; on one hand, a longing to recover the dead Madonna so strong that it arranged its own impossible fulfillment; on the other, a bitter resentment that outlived the mother herself and continued to pour forth long after the original wrong could be redressed. With deeply mixed motives, Woolf resurrects her mother—to recover her magical presence in an act of love, to repudiate her in an act of self-justification, and to control her in an act of power, undoing the terrible fact of her death.

In one way, I hesitate to use this incident, a psychotic break, as an image of Woolf's experience, because the melodrama of madness has too easily obscured more sober and accurate assessments of her life and work (it is sad that Phyllis Rose should have to remind us of Woolf's productivity, overshadowed by the spectres of insanity and incapacity which compose her caricature, in "The Invalid Lady of Bloomsbury").[3]

3. Phyllis Rose, *Woman of Letters: A Life of Virginia Woolf* (New York, 1978), xii.

Yet the incident is, in some ways, especially appropriate precisely because of its origin in insanity. Madness is not art, of course, but both restructure reality in response to deep needs and desires. The imagination which, in its psychotic aspect, hallucinated Julia Stephen was equally drawn to her in its artistic one, re-imagining the mother, the daughter, and the bond between them in a variety of guises, and with the same mixture of motives. Woolf's madness is not part of my investigation—a "diagnosis" of her psychological condition would be reductive and presumptuous[4]—but I am interested in the displaced acts of recovery, repudiation, and control which animate her writing, in the diverse symbolic forms into which she casts the psychological experience of daughterhood, even when she is not writing "about" mothers and daughters in a literal sense.

Mother-daughter issues appear in two major, translated forms: diffuse states of consciousness and identity—the hallmark of Woolf's unusual characterizations—and the process of inheritance. These subjects are particularly intriguing in relation to art, both for the artist-figures Woolf creates in her fiction and for her own aesthetic experience. The creative process, the nature and rewards of art, the relation of subject and object, the value of a literary tradition, the conflict between the female artist and cultural stereotypes of women—all these recapitulate in some way Woolf's maternal obsession. Sometimes crippling in Woolf's psychological life, it is also a wellspring of creativity, infusing her work with an essential coherence beneath experiment and innovation.

Because Woolf herself was never a mother—the tangled history of her decision not to have children, made, evidently, more by her sister Vanessa and her husband Leonard than herself, on the grounds that motherhood would only exacerbate her mental instability—it is tempting to assert that her work is her child, her artistic creativity a compensatory form of procreation. At least to some extent, Woolf herself regarded it this way, almost compulsively comparing her career as a writer to her sister Vanessa's actual motherhood. Although the equation is obviously simplistic, it does suggest the intertwining of aesthetic and psychological motives characteristic of Woolf's distinctive art. At the

4. An exception to the generally reductive treatments of Woolf's mental state is Susan M. Kenney and Edwin J. Kenney, Jr., "Virginia Woolf and the Art of Madness," *Massachusetts Review,* XXIII (1982), 161–85.

very least, Woolf has become a literary foremother to later women writers and critics, the kind of model whose existence, she asserts in *A Room of One's Own*, is essential for continued female achievement. One of the great satisfactions which I have gained from this inquiry has been imagining the pleasure she would have taken from this metaphorical maternity.

Many people contributed to this book with their help and support, and I am happy to have the opportunity to thank them. Daniel Albright offered incisive criticism as well as encouragement. With extraordinary generosity, Joanne Trautmann Banks read the entire manuscript and suggested many useful changes. Friends and colleagues at Dickinson College helped me in ways too numerous and diverse to list here, but I wish to mention two groups in particular: the Research and Development Committee for its financial support, and the Zatae Longsdorff Reading Group for its wide-ranging and enlivening discussion of feminist issues.

Most of all, I wish to thank Sharon O'Brien for her sustaining friendship. Her own scholarship has served as an example to me, and her support, both intellectual and personal, has been invaluable.

Abbreviations

AROOO	*A Room of One's Own.* New York, 1957.
Books and Portraits	*Books and Portraits.* Edited by Mary Lyon. New York, 1977.
BTA	*Between the Acts.* New York, 1941.
CE I–IV	*Collected Essays.* 4 vols. Edited by Leonard Woolf. New York, 1967.
Contemporary Writers	*Contemporary Writers.* Edited by Jean Guiguet. New York, 1965.
Diary I–V	*The Diary of Virginia Woolf.* 5 vols. Edited by Quentin Bell and Anne Olivier Bell. New York, 1977–84.
HH	*A Haunted House and Other Stories.* New York, 1972.
JR	*Jacob's Room.* New York, 1950.
Letters I–VI	*The Letters of Virginia Woolf.* 6 vols. Edited by Nigel Nicolson and Joanne Trautmann. New York, 1975–80.
M	*Melymbrosia: An Early Version of The Voyage Out.* Edited by Louise DeSalvo. New York, 1982.
MB	*Moments of Being.* Edited by Jeanne Schulkind. New York, 1976.
MD	*Mrs. Dalloway.* New York, 1953.
MDP	*Mrs. Dalloway's Party.* Edited by Stella McNichol. New York, 1973.
N&D	*Night and Day.* New York, 1948.
O	*Orlando.* New York, 1956.
PH	*Pointz Hall: The Earlier and Later Typescripts of Between the Acts.* Edited by Mitchell A. Leaska. New York, 1983.
TG	*Three Guineas.* New York, 1965.
TM	*The Moment and Other Essays.* Edited by Leonard Woolf. New York, 1949.
TTL	*To the Lighthouse.* New York, 1954.

TTL/H	*To the Lighthouse: The Original Holograph Draft.* Edited by Susan Dick. Toronto, 1982.
TVO	*The Voyage Out.* New York, 1948.
TW	*The Waves.* New York, 1950.
TW/H I–II	*The Waves: The Two Holograph Drafts.* Edited by J. W. Graham. Toronto, 1976.
TY	*The Years.* New York, 1966.
TY/H I–VI	*The Years:* Holograph Notebooks I–VI. MS in Henry W. and Albert A. Berg Collection, New York Public Library, New York City.

I

THE MOTHER-DAUGHTER RELATIONSHIP

1

The Empty Center

"THE DEAD, so people say, are forgotten, or they should say, that life has for the most part little significance to any of us. But now and again, on more occasions than I can number, in bed at night, or in the street, or as I come into a room, there she is; beautiful, emphatic, with her familiar phrase and her laugh; closer than any of the living are, lighting our random lives with a burning torch, infinitely noble and delightful to her children" (*MB*, 40). "She" is Virginia Woolf's mother, Julia Duckworth Stephen, an extraordinary, continuing influence even after her death. Well into her forties, until the writing of *To the Lighthouse*, Woolf reports, "I could hear her voice, see her, imagine what she would do or say as I went about my day's doings" (p. 80). Both psychologically and aesthetically, Julia Stephen is Woolf's center, shaping not only experience and memory but consciousness itself, the "invisible presence" who inspires and inhabits Woolf's art (p. 80).

The mother-daughter relationship dominates Woolf's imagination, never more strongly than when she considers her identity as an artist. Speaking as a writer, she announces, "We think back through our mothers if we are women" (*AROOO*, 79), and her use of the word "mothers" is not entirely metaphorical. She refers, of course, to literary predecessors such as George Eliot, Jane Austen, and the Brontës, but also to those women who, although they did not achieve fame, are nevertheless the foundation on which female achievement rests:

> The extraordinary woman depends on the ordinary woman. It is only when we know the conditions of the average woman's life—the number of her children, whether she had money of her own, if she had a room to herself, whether she had help in bringing up her family, if she had ser-

vants, whether part of the housework was her task—it is only when we can measure the way of life and the experience of life made possible to the ordinary woman that we can account for the success or failure of the extraordinary woman as a writer. ("Women and Fiction," CE II, 141)

Woolf seeks to recover "our mothers, our grandmothers, our great-grandmothers," those women who actually gave birth and nurtured, who passed on the self-images and values of womanhood on which the extraordinary woman draws, and which she celebrates and criticizes—but never ignores—in her work. As Woolf's vocabulary suggests, her identity as a writer is bound up in her identity as her mother's daughter.

This assertion may seem strange given so literary and domineering a father. Indeed, Leslie Stephen offers a powerful influence as both teacher and model. He guided Woolf carefully through his extensive library when she was a girl; later, she was sufficiently impressed by his literary stature to consider him in her own criticism. Many of Woolf's critics have emphasized Sir Leslie's role in forming his daughter as a writer (and, by setting a poor example of male identity, securing her commitment to feminism).[1] While her father provided her with a link to the literary and intellectual establishment, her mother shaped Woolf in equally important and perhaps more pervasive ways, as recent biographers have asserted. In *Woman of Letters*, Phyllis Rose says, "Of the two relationships, I will continue to suggest that the one with her mother was the more significant in Virginia Woolf's psychic life." Jean Love asserts, "Her relationship with her mother . . . next after her need to be a writer and artist and to fight against madness, was the strongest motive in her life."[2] Woolf herself, in her 1939 memoir "A Sketch of the Past," calls Julia Stephen the "centre" of her childhood existence (MB, 81, 84).

It may be useful to recount briefly the life of this woman who exerted so profound an influence over her daughter.[3] Julia Duckworth Stephen, née Jackson, was born in 1846. Her maternal line, the Pattles, was fa-

1. Herbert Marder, *Feminism and Art: A Study of Virginia Woolf* (Chicago, 1968); Rose, *Woman of Letters*.

2. Rose, *Woman of Letters*, 161; Jean O. Love, *Sources of Madness and Art* (Berkeley, 1977), I, 16 (2 vols. projected).

3. This portrait of Julia Stephen is compiled from Rose, *Woman of Letters*; Love, *Sources of Madness and Art*; Quentin Bell, *The Biography of Virginia Woolf* (2 vols.; London, 1972), I; and Elizabeth French Boyd, *Bloomsbury Heritage: Their Mothers and Their Aunts* (New York, 1976).

mous for its great beauty, which she inherited. At the age of twenty-one she married Herbert Duckworth, a barrister (having refused the artists Thomas Woolner and Holman Hunt), and was "as happy as anyone can be" (MB, 89). She bore three children, George, Stella, and Gerald. In 1871, after only four years of marriage, Herbert Duckworth died, entirely unexpectedly, while picking a fig for her. The shock devastated Julia; she never again found, or allowed herself, a deep, uncomplicated happiness. At least in part to take her mind from her own grief, she threw herself into nursing the sick and comforting the afflicted. Having known Sir Leslie Stephen and his first wife for some time, she naturally consoled him when he was widowed; in 1878 they married. Although he adored her, Julia found her second husband far more moody, demanding, and irascible than Herbert Duckworth. She also took on Leslie's retarded daughter from his first marriage; soon, Vanessa, Thoby, Virginia, and Adrian were added to the household, bringing the number of children to eight. Although the marriage was in some ways tense and wearing, Julia embraced its responsibilities and rewards conscientiously and gracefully. She died young, at forty-eight, from influenza.

These are the bare bones of Julia Stephen's life. Physically arresting and strong in character, she was, according to Phyllis Rose, "a remarkable person" in life.[4] After death, she became even more compelling, exalted into "an apotheosis of motherhood" by Leslie Stephen in his morbid memoir *The Mausoleum Book*.[5] The legend of Saint Julia, beauty and goodness incarnate, sacrificing herself in the service of others, lodged itself firmly in Woolf's imagination; she says that she was "obsessed" with her mother and with her mother's legacy all of her life (MB, 80). The Julia Stephen whom Woolf portrays in her memoirs is not merely a remarkable person but an ideal, an image of female perfection. Over and over again, Woolf reports that her mother was breathtakingly beautiful and almost seemed defined by this quality; she questions whether Julia Stephen, "she herself," can be considered "apart from her beauty" (p. 68). Coupled with Julia's physical attributes were equally compelling personal qualities. Her actual and prolific motherhood

---

4. Rose, *Woman of Letters*, 10; see also Noel Annan, *Leslie Stephen: His Thought and Character in Relation to His Time* (London, 1951), 100.

5. Annan, *Leslie Stephen*, 99.

Burne-Jones's *Annunciation*
Courtesy Aldo Zegna di Monterubello Collection

blended imperceptibly into more public caretaking as she nursed sick friends and relatives and performed extensive charity work. After her death, Woolf recalls, she left behind her a trail of supplicants, many unknown to the rest of the Stephen family, who had turned to her for aid (p. 38).

At home, Julia harmonized the disparate strands of the Stephen household. Sons and daughters—especially daughters—were initiated into the decorous social life of the drawing room (*MB*, 183). Even when Leslie was at his most impossible, Julia managed to maintain peace, placating with the balm of female flattery either Leslie or the person he had offended. Julia's vocation was to soothe, to pacify, to nurture. As if to seal all the implications of her life and personality into a single image, Burne-Jones chose her as his model for the Madonna in his *Annunciation*. Beauty, grace, maternity, and goodness crystallize in this figure. It suggests, too, the symbolic quality of Julia's motherhood, the perfection with which she not only fulfilled but became the role. Woolf describes her as possessing "the natural quality that a mother [has]—she seemed typical, universal," not in the sense of being ordinary but of being almost archetypal (p. 82).

Woolf could never reduce her mother to one of many actors in a biography. Julia retains an importance beyond that of any individual human being; she is a force, a mystical power, a "general presence rather than a particular person" (*MB*, 83). Woolf recalls:

> And of course she was central. I suspect the word "central" gets closest to the general feeling I had of living so completely in her atmosphere that one never got far enough away from her to see her as a person . . . She was the whole thing; Talland House was full of her; Hyde Park Gate was full of her. I see now, though the sentence is hasty, feeble and inexpressive, why it was that it was impossible for her to leave a very private and particular impression upon a child. She was keeping what I call in my shorthand the panoply of life—that which we all lived in common—in being. (p. 83)

Not simply an individual mother, however beloved, Julia is the source of unity and security. She presides over an image of life which is glorious, shining, enclosing, and protecting like a panoply (literally, a complete suit of armor; metaphorically, a beautiful, protective array or covering), a goddess of order in a child's world. Woolf's memory of Julia, written forty-seven years after her death, is specifically infantile, reconstructing the time when the mother is the child's whole environment.[6] In Woolf's mind, Julia remains this idealized figure as if no other understanding of her had intervened since childhood.

Woolf's vivid, sensual descriptions of the natural world at St. Ives are also part of these infantile memories; like the memory of Julia herself, they are "still more real than the present moment" (MB, 67). Her physical surroundings envelop her in a unified field of sense impressions like the mother's nurturant atmosphere; in these memories, Woolf writes, "I am hardly aware of myself, but only of sensation" (p. 67). She recounts two separate but similar experiences, one of "ecstasy," in which consciousness plays a more major role, and one of "rapture," in which the body is more important (in this distinction Woolf follows the OED definitions of the words); the memories, however, resemble each other at least as much as they diverge. The ecstatic moment takes place when Woolf lies "half asleep, half awake" in her bed; she hears the waves breaking on the shore and the rooks cawing, but these sense impressions are muffled and fused, not clear and individuated: "The sound seems to fall through an elastic, gummy air; which holds it up, which prevents it from being sharp and distinct . . . The rooks cawing is part of the waves breaking—one, two, three—and the splash as the wave drew back and then it gathered again" (p. 66). The blurred coalescence of sounds and sights; the image of waves, familiar in Woolf's work as an evocation of union; and Woolf's own trance-like state halfway between sleeping and waking give the impression of a mind just coming to human consciousness, perhaps retaining a sense of the womb but beginning slowly to distinguish another world.

The second memory, one of rapture, is, in Woolf's words, "more robust; it was highly sensual" (MB, 66). Again, the memory gives the impression of having taken place before the full advent of a perceiving, distinguishing, and classifying mind, but the emphasis here is on the body's receptiveness to impressions:

> It still makes me feel warm; as if everything were ripe; humming; sunny; smelling so many smells at once; and all making a whole that even now makes me stop— . . . The garden gave off a murmur of bees; the apples were red and gold; there were also pink flowers; and grey and silver leaves. The buzz, the croon, the smell, all seemed to press voluptuously against some membrane; not to burst it; but to hum round one such a

6. Love, *Sources of Madness and Art*, 224, 234.

complete rapture of pleasure that I stopped, smelt; looked. But again I cannot describe that rapture. It was rapture rather than ecstasy. (p. 66)

Although different in their emphasis—one vague and almost submarine, recording a state of consciousness, the other clearer and more intense, favoring the body—these memories share important characteristics. They both mingle sight and sound into a more general synesthetic impression. Along with the memory of Julia herself, they also share the image of a protective enclosure, a sort of organic panoply. In the first, Woolf feels herself "lying in a grape and seeing through a film of semi-transparent yellow"; in the second, she feels sensation "press voluptuously against some membrane; not to burst it; but to hum round one" (p. 66). The membrane does not exactly separate Woolf from the outside world; rather, it is the site of her interaction with that world, the point at which infant and environment meet. A sensitive conductor of sight, sound, and touch, it provides the infant the simultaneous experience of protection and wholeness.

Woolf symbolizes that protection and wholeness in a flower which she regards as a child in St. Ives. Inscribed in the flower is the mother-infant relationship, a special unity which Woolf understands in a moment of intense revelation: "'That is the whole,' I said. I was looking at a plant with a spread of leaves; and it seemed suddenly plain that the flower itself was a part of the earth; that a ring enclosed what was the real flower; part earth; part flower" (MB, 71). A product of Mother Earth's fertility as the infant is the product of the mother's, the flower remains part of the original source of its life; the whole encompasses the nurturer and the nurtured, not in any ways separable, unified by the panoply of the enclosing ring. We can begin to construct the significance of the flower as a symbol by noting Woolf's first conscious recollection: "I begin: the first memory. This was of red and purple flowers on a black background—my mother's dress; and she was sitting either on a train or in an omnibus, and I was on her lap. I therefore saw the flowers she was wearing very close" (p. 64). Woolf unfolds the scene from sense impression to emotional content: first the sight of the flowers, then the generalized understanding that the flowers are connected to the mother, then the feeling of maternal closeness and care in sitting on her lap. The flowers lead inevitably, in the movement of the recollecting mind, to maternal nurturance in an instinctive chain of desire. Later in the memoir, Woolf connects her revelation of the flower with a more abstract realization, her "conception . . . that one's life is not confined to one's body and what one says and does" (p. 73). Reflecting on the flower, Woolf understands herself as being part of the wholeness which originates in the mother.

But, of course, there is a darker side to Woolf's childhood, a less happy reality which grows out of the very grounds of Julia's deification. Julia was human after all, and inevitably could not fulfill her daughter's absolute, infantile desires. Immediately following her memory of the panoply of life, Woolf remarks, "I see now that she was living on such an extended surface that she had not time, nor strength, to concentrate, except for a moment if one were ill or in some child's crisis, upon me, or upon anyone" (MB, 83). Jean Love speculates that Julia must have mothered her infants well enough to leave Woolf with a taste of maternal love but thereafter spread herself too thin to fulfill the need she aroused. She weaned her daughter Virginia at ten weeks, an unusually early separation.[7] Whatever the nature and quality of Julia's actual mothering, Woolf's memoirs record frustration as well as pleasure.[8] In the midst of her idealized portrait, Julia appears as "sharp . . . severe," "aloof," and "stern" (pp. 82, 88, 96). This theme of maternal absence and inaccessibility was completed by Julia's early death when Woolf was thirteen, exhausted by charity work and her husband's demands, according to the family mythology. Woolf immediately suffered her first mental breakdown. Woolf's insular adolescence enmeshed her almost exclusively in family relationships, and the death of her half-sister Stella, surrogate mother to the Stephen children after Julia's death, gave Woolf no release from her obsession.[9]

For the rest of her life, Woolf sought compensation for the loss of maternal love. She sought in her sister Vanessa, in female friends and mentors (and, according to some accounts, in Leonard Woolf) a re-enactment of the mother-child relationship and its nurturance.[10] Dur-

7. Ibid., 109.

8. Nancy Chodorow and Susan Contratto argue persuasively against accepting infantile longings as absolute and legitimate needs and against taking unfulfilled longings as proof of maternal insufficiency; see "The Fantasy of the Perfect Mother," in Barrie Thorne and Marilyn Yalom (eds.), Rethinking the Family: Some Feminist Questions (New York, 1982), 54–75.

9. Louise A. DeSalvo, "1897: Virginia Woolf at Fifteen," in Jane Marcus (ed.), Virginia Woolf: A Feminist Slant (Lincoln, Neb., 1983), 78–108.

10. Jane Lilienfeld, "Reentering Paradise: Cather, Colette, Woolf and Their Mothers," in Broner and Davidson (eds.), The Lost Tradition, 170; and Joanne Trautmann

ing a rough Channel crossing, she sits in Vanessa's lap; she is twenty-three years old (*Letters* I, 186–87). To Violet Dickinson she writes, "Would you like to feel the Wallaby snout on your bosom?" ["Wallaby" was one of Woolf's names for herself in their correspondence] (p. 96). Her relationship with Vita Sackville-West, overtly sexual and undertaken when Woolf was middle-aged, is tinged with infantile needs despite the fact that Woolf is ten years Vita's senior. She appreciates the "maternal protection" provided by Vita (*Diary* III, 52) and even resurrects the image of herself as a small animal cuddled at the maternal breast which she used, decades earlier, with Violet Dickinson: "Open the top button of your jersey and you will see, nestling inside, a lively squirrel, with the most inquisitive habits, but a dear creature all the same— your Virginia" (*Letters* III, 233). It is not hard to imagine that Woolf's early weaning and a pervasive emotional hunger underlie this language.

Julia appears to have made an extraordinary imprint on her daughter, in part because of her own compelling presence and in part because of Woolf's gifts as a writer. But if the intensity of Woolf's memories is unusual, the essential nature of this relationship is not unique. It conforms closely to psychoanalytic descriptions of the pre-Oedipal period, when all children are tightly bound to the mother. Woolf's "conception . . . that one's life is not confined to one's body" corresponds to the "oceanic consciousness" of the infant described by Freud in "Civilization and Its Discontents," a consciousness which can persist throughout life alongside the "more sharply demarcated ego-feeling of maturity": "Originally the ego includes everything; later it separates off an external world from itself . . . [this earlier primary ego-feeling] is a much more inclusive—indeed, an all-embracing—feeling which corresponded to a more intimate bond between the ego and the world around it . . . ideational contents appropriate to it would be precisely those of limitlessness and of a bond with the universe."[11]

I wish to pursue the psychological basis for this state of consciousness because it sheds light on some of Woolf's most consistent aesthetic preoccupations and reveals in the process the pervasive ways in which

[Banks], *The Jessamy Brides: The Friendship Between Virginia Woolf and Vita Sackville-West* (University Park, Pa., 1973), 22.

11. Sigmund Freud, "Civilization and Its Discontents," in *The Standard Edition of the Complete Psychological Works* (24 vols.; London, 1962), XXI, 65.

Woolf may be said to "think back through her mother" when she writes. The mother, of course, dominates these early years; the infant's sense of oneness with the environment which Freud describes derives from the mother's apparently automatic responses to its needs. This stage of development is crucial to all individuals, but psychoanalysts argue that it is more important for girls because they have greater difficulty than boys in leaving it behind. Freud is the first to make this argument, observing, "In short, we get the impression that we cannot understand women unless we appreciate this phase of their pre-Oedipal attachment to their mother."[12]

Constructing a detailed picture of this pre-Oedipal attachment, object-relations psychologists describe a sense of self formed in relationship, unlike our usual conception of an individual identity which defines itself by separating the "me" from the "not-me." In the early weeks and months of life, the infant gains a sense of "continuity of being" from the mother's responses, including holding, fondling, and smiling as well as feeding. From this recognition and approval, infants gain a sense of ontological validity, finding their existence confirmed by "getting themselves back from the environment."[13] Later, the mirror may replace the mother as the source of this confirmation.[14] Infant and mirror become interdependent, each creating the other: the infant's presence makes the image, the image records the infant's presence and gives her a sense of herself. Enriched by close communion with mother and mirror, the self is affirmed by relationship, reciprocity, mutuality, and reflection.

When mother and child are of the same sex, these conditions are reinforced, resulting in the mother-daughter attachment which Freud observed and which feminist theorists such as Nancy Chodorow have explored more fully. Chodorow argues that pre-Oedipal issues persist with special tenacity in a daughter because gender identification with

12. Freud, "Femininity," *Complete Psychological Works*, XXII, 119.

13. D. W. Winnicott, *The Maturational Processes and the Facilitating Environment* (New York, 1965), 54.

14. D. W. Winnicott, "The Mirror Role of the Mother and Family in Child Development," *Playing and Reality* (London, 1971), 112; Jacques Lacan, "The Mirror Stage as Formative of the Function of the I as Revealed in Psychoanalytic Experience," *Ecrits*, trans. Alan Sheridan (New York, 1977), 1–7; Luce Irigaray, "And the One Doesn't Stir Without the Other," trans. Helene Vivienne Wenzel, *Signs*, VII (1981), 61. Woolf's anxiety about looking in mirrors, intensified but not created by being fondled by her half-brother while she looked at her reflection, seems relevant here (*MB*, 68).

the mother makes total separation almost impossible: the sense of sameness always counters the sense of difference. Because of this extended, unresolved relationship, more women than men tend to experience "boundary confusion and a lack of separateness from the world"—the sense of wholeness described by Woolf in her memoirs.[15] Women are more likely to feel a part of their environment and more closely tied to other people throughout life, to be more empathic and less autonomous than men. Particularly if they experience inadequate early mothering, women may also continually seek to recreate the mother-daughter dyad in other forms such as female friendships, lesbian relationships, and motherhood itself, which restores the symbiotic bond.[16]

Woolf's close attachments to mother-figures such as Violet Dickinson and her sister Vanessa, her affair with Vita Sackville-West, her constant search for "that maternal quality which of all others I need and adore" (*Diary* IV, 188), and her sense of herself as "bound . . . from the first moment of consciousness to other people" (*MB*, 52) all suggest the applicability of Chodorow's argument. It is not difficult to see why Woolf invokes her mother's magic simply by announcing her presence—"there she is" (p. 40)—or why that phrase should recur as the seal of maternal magic for her most compelling mother-figures, Clarissa Dalloway and Mrs. Ramsay:

It was Clarissa herself, he thought, with deep emotion. (*MD*, 74)

there she was, however; there she was. (p. 115)

It was Clarissa, he said.
For there she was. (p. 296)

there it was [the essence of life] . . . she held it in her hands. (*TTL*, 181)

There she sat. [Lily has her vision of Mrs. Ramsay] (p. 300)

15. Nancy Chodorow, *The Reproduction of Mothering: The Sociology of Gender* (Berkeley, 1978), 110. Because Chodorow retains the language of traditional psychoanalytic theory, I use it as well, although with some misgivings about its implications. The term "pre-Oedipal," for instance, suggests that the stage is merely a prelude to the more mature, central Oedipal stage—precisely the assumption which feminist theory questions. Nevertheless, this is not the place to devise a complete revisionist vocabulary, so I have let these somewhat misleading terms stand.

16. For a discussion of romantic attachments between women, see Lillian Faderman, *Surpassing the Love of Men: Romantic Friendship and Love Between Women from the Renaissance to the Present* (New York, 1981); and Carol Smith-Rosenberg, "The Female World of Love and Ritual: Relations Between Women in Mid-Nineteenth Century America," *Signs*, I (1975), 1–21. The language of these attachments, mingling the nurturant and the erotic, resembles Woolf's own in her youthful letter to Violet Dickinson.

These short, simple sentences have as their whole business locating the mother-figure in space, suggesting the almost talismanic significance invested in her existence. Her presence anchors the universe.

Almost inevitably, such an intense attachment induces ambivalence. Pursuing this early bond in later life, women may feel a desperate need for closeness and even fusion, experiencing a powerless dependence as well as intimacy. Jane Flax explains this ambivalence as a conflict between nurturance and autonomy, one pole apparently offering security with the danger of infantilism; the other, selfhood with the danger of loneliness.[17] Karen Elias-Button argues that the daughter is trapped by contradictory needs: as she moves toward maturity, she attempts to be like the mother, to imitate her as a model of womanhood, but she must also distinguish herself from her mother in order to separate and win a sense of unique identity. To the daughter, the mother represents "the childhood she must move away from as well as the adulthood she must journey toward and eventually accept."[18] Thus, the daughter's sense of self depends on identifying both with and against the mother.

At its most obsessive, this ambivalent relationship absorbs the daughter's attention, shapes her consciousness, and directs her life. With a sensitivity born, perhaps, of her own situation, Woolf noted the damaging effects of a too-close maternal tie in her half-sister Stella, whose attachment to Julia Stephen eclipsed all other bonds and even her own individuality: "All her triumphs were mere frippery on the surface of this constant preoccupation with her mother. It was beautiful, it was almost excessive; for it had something of the morbid nature of an affection between two people too closely allied for the proper amount of reflection to take place between them; what her mother felt passed almost instantly through Stella's mind; there was no need for the brain to ponder and criticize what the soul knew" (MB, 43). Mother and daughter enjoy a telepathic understanding, a symbiosis of consciousness, yet Woolf realizes that the very closeness of their communion threatens Stella's selfhood. The word "morbid" hints at a truth which Woolf explores more fully elsewhere, particularly in The Voyage Out; taken to its ultimate implication, the desire for union with the mother is a desire for dissolution.

17. Jane Flax, "The Conflict Between Nurturance and Autonomy in Mother-Daughter Relationships and Within Feminism," Feminist Studies, IV (1978), 171–89.

18. Karen Elias-Button, "The Muse as Medusa," in Broner and Davidson (eds.), The Lost Tradition, 198.

Despite its dangers, this complex relationship retains an irresistible attraction for Woolf, drawing her into its orbit not only as a daughter but as a writer. Her desire to create is also, in part, the desire to restore the Eden of St. Ives and the security of the mother's presence.[19] Woolf explicitly identifies her "conception," her sense of wholeness, as a motivation for art—in fact, what makes writing "necessary" (MB, 73). After calling the revelation of the flower "the strongest pleasure known to me," Woolf goes on to say, "It is the rapture I get when in writing I seem to be discovering what goes with what; making a scene come right; making a character come together" (pp. 72–73). One hesitates, of course, to psychoanalyze creative effort as if it were compulsive hand-washing, and the question of why a writer writes cannot be reduced to a single dynamic, whether psychological, political, or aesthetic. Nevertheless, it seems clear that Woolf herself associates her writing with moments of consciousness from childhood which revolve around the mother. I would assert that the need to recover the mother is one important motive for Woolf's writing—one among many complex motives.

Again, psychoanalytic theory can elaborate the implicit values of Woolf's memoirs. D. W. Winnicott, for example, emphasizes the role of the infant's imagination in managing its separation from the mother, arguing that the baby fills the "potential space" between itself and the mother with playing and symbols in order to cope with its increasing autonomy. Winnicott's discussion of the transitional object—the blanket or teddy-bear, for instance, which the child carries everywhere—is particularly suggestive, for that object seems to be the forerunner of art. Because it is always present for the child, it stands for the omnipresent mother of infancy without *being* her, thus providing the child's first experience with the symbolic.[20] In the same vein, Anthony Storr speculates that a sense of maternal loss may strengthen the impulse to recapture the state of wholeness which too quickly evaporates. Storr claims that "part of the compulsion to create may be motivated by the idea of making restitution for what has been destroyed."[21] Freud himself considered language a token of loss and an attempt at restoration, describing writing as "the voice of an absent person." He explores these

19. See also Claire Kahane, "The Nuptials of Metaphor: Self and Other in Virginia Woolf," *Literature and Psychology,* XXX (1980), 72–82.
20. Winnicott, *Playing and Reality,* 100, 109.
21. Anthony Storr, *The Dynamics of Creation* (New York, 1972), 151–55.

functions in the famous anecdote in which a young child, troubled by his mother's inattention, hides a toy, saying "fort" ("gone") and then recovers it, exclaiming "da" ("There"), thus controlling the experience of separation.[22]

Woolf herself often grounds creative effort in the desire for restitution by revealing the sense of loss in which art originates. When the "centre" of the unifying maternal presence becomes a "centre of complete emptiness" with her death, as it does in the autobiographical *To the Lighthouse*, art is born as a source of compensation. Lily Briscoe's attempt to paint Mrs. Ramsay after her death is also a central attempt in Woolf's work: to recover the dead mother, to fill this empty center: "It had seemed so safe, thinking of her. Ghost, air, nothingness, a thing you could play with easily and safely at any time of day or night, she had been that, and then suddenly she put her hand out and wrung the heart thus. Suddenly, the empty drawing-room steps, the frill of the chair inside, the puppy tumbling on the terrace, the whole wave and whisper of the garden became like curves and arabesques flourishing round a centre of complete emptiness" (*TTL*, 266). Woolf recurrently evokes this awareness of absence: J. Hillis Miller calls her novels "the place of death made visible"; Geoffrey Hartman finds this need to fill the empty center essential to her art, calling her writing an attempt at "interpolation" rather than "mimesis."[23] The original loss, for Woolf, is the loss of the mother, the "centre" of St. Ives and childhood who is no longer present and who can only be approached through the compensatory gestures of art.

Indeed, in some ways this passage describes this aspect of Woolf's art perfectly: around the empty center of loss, she weaves an imaginative reconstruction of the mother, celebrating the drawing room of her unifying parties, the garden of civilized fertility, and the flowers with which she beautifies the domestic world. In fact, in "A Sketch of the Past," Woolf remarks that if she were a painter she would attempt to recreate her infantile sensations at St. Ives with "curved petals . . .

22. Freud, "Beyond the Pleasure Principle," *Complete Psychological Works*, XVIII, 14–17.

23. J. Hillis Miller, "Virginia Woolf's All Soul's Day: The Omniscient Narrator in *Mrs. Dalloway*," in Melvin Friedman and John B. Vickery (eds.), *The Shaken Realist: Essays in Honor of Frederick J. Hoffman* (Baton Rouge, 1970), 127; Geoffrey Hartman, "Virginia's Web," in Thomas Vogler (ed.), *Twentieth Century Interpretations of "To the Lighthouse"* (Englewood Cliffs, 1970), 78.

curved shapes" (MB, 66) like Lily's curved arabesques. The memoirs themselves form the verbal equivalent of those shapes in attempting to render childhood experiences and to bring back the mother by writing about her, as Lily does by painting. In turn, Lily expresses most clearly the writer's aspiration to "make a phrase to cover the blankness" (TTL, 271). This fundamental condition, this original loss, recalls Woolf's characteristic means of praising the mothers whom she creates in fiction: "There she is." Issues of absence and presence, the pairing of the empty center and the mother who is "there," structure Woolf's fictional worlds from her first novel to her last. In The Voyage Out, Rachel Vinrace expresses her longing for mother-love by saying "I want—," the missing syntactical object of the sentence invoking the missing object of her emotions (p. 60); in Between the Acts, the audience locates its bathetic "mother," the author of the pageant who should serve as its unifying center (p. 198), by saying, "There she is, Miss La Trobe" (p. 122).

In The Waves, Rhoda describes human response in the face of emptiness; she experiences a musical performance in terms which W. H. Auden has taken as a description of all art:[24] "There is a square; there is an oblong. The players take the square and place it upon the oblong. They place it very accurately; they make a perfect dwelling-place. Very little is left outside. The structure is now visible; what was inchoate is here stated; we are not so various or so mean; we have made oblongs and stood them upon squares. This is our triumph; this is our consolation" (TW, 288). This austere description of human effort contains the motive of Woolf's creative impulse. The central act is managing loss—filling the empty center, making space into a "dwelling-place" by shaping it, enclosing it, transforming it from negativity into a secure environment (Woolf's descriptions of books as buildings and rooms echo this symbolism; see Diary III, 13, 24; AROOO, 123, 134; CE II, 2). The emotions which Rhoda's building evokes also speak to this underlying sense of loss. The two terms of the accomplishment, triumph and consolation, recurrently cluster around the artist's work: Clarissa, Lily Briscoe, and Miss La Trobe all experience the "triumph" of creation, certainly the more expected reaction. But consolation informs these efforts too: Lily's recognition that "the sight, the phrase had its power to console" (TTL, 270) and Woolf's own "theory," explored in her diary as she wrote To the Lighthouse, her most straightforward attempt to re-

24. W. H. Auden, The Dyer's Hand (New York, 1962), 61.

populate the empty center of her mother's absence, that "there is consolation in expression" (*Diary* III, 81). The pairing of these words expresses the artistic impulse and experience as a whole: triumph at having managed the loss, and consolation for what was lost.

Art offers substitute satisfactions, then, but the privacy and tenuousness of moments of artistic "vision," the dubiousness with which all of Woolf's artists regard their achievements, always imply that art has not quite attained its object—that, almost inevitably, it disappoints. Woolf's own momentary sense of failure after having completed *To the Lighthouse* suggests this disappointment. Contrasting her own talent for art with her sister Vanessa's motherhood, she experiences a "blankness," thinking again and again of the phrase, "Where there is nothing" (*Diary* III, 111). In the holograph version of the novel, Lily herself states the need to create something "where there was nothing" at the beginning of Part 3, when she feels Mrs. Ramsay's absence (*TTL/H*, 238). Woolf's diary entry takes her back to the time before the art work has been created, as if to say that her completed novel, like Lily's as yet unfinished painting, has not filled the space. It seems psychologically significant that Woolf would excise this phrase in the published version but continue to dwell on it, as if the phrase were too threatening to include but too powerful to forget. Vanessa's actual motherhood can meet the emotional needs left by the absent mother, unifying a world fragmented by her death, but Woolf's art only marks the spot where the mother used to be; the verbal sign "There she is" only screens the emptiness "where there is nothing." Perhaps this is why Woolf so carefully creates for Lily Briscoe, artist-daughter, a wish-fulfilling completion of the space in her art: a triangular shadow miraculously appears on the steps of the Ramsay house, the perfect shape to fill the triangle which Lily has outlined on her canvas to represent Mrs. Ramsay—as if Woolf were achieving the reparation of the mother through Lily. The "stroke of luck" (*TTL*, 299) which Woolf magnanimously grants Lily is what she herself desires in her memoirs, for she says that "unless I had some wonderful luck," she will never recreate in prose the "ecstasy" which she felt at St. Ives (*MB*, 65). Although the magical nature of the completion may seem to denigrate the artist by taking the triumph out of her hands, the stroke of luck is actually part of the desired recovery, for it mimics the perfect responsiveness of the maternal environment and recaptures the time when infant and mother seemed one.

Explaining her motive in writing her memoirs, Woolf writes: "I feel that strong emotion must leave its trace; and it is only a question of discovering how we can get ourselves again attached to it, so that we shall be able to live our lives through from the start" (*MB*, 67). In memoirs and fiction, essays, diaries, and letters, Woolf returns again and again to the strong emotions which her mother aroused—longing and frustration, adoration and loneliness—attempting to live her life through from the start, to retell the myth of her golden childhood, to recover the panoply of her mother's presence, to confront and accept the loss of the mother by articulating it in art. This is her triumph, her consolation.

2

The Body of Our Mother

ONE OF WOOLF'S most powerful means of recovering the mother is to recreate the sense of pre-Oedipal wholeness in her novels. This wholeness appears most obviously in the states of merging and diffusion which are among the most compelling experiences in Woolf's works. When Clarissa Dalloway senses herself as "part of people she never met" in *Mrs. Dalloway* (p. 14), when Mrs. Ramsay enters a trance-like state in which she "became the thing she looked at" (*TTL*, 97), when Lily Briscoe longs for a "device for becoming, like waters poured into one jar, inextricably the same, one with the object one adored" (p. 79), they all participate in the desire to efface the boundaries between the me and the not-me, to enter into a radical communion with environment and Other. *The Voyage Out* and *The Waves*, in particular, are infused with the implicit memory of an earlier wholeness which makes all ensuing development "a second severance from the body of our mother," as Bernard says in *The Waves* (p. 261).

Often considered the quintessential expression of Woolf's special gifts, *The Waves* structures its characterizations from this remembered wholeness. It presumes an original mass which includes all the characters, who become individuals painfully and grudgingly.[1] "We suffered terribly as we became separate bodies," Bernard reports (*TW*, 344), feeling his "second severance" when he leaves for school with name tags on his possessions, markers of his individual identity. He, the artist, insists most strongly on the persistence of that sense of life, repeatedly

---

1. For a parallel discussion, one which describes the individual as an undifferentiated mass, see Daniel Albright, *Personality and Impersonality: Lawrence, Woolf, and Mann* (Chicago, 1978), 97–98.

20

asserting the interpenetration of his identity with the others: "we are not single, we are one" (p. 221). The image of the waves which is the book's title implies this notion of a common body: from the undifferentiated mass of the ocean, waves rise as distinct forms, but they remain a part of the mass, rising and subsiding in an endless rhythm of apparent separation and re-fusion; in fact, in an early draft, the characters are born from the ocean, as "every wave . . . cast a child from it" (*TW/H* I, 10). To Bernard, the friends never quite break free from each other; they seem to him "a six-sided flower" (*TW*, 335), and when they meet at Hampton Court, they reconstitute the single complete person who had become fragmented into their individuality (p. 369).

In this novel, we are always conscious of what Woolf calls "embryo lives," those potential selves which can exist only "before 'I' suppressed them" ("On Being Ill," *CE* IV, 199). *The Waves* seems to trace those lives in its six characters, who are identified almost as types—Susan the earth mother, Neville the scholar, Louis the businessman—but who are nevertheless pulled more strongly toward their common origin than toward autonomous identity. In the early stages of planning the novel, Woolf conceived it as a biography, "some semi-mystic very profound life of a woman" contained in the image of the flower, which recalls the mother's presence and Woolf's conception of "wholeness" in *Moments of Being*, as well as Bernard's sense of the characters as a six-sided flower (*Diary* III, 118). Woolf also imagined it as an autobiography, leading Jean Guiguet to assert that the novel's six speakers "are not six voices in search of characters, but a single being in search of voices."[2] It is as if many lines of human development emanate from a common origin, like embryo lives growing to fruition within the boundary of a different kind of self from the conventional "I"—what D. H. Lawrence also rejected as "the old stable *ego*—of the character"—one which is manifold and all-embracing.[3] The defining metaphors of this arrangement, "embryo lives" and "the body of our mother," neatly mesh, although they appear in different places. They suggest the underlying experience which might shape this new conception of selfhood, some dim memory of the pre-natal unity which Woolf calls "ecstasy" in *Moments of Being*.

2. Jean Guiguet, *Virginia Woolf and Her Works*, trans. Jean Stewart (New York, 1966), 285.

3. Harry T. Moore (ed.), *The Collected Letters of D. H. Lawrence* (2 vols.; New York, 1962), I, 282.

As in *Jacob's Room*, Woolf explores new modes of characterization by placing a shadowy male presence at the center of the novel. But whereas in *Jacob's Room* the surrounding presences simply outline the spot where Jacob stands, inscrutable and adored—they *are* Jacob's room, his defining environment, as they describe and analyze him— here they become the focus of interest in their own right, brought into the foreground because the "I" of the charismatic hero who would out-shine and subsume them has perished. Percival, identified by his name as the heroic quester, dies a bathetic death in a polo game while en-gaged in a mission of empire-building; into the vacuum of his loss rush these six interconnected lives, replacing one form of personality with another.[4] Ironically, in *The Waves*, the grail quest for spiritual wholeness is fulfilled not by Percival but by his six friends, whose unity is symbol-ized by the water which, in the legend, revitalizes the wasteland. In a sense, too, the narrative has turned inside out from *Jacob's Room* to *The Waves*, emphasizing the interpenetration of voices rather than their sepa-rateness. In *Jacob's Room* not only the characters but the narrator herself is individuated: she is a woman and ten years older than her subject, differences which prevent her from entering fully into his mind (*JR*, 94); she, like the other characters, stands outside the magic circle of Jacob's personality, peering in. In *The Waves* she appears to be on the inside of the novel, at its center, projected out through her characters.

Significantly, the character who is powerless to recover the sense of wholeness commits suicide: Rhoda recognizes that, unlike Bernard's ex-periences, her own are "all violent, all separate," that she lacks the abil-ity "to run minute to minute and hour to hour, solving them by some natural force until they make the whole and indivisible mass that you call life" (*TW*, 265). Using the image of a loop, kin to the maternal sym-bols of panoply and envelope, she describes her alienation as she stares at a problem in mathematics on the schoolroom blackboard: "Look, the loop of the figure is beginning to fill with time; it holds the world in it. I begin to draw a figure and the world is looped in it, and I myself am outside the loop; which I now join—so—and seal up, and make entire. The world is entire, and I am outside of it" (p. 189).

Memories She suffers the ontological doubts of someone without a sense of "con-tinuity of being," feeling not only shut out but unreal, non-existent.

4. Susan Gorsky, "'The Central Shadow': Characterization in *The Waves*," *Modern Fiction Studies*, XVIII (1972), 449–66.

When she looks in the mirror, she sees "my face" but nevertheless feels "I have no face" (*TW*, 203), recalling the importance of the reflecting mother and mirror in securing an infant's sense of self; she finds that "no echo comes when I speak" (p. 374). Rhoda's need to imitate in order to function properly, "to look first and do what other people do when they have done it" (p. 204), bespeaks a hunger for confirmation from the environment. Powerless to combat her sense of isolation, she drowns herself, a form of suicide that implies a return to the womb and to the formless state before birth. Bernard the artist may imaginatively re-experience this union through his relationship to other characters and through his art, as I will argue later, but Rhoda prefers "the thing itself," as she says of Percival's death, relinquishing her individuality in the dissolution of drowning.

Rachel Vinrace also attempts a return to the mother in *The Voyage Out*, first through heterosexual love and, when that alternative proves unsatisfactory, through a watery delirium which resembles Rhoda's death by drowning. Woolf's first novel is intensely preoccupied with the psychological issues which underlie her sense of self as a daughter and an artist; in some ways, it is as autobiographical as *To the Lighthouse* and suggests the psychological origins of the motive for fusion which informs *The Waves* as well as the characterization of Rhoda. Rachel recognizes that her loneliness results from her mother's death, an explanation which is at most implied by the nature and imagery of Rhoda's meditations (indeed, *The Waves* does not invite us to speculate about the particular psychological origins of any state of mind, as the more conventional *The Voyage Out* does, because of its unusual mode of characterization). When Mrs. Dalloway, a passenger on her father's ship, mentions Rachel's mother, Rachel tacitly acknowledges her loss:

> She was overcome by an intense desire to tell Mrs. Dalloway things she had never told anyone—things she had never realized until this moment.
> "I am lonely," she began. "I want—" She did not know what she wanted, so that she could not finish the sentence; but her lip quavered. (*TVO*, 60)

Rachel, like Rhoda, has only a shadowy sense of her own identity and, again, what is left unexplained in *The Waves* is explicitly tied to the figure of the mother in *The Voyage Out*, in which Rachel's mother, present in memory, determines not only *who* she is, but *that* she is: "She was like her mother, as the image in a pool on a still summer's day is like the vivid flushed face that hangs over it" (p. 25). Rachel exists only as a reflection. This image is a pathological variant of the mirroring relationship between mother and infant, in which the child verifies its existence by watching its mother's responses.[5] By implication, it raises the question: what does a reflection do when its original dies? The possible answers—seek a new original or die—are provided by *The Voyage Out*. The reference to flowers, symbol of the mother in *Moments of Being*, reveals Rachel's morbid attachment to her mother's memory: she remembers the wreaths at the funeral so vividly "that now any flower-scent brought back the sickly-horrible sensation" (p. 35).

Rachel first attempts to recover the mother—to seek a new original—through her love affair with Terence Hewet. Although their relationship is often perceived as part of her emotional growth,[6] Rachel's desires suggest a movement in the opposite direction, regression. Rachel and Terence share, not passion, but a drowsy, timid, childish sensuality which regularly devolves into still, silent trances: "He was afraid to kiss her again. By degrees she drew close to him, and rested against him. In this position they sat for some time. . . . She raised herself very slowly. When she was standing up she stretched her arms and drew a deep breath, half a sigh and half a yawn. . . . They walked in silence, as people walking in their sleep" (*TVO*, 271–72). In fact, when Terence proposes to her, Rachel falls into a sort of trance and sees not her fiancé but her aunt Helen Ambrose, who appears in her most maternal, nurturant aspect: "she realized . . . Helen's soft body, the strong and hospitable arms, and happiness swelling and breaking in one vast wave" (pp. 283–84). Helen's unnecessary and even bizarre presence in this scene underscores the double focus of Rachel's desire, and the echo of her mother's name, Theresa, in that of her lover re-

5. Winnicott, *Playing and Reality*, 111–18.
6. Frederick P. W. McDowell, "'Surely Order Did Prevail': Virginia Woolf and *The Voyage Out*," in Ralph Freedman (ed.), *Virginia Woolf, Revaluation and Continuity: A Collection of Essays* (Berkeley, 1980), 29; Allen McLaurin, *Virginia Woolf: The Echoes Enslaved* (Cambridge, England, 1973), 76–77; Michael Rosenthal, *Virginia Woolf* (New York, 1979), 50; Josephine O'Brien Schaefer, *The Three-fold Nature of Reality in the Novels of Virginia Woolf* (London, 1965), 44. The exceptions are Mitchell Leaska, "Virginia Woolf's *The Voyage Out*: Character Deduction and the Function of Ambiguity," *Virginia Woolf Quarterly*, I (1973), 18–41; JoAnn S. Frye, "*The Voyage Out*: Thematic Tensions and Narrative Techniques," *Twentieth Century Literature*, XXVI (1980), 404.

inforces the idea that Rachel turns to a romantic relationship as a sub-stitute for mothering. In an early version of the novel, the connection is even more explicit: in the midst of Terence's declaration of love, Rachel cries, "My mother is dead!" (M, 197–98). Her confidante Mrs. Dalloway promises this substitute mother when Rachel hesitantly ad-mits her loneliness: "I know . . . When I was your age, I wanted too. No one understood until I met Richard [her husband]. He gave me all I wanted. He's man and woman as well" (TVO, 61). Richard Dalloway proves no comforting maternal substitute for Rachel: when he kisses her suddenly, he confronts her with an aggressive sexuality that she finds deeply disturbing. Yet the imagery of the nightmare provoked by his kiss hints at the needs which underlie Rachel's heterosexual experi-ence. She dreams of a deformed man who is clearly a figure of threaten-ing male sexuality, probably drawn from Woolf's own experiences with her half-brother (MB, 68–69), but the rest of the imagery, tunnels and a damp, oozing vault, suggests the female body and a return to the womb (TVO, 77). Terence, with "something of a woman in him" (p. 302), offers Rachel a less dangerous way to realize Mrs. Dalloway's promise of a lover who is "man and woman as well."

Far from moving Rachel along a line of development toward conven-tional social maturity, as the usual *bildungsroman* reading of the novel claims, Terence's love allows her to retire from the world into a som-nambulent state. The Orphic qualities of enchantment and sleep per-vade her "daze of happiness," a state which presents a charmed retreat from individuality and loneliness. Seeking a union so complete that she and Terence cease to be separate individuals, Rachel objects not to Terence's closeness but to his not being close enough. She wonders, "Would there ever be a time when the world was one and indivisible? Even with Terence himself—how far apart they could be, how little she knew what was passing in his brain!" (TVO, 296). Rachel achieves her ideal in occasional, momentary flashes of wholeness that owe little to heterosexual passion: "Merely to be so close soothed them, and sitting side by side the divisions disappeared, and it seemed as if the world were once more solid and entire" (p. 303); "They had ceased to be little separate bodies; they had ceased to struggle and desire one another. There seemed to be peace between them. It might be love, but it was not the love of man for woman" (p. 315). The rejection of "the love of man for woman" and sexual desire, the soothing and peaceful state which takes its place, the desires to heal all breaches "once more"—all suggest a nostalgic longing for infantile unity, before consciousness of individual identity intrudes.

Thus, when Rachel and Terence declare their love, they immerse themselves in the womb-like atmosphere of the interior jungle, a space both erotic and feminine. The jungle inscribes Rachel's desire for regression in her surroundings: the path of "springy moss" which they follow narrows until they are enclosed, "hedged in" by vines and shaded by trees which form an "immense umbrella of green." Sometimes the jungle even seems to be "at the bottom of the sea," a submarine quality which suggests the amniotic fluid of the womb. The "close" atmosphere (TVO, p. 270), which permits only muffled sounds of "murmuring" and dim shafts of light, and lulls them into a somnambulent silence (p. 283), recalls Woolf's infantile memories of St. Ives, particularly the trance-like ecstasy between sleeping and waking. Nature in The Voyage Out not only offers the sensual protection of a maternal environment but also provides a model for the unity that Rachel seeks: "Changing only with the change of the sun and the clouds, the waving green mass had stood there for century after century, and the water had run between its banks ceaselessly, sometimes washing away earth and sometimes the branches of trees" (p. 264). The undifferentiated "mass" of green, the communion of water with earth and branches, the freedom from rigid, articulated forms, mark nature as the symbol of primitive union to which the lovers aspire. Personified in myth, nature is the Great Mother.

In contrast to nature, unfortunately but inevitably, human beings become detailed and individuated, detached from "the body of our mother" into separate selves. Standing in front of a magnolia tree, St. John Hirst—who has declared his repulsion from the female breast (TVO, 184) and, symbolically, from the body of the mother—is wholly differentiated from nature: "There was something curious in the sight. Perhaps it was that the heavy wax-like flowers were so smooth and inarticulate, and his face—he had thrown his hat away, his hair was rumpled, he held his eyeglasses in his hand, so that a red mark appeared on either side of his nose—was so worried and garrulous" (pp. 208–209). The wealth of idiosyncratic detail describing Hirst's appearance, unusual in The Voyage Out, is part of the general contrast between "inarticulate" and unarticulated nature and the "garrulous" human being whose original amorphous body has not only severed itself from the body of the mother but has become articulated into rumpled hair and red marks.

26

The double meaning of "articulate," involving precision in both form and language, is not accidental but is part of a philogenetic myth which corresponds to the ontogenetic tragedy of individuation. The race as a whole, with its increasingly complex language and civilization, has become estranged from a state of perfect unity as it has developed: "One town had risen upon the ruins of another town, and the men in the towns had become more and more articulate and unlike each other" (p. 264).

This view of language as estranging informs the odd, incantatory encholalia which Rachel and Terence use together, repeating each other's sentences in a kind of mirror-talk:

"We sat upon the ground," he recollected.
"We sat upon the ground," she confirmed him. (*TVO,* 282)
Aloud to Terence she spoke. "This is happiness."
On the heels of her words he answered, "This is happiness." (p. 283)

Given the desire for union, repetition offers the most perfect form of language. Making the Other as much like the Self as possible, it effaces any variety in word choice and sentence structure, and therefore of thought, which might call attention to a difference in consciousness. While the narrator reports that they go on to discuss their differences once they have agreed to marry, at their most intense moments of feeling they rely on this mirror-language, which suggests not merely likeness but sameness and recalls Rachel's status as a reflection seeking an original.

Yet even this language implies estrangement. The lovers abandon it to "murmur inarticulately" (*TVO,* 280), and, as they move closer to their desired union, language detaches itself from the needs of human communication and is finally absorbed into the pre-verbal noises of nature: "Voices crying behind them never reached through the waters in which they were now sunk. The repetition of Hewet's name in short, dissevered syllables was to them the crack of a dry branch or the laughter of a bird" (p. 283). Finally, their words resolve themselves in silence: "Long silences came between their words" (p. 283); "silence weigh[ed] upon them" (p. 270); "The silence was again profound" (p. 271); "He was silent for a moment. Silence seemed to have fallen upon the world" (p. 271); "They walked on in silence" (p. 272). In later works, Woolf uses silence to emphasize an emotional bond between lovers who understand each other without speech: when Katharine and Ralph discover their shared vision of life in an image rather than in words (N&D, 493), when Clarissa intuits Richard's unspoken declaration of love in *Mrs. Dalloway* (p. 179), when Mr. Ramsay does the same with Mrs. Ramsay (*TTL,* 185–86), these telepathic moments signal a triumph of empathy. But in *The Voyage Out,* inarticulate murmurs and silence are part of a larger movement back to the womb, to dissolution and death.

The mythic association of Helen with the Great Mother reinforces this trajectory toward death. Described as a "great stone woman" (*TVO*, 135), she presides in this aspect, larger than life, over two key moments in Rachel's experience: the proposal scene, where she is "large and shapeless" and inexplicably fells Rachel with a gesture like "a bolt from heaven" (p. 283), and at Rachel's deathbed, where she seems "of gigantic size" (p. 347). Taken together, these moments suggest the enormous and dangerous power of the Great Mother: as the incarnation of nature and female immanence—the sexuality implied by the marriage proposal—she also contains the seed of death.[7] Helen's resemblance to a specific avatar of the Great Mother, the Fates who spin, weave, and sever the thread of life, seals this implication. (The association apparently has a psychological as well as mythological origin: Woolf remembers her own mother "like some wise Fate, [watching] the birth, growth, flower and death of innumerable lives around her"; see *MB*, 34.) Working her embroidery throughout the novel, Helen possesses "the sublimity of a woman's [figure] of the early world, spinning the thread of fate" (*TVO*, 208). She begins her trip on the *Euphrosyne* embroidering a prophetic pattern, a jungle scene including a river, deer, and dancing natives (p. 33). The scene foreshadows the later trip of the hotel party down the river to the interior of the continent, where they see deer grazing and visit a native village (pp. 279–85); on the trip, Rachel evidently contracts the fever which kills her. The Fates' last task, cutting off human life, may lie behind Rachel's recurring delirious vision of an "old woman slicing a man's head off with a knife" as she lies dying (pp. 333, 339). Their story is the mythological version of "Civilization and Its Discontents": once we leave the womb, we only truly return to the mother in death.[8]

7. Erich Neumann, *The Great Mother: An Analysis of the Archetype,* trans. Ralph Manheim (New York, 1955); Jane Harrison, *Mythology* (1924; rpr. Ann Arbor, 1979), 62–101.

8. This pattern may derive from the myth of Orpheus, a mystical musician like Rachel, who was beheaded by angry women and whose head was finally enshrined at

Rachel is finally defeated in her desire to merge with Terence by the fact of their separate adult bodies, as the mirror reveals to them the fact of their individuality: "It chilled them to see themselves in the glass, for instead of being indivisible they were really very small and separate, the size of the glass leaving a large space for the reflection of other things" (TVO, 303). The glass is to water as the heterosexual affair is to mother-infant love: a crude and frustrating approximation. The hard surface of the glass arouses but cannot fulfill the possibility of communion; unlike water, it offers no possibility of actual merging but acts as a symbol of unconsummated desire, the inevitably imperfect reconstruction of pre-natal oneness.

Rachel's death offers the only solution to this estrangement. Although it is often regarded as either a senseless tragedy or an escape from the dependence and sexual threat presented by her engagement,[9] it actually achieves "the union which had been impossible while they lived" (TVO, 353). In imagery a death by drowning, like Rhoda's suicide in The Waves, the delirious fatal illness submerges Rachel beneath the surface of a hallucinated pond, where she huddles like a fetus in the womb: "She fell into a deep pool of sticky water, which eventually closed over her head. She saw nothing and heard nothing but a faint booming sound, which was the sound of the sea rolling over her head. While all of her tormentors thought that she was dead, she was not dead, but curled up at the bottom of the sea" (p. 341).

The sense of being at the bottom of the sea recalls the submarine environment of the Amazon jungle where Rachel and Terence declare their love, as well as Woolf's memory of infantile ecstasy at St. Ives, where sounds also filtered dimly through a heavy, "gummy" atmosphere, the equivalent of the sticky pool, and waves broke endlessly on shore (MB, 66). Rachel's delirious hallucination underscores her desired

---

Lesbos by the Muses, one of whom was Orpheus' mother. Harrison asserts that the murderers are avatars of the Muses, linking the destructive and the adoring mother-figures. As a whole, the myth enacts the return to the mother through death. See Jane Harrison, *Prolegomena to the Study of Greek Religion* (1903; rpr. New York, 1966), 462–63.

9. McDowell, "'Surely Order Did Prevail,'" in Freedman (ed.), *Revaluation and Continuity*, 92; Schaefer, *The Three-fold Nature of Reality*, 44; Nancy Topping Bazin, *Virginia Woolf and the Androgynous Vision* (New Brunswick, N.J., 1973), 51; Madeline Moore, "Some Female Versions of Pastoral: *The Voyage Out* and Matriarchal Mythologies," in Jane Marcus (ed.), *New Feminist Essays on Virginia Woolf* (Lincoln, Neb., 1981), 91; Louise A. Poresky, *The Elusive Self: Psyche and Spirit in Virginia Woolf's Novels* (Newark, Del., 1981), 25.

reunion with her mother, for it recapitulates the dream in which Richard Dalloway, deceptively offered as a mother-substitute, kissed her. Again Rachel sees a damp-walled "cavern" and "tunnel," now inhabited by a woman, the "real" figure behind the deformed man in her original dream, who fits consistently with the surrounding female imagery (*TVO*, 331). Rachel's return to the body of her mother is the culmination of her voyage out, a journey by sea into the female depths of the Amazon jungle, and finally back into the womb.[10]

Woolf never again treats regression so longingly and extensively. The morbid desire which dominates *The Voyage Out* in characterization, plot, imagery, and setting becomes localized in a single character, Rhoda, in *The Waves*, while the imagery of pre-Oedipal states of consciousness and original fusion is generally detached from obsessive emotional need. One can only speculate, but the events of Woolf's life as she wrote and finished the novel suggest that Rachel's desires may have approached Woolf's own, and that the parallel must have seemed vivid and dangerous. Having lost her maternal sister Vanessa to marriage, Woolf embarked on an extended flirtation with Vanessa's husband, Clive Bell. While Bell was not a mother-substitute for Woolf, he acted not only as a male admirer but also as a conduit back to Vanessa: "Kiss Dolphin's [Vanessa's] nose—if it isn't too wet— . . . Whisper in your wife's ear that I love her" (*Letters* I, 362).[11] Shortly after her own marriage to Leonard Woolf, to whom she turned for "maternal" support (*Diary* III, 52), Woolf had a major nervous breakdown during which she hallucinated her mother's presence. As a woman in her late twenties and early thirties, then, Woolf seems to have found heterosexual love entwined with desire for the mother, just as Rachel does.

In later works, Woolf purges the regressive paradigm of its most

10. Imagery and theme ally *The Voyage Out* to other works by women writers; it may owe more to an as yet uncharted genre of female regression than to the traditional *bildungsroman*. Its nearest relation is *The Awakening* by Kate Chopin (1899; rpr. New York, 1976), in which Edna Pontellier, vacationing on a subtropical island, embarks on a love affair which induces in her a desire for sleep, silence, and dissolution; eventually she drowns herself. It also bears some resemblance to Sylvia Plath's *The Bell Jar* (New York, 1972), particularly Esther's suicide attempt, described in imagery reminiscent of the caves and tunnels of Rachels' dreams. After making several trips to the ocean, Esther takes sleeping pills and crawls into a tunnel in her mother's basement; she awakens crying "Mother" (139).

11. Louise DeSalvo, "Sorting, Sequencing, and Dating the Drafts of Virginia Woolf's *The Voyage Out*," *Bulletin of Research in the Humanities*, LXXXII (1979), 274.

frightening overtones. It is hard not to see *Night and Day*, her next novel, as reacting against *The Voyage Out* and the issues of separation, fusion, and identity which that book raises. While sharing these issues with *The Voyage Out*, *Night and Day* domesticates them. Questions of existence are tamed into questions of identity—"Am I?" becomes "Who am I?"—and the life-and-death implications which *The Voyage Out* finds in human relationships become matters of happiness and fulfillment. Careful redirections of feeling replace the compulsions of unconscious longings; myth gives way to literature as Shakespearean forms of romantic comedy and misdirected love rather than the Fates and the Great Mother determine the plot. Society rather than nature dominates: the Amazon jungle dwindles to a botanical garden. *Night and Day* grounds itself much more firmly in the everyday and the empirical, escaping the world of *The Voyage Out* in which no middle ground, no saving compromise is possible.

Although Woolf finds positive uses for pre-Oedipal states, notably in her conception of *The Waves*, *Night and Day* responds to the dangers of regression in *The Voyage Out* by repudiating the mother-daughter bond as an impediment to selfhood. Katharine Hilbery symbolically rejects that bond when she rejects her mother's choice of suitor, the colorless William Rodney (who resembles Terence Hewet in his vague, fussy character and his literary pretensions) and chooses instead her father's protégé Ralph Denham. These suitors represent the two paths open to Katharine: she can marry William, which "will make no difference" in her life, leaving her trapped close to home (*N&D*, 143), or she can marry Ralph and break free of her mother's hold. While the novel's major action centers on Katharine's romantic entanglements, her relationship to her mother influences her shift of allegiance from William to Ralph, just as mother-love underlay romantic love in *The Voyage Out* (although with opposite consequences: Rachel returns to the womb; Katharine begins to chart an independent course for herself).

The novel opens as Katharine Hilbery, competent but remote, pours tea in her mother's drawing room, acting as factotum in her mother's social life. The role of hostess' assistant, which clearly holds few charms for Katharine, is a specific version of the larger and equally constricting role of daughter. Katharine is enmeshed in the sort of stifling attachment which Luce Irigaray, French feminist critic, describes in her discussion of the mother-daughter relationship, "And the One Doesn't Stir Without the Other": "You take care of me, you keep watch over me.

31

You want me always in your sight in order to protect me. You fear that something will happen to me. Do you fear that something will happen? But what could happen that would be worse than the fact of my lying supine day and night? Already full grown and still in the cradle. Still dependent upon someone who carries me, who nurses me."[12] Katharine's apparent strength of character is superficially distinct from the passivity implied by this passage, but she is nevertheless imprisoned and paralyzed as a daughter. Despite her charms, Mrs. Hilbery embodies negative tendencies of the maternal as well as positive ones, frustrating Katharine's growth. Some of the early imagery makes this point: the web, usually a symbol of communal experience and the woman's ability to spin an all-embracing, unifying atmosphere, becomes in Mrs. Hilbery's hands a form of entrapment: "It was like tearing through a maze of diamond-glittering spiders' webs to say good-bye and escape, for at each moment Mrs. Hilbery remembered something about the villainies of picture framers or the delights of poetry" (N&D, 22).

In the same way, Mrs. Hilbery prevents Katharine from living a life of her own, from saying "good-bye" to her mother, simply by relying on her. Mrs. Hilbery depends on her daughter's "authoritative good sense" to send her to bed on time (N&D, 425), while Katherine finds it necessary "to counsel and help and generally sustain her mother" (p. 44). Mother and daughter have apparently exchanged roles—"And why shouldn't Mrs. Hilbery be sometimes the daughter of Katharine," Woolf asks while writing the novel (Diary II, 121)—but Katharine's authority does not grant her self-determination. The role reversal simply redistributes the terms of a stifling interdependence rather than undoing the relationship itself. Katharine's competence chains her to her mother as tightly as incompetence would have bound her to a more masterful parent.

Assisting in Mrs. Hilbery's labor of Sisyphus, the endless biography of the family patriarch which becomes a symbol of the mother's own unrelenting needs, Katharine expends her energy in a silent rebellion which is not sufficient to free her, although the intensity of her emotion testifies to the strength of that desire:

> How impotent they were, fiddling about all day long with papers! And the clock was striking eleven and nothing done! She watched her mother, now rummaging in a great brass-bound box which stood by her table,

12. Irigaray, "And the One Doesn't Stir Without the Other," 60.

but she did not go to help her. Of course, Katharine reflected, her mother had now lost some paper, and they would waste the rest of the morning looking for it. . . .

Katharine looked at her mother, but did not stir. . . . She had suddenly become very angry, with a rage which their relationship made silent, and therefore doubly powerful and critical. She felt all the unfairness of the claim which her mother tacitly made to her time and sympathy, and what Mrs. Hilbery took, Katharine thought bitterly, she wasted. Then, in a flash, she remembered that she had still to tell her about Cyril's misbehavior. Her anger immediately dissipated itself; it broke like some wave that has gathered itself high above the rest; the waters were resumed into the sea again, and Katharine felt once more full of peace and solicitude, and anxious only that her mother should be protected from pain. She crossed the room instinctively, and sat on the arm of her mother's chair. Mrs. Hilbery leant her head against her daughter's body. (*N&D*, 115–16)

The very act of separating from her mother sparks a guilty reaction in the opposite direction, as Katharine resumes her maternal posture at the end of her thoughts. She re-enters their symbiotic relationship—her mother losing and she finding, her mother needing protection and she protecting—as the wave of her anger momentarily appears as a separate form but sinks back into unity with the sea, symbol of infantile union, reflected in the physical closeness of mother and daughter as Mrs. Hilbery "leant her head against her daughter's body."

This interdependence prepares the way for what is at first glance a surprising turn of events, a moment of explicit regression which Katharine experiences at the end of the novel. When Katharine announces her love for Ralph—that is, when she announces her intention to break free of her mother—she suddenly feels a desire for "the mother of earliest childhood" (*N&D*, 482). Mrs. Hilbery appears in Katharine's imagination as a mythic figure towering over a young child, like Helen in *The Voyage Out*. Katharine feels that "instead of being a grown woman, used to advise and command, she was only a foot or two raised above the long grass and the little flowers and entirely dependent upon the figure of indefinite size whose head went up to the sky, whose hand was hers, for guidance" (p. 485). In this fantasy, Katharine momentarily escapes the implications of her love affair with Ralph, moving back into the safe womb of dependency on her mother— which is in fact her state of affairs throughout the novel, thinly disguised by the role reversal which gives her a deceptive aura of independence.

Such a bald representation of the underlying truth of the relationship

allows Katharine to confront her secret complicity in her imprisonment and finally reject it as she decides to marry Ralph. Abjuring her
earlier angry silence, Katharine chooses in the midst of her fantasy to
voice her desire for autonomy; although she is charmed by her mother's
romantic depiction of love as a boat trip down a river—a suggestive
echo of regressive desire in *The Voyage Out*—Katharine insists "but we're
different," for she and Ralph maintain a distance from each other despite
their attachment (*N&D*, 484). Woolf carefully preserves Katharine's independence in the "lapses" of attention which take her beyond Ralph's reach
and the claims of intimacy (p. 473). Katharine's sense of connection always includes a sense of separateness as well; she and Ralph are "alone
together," and being together means that "someone shared her loneliness" (pp. 398, 492). Although they discover the depths of their likeness in a shared image, the little dot with flames around it (p. 493), this
intuitive non-verbal intimacy is balanced by moments of apartness,
which they discuss in a "common language" (p. 473) rather than attempt to conquer their separateness and achieve the silent communion
of Terence and Rachel. In choosing Ralph, Katharine doubly escapes
regression: she finds a relationship which permits her independence,
and she rejects her mother's choice of suitor. The promise that she will
leave her parents' house, although not fulfilled in the novel, constitutes
the final step toward adulthood.

Nonetheless, mother gets her wish for a dependent daughter in the
figure of Cassandra. At the level of plot, Cassandra's appearance in the
Hilbery household precipitates the realignment of affections: William's
incipient attraction for her emerges, leaving Katharine free to pursue
Ralph. Symbolically, she adopts Katharine's role as daughter by taking
over her room in her parents' home: making herself at home in the bedroom, reading what Katharine reads before bed, regarding herself in
Katharine's mirror, "finger[ing] what her cousin was in the habit of fin-
gering" (*N&D*, 342–43). Finally, Cassandra takes the engagement ring
which William gave to Katharine and which, as Katharine notes, "will
fit you without any alteration" (p. 495). Cassandra is a kind of alter ego
for Katharine, as her quick appropriation of Katharine's possessions suggests, attracting the possessive impulses of William and Mrs. Hilbery
like a lightning rod so that Katharine may reach maturity. Indeed, Cassandra responds perfectly to those impulses, being more malleable, romantic, and disorganized than Katharine, slipping easily into the roles
of lover and daughter in which Katharine chafed. She professes the

rhapsodic interest in literature which Katharine lacks, along with a flattering ignorance which permits William to assume the role of man of letters, tutoring the unformed but adoring novice. In her inconclusive, dilettantish swings from one enthusiasm to another, Cassandra is also the perfect match for Mrs. Hilbery and her own distracted labors. When, at the end of the novel, Cassandra returns to the Hilberys because she has missed her train and lost her luggage, she enjoys a true homecoming, finding a mother who is her equal in misplaced possessions and unfinished business. Mrs. Hilbery announces the new family grouping: "Where's Katharine, I say? I go to look, and I find Cassandra!" Satisfied with her substitute daughter, she "put her arm around Cassandra and drew her upstairs" (p. 496).

These important differences between Katharine and Cassandra make Cassandra Katharine's foil as well as her double, but she does accept roles which, despite their frustrations, Katharine finds difficult to discard. Like the scene which reveals Katharine's desire for "the mother of earliest childhood," Cassandra's role makes explicit a dependence which is implicit in Katharine's inability to relinquish her unsatisfying relationships with William and her mother. In the slow, Shakespearean minuet of shifting alliances, Woolf subtly represents the psychological process of resolving ambivalence, especially ambivalence about the mother, whose desire to keep her daughter within her orbit determines, for Katharine, the value and attractiveness of her competing suitors.

I have emphasized Katharine's implicit dependence to demonstrate how *Night and Day*, often regarded as an anomaly in Woolf's development, in fact continues to explore the problems of *The Voyage Out.* Clearly, the transformations of that first novel, as well as the elements which Woolf retains, are part of this development. Thus, *Night and Day* is also significant in reversing, on the surface, the dynamic of regression. Here, the most explicit and conspicuous emotional need for closeness is found in the mother, not in a lonely daughter who seeks her absent parent. Woolf's emphasis on maternal possessiveness shifts the balance of power away from the mother by making her a less appealing figure to the reader and less desired by her fictional children. This possessiveness recurs throughout Woolf's work, in Mrs. Flanders' cry "come back, come back, come back to me" (*JR*, 90), Clarissa's uncharacteristic egotism in pronouncing her daughter "My Elizabeth" (*MD*, 71), in Mrs. Ramsay's wish that her children remain young forever

(*TTL,* 89–90), in Susan's maternal grasping "like a net folding one's limbs in its meshes" (*TW,* 363). After these first two novels, Woolf does not again confront the daughter's regressive urges until the autobiographical *To the Lighthouse;* with that confrontation, she cures the "obsession" which made Julia Stephen an "invisible presence" and a constant imaginary companion throughout much of her adult life.

The theme of regression is only one manifestation of Woolf's intense preoccupation with the mother and the childhood world which she protects. Not only Woolf's subject matter but her conception of the process, nature, and purpose of creative effort is grounded in this preoccupation; it forms part of her motive for writing and for participating in diverse aesthetic experiences. Woolf sees a work of art as a place of merging and wholeness; her imagination fuses components of the aesthetic experience which analysis would distinguish. In an epiphanic moment, she realizes "that the whole world is a work of art; that we are parts of the work of art. Hamlet or a Beethoven quartet is the truth about this vast mass that we call the world. But there is no Shakespeare, there is no Beethoven; certainly and emphatically there is no God; *we are the words; we are the music; we are the thing itself*" (*MB,* 72; my italics). Art and artist are both incorporated into the perceiving consciousness, which becomes the work. In place of a chain of production and consumption in which the artist makes an artifact and the audience regards it, Woolf posits a web of identification between art and its context—the world, the artist, and the viewer. Significantly, she reaches this insight by reflecting on her own artistic efforts and the "rapture" of "discovering what belongs to what" in her writing, an experience which she traces to the revelation of the maternal flower at St. Ives— actually a unity of earth *and* flower, as the work of art includes artist and audience—which symbolizes for her another rapture of wholeness.

Particular books and the act of reading recall to Woolf a child's sense of wholeness; she often describes her own writing process with metaphors of tunneling, burrowing, and making caves, suggesting a return to the womb. "Sometimes I feel like a happy animal in its own burrow—weather tight and safe," she writes while re-reading *The Voyage Out (Letters* I, 344; see also *Diary* II, 263, 272). Her memories of reading often locate themselves in childhood, before the wedge of critical intelligence separates fact from fiction and denies the power of the imagination to dissolve boundaries and erase the separateness of the external world. Describing such an encounter with literature, Woolf writes, "Instead of being a book it seemed as if what I read was laid upon the landscape, not printed, bound, or sewn up, but somehow the product of trees and fields and the hot summer sky, like the air which swam, on fine mornings, round the outlines of things" ("Reading," CE II, 13). The book is not an individual object guarding its own discreteness—"bound, or sewn up"—but a point of entry into the natural world. Like air, the book surrounds all objects, becoming a medium for their continuity, creating the atmosphere which unifies the field.

But most significant are the ideas of nurturance and symbiosis which thread through Woolf's encounters with both literature and painting, ideas which crystallize around the mystical, maternal image of the flower. In "The Patron and the Crocus," the flower represents pure art, unseen by an audience; Woolf devotes the essay to the terms on which the patron—who, as we shall see, is the nurturer—and the flower should be united. Woolf describes the relationship between the artist and the patron as one of radical interdependence: "They are twins indeed, one dying if the other dies, one flourishing if the other flourishes" (CE I, 152). Woolf demands from the patron nothing less than perfect, total responsiveness: "He is now ready to efface himself or assert himself as the writer requires." She adds, significantly, "He is bound to them by a more than maternal tie." At the heart of this symbiotic theory of patronage is the dream of infantile omnipotence, projected by a mind which has already experienced maternal loss: this professional relationship will actually fulfill the failed promise of the actual maternal one; the actions of *this* nurturer will be entirely governed by her needs. It is the need for "more than" her mother which accounts for the jarring presence of a *patron*, father, in a maternal role; it is a deliberate turning away from the figure which rejected Woolf, a search for satisfaction in an overtly different and therefore more promising form. But despite this dissonance in vocabulary, the relationship which Woolf seeks is clearly that of infant and mother.

Woolf elaborates this dream of symbiosis in "Walter Sickert," one of her most remarkable essays. She likens the art gallery in which Sickert's paintings hang to a primeval forest in its "stillness, warmth and seclusion" (CE II, 234), like the womb-like Amazon jungle of *The Voyage Out*. Woolf imagines that, as visitors enter the jungle-gallery, they revert to a more primitive form of life, becoming insects with enormous eyes the better to regard the paintings. Along with this philogenetic regression, Woolf suggests an ontogenetic one as well, describing the viewer's intense interest in Sickert's paintings as a primitive insect's symbiotic union with flowers. The twin-like relationship of patron and artist is recapitulated here by the "twinning" of flower and insect, the maternal flower feeding the insect and even letting the insect imbibe its color: "These little creatures [the insects] drink crimson; then flitting on to violet; then to a vivid green, and becoming for a moment the thing they saw—red, green, blue, whatever the color of the flower might be" (p. 234). The passage combines the ideas of nurturance and wholeness as the boundaries between insect and flower, nurturer and nurtured dissolve. When the sustenance is exhausted, both flower and insect die simultaneously in perfectly attuned life cycles.

Woolf as viewer seems to participate in a similar relationship, regarding the paintings with an intense sight which makes all sense experience almost tactile—or, alternatively, with the child's consciousness which conflates the senses, experiencing the colors as both erotic and nurturant: "colors warmed, thrilled, chafed, burnt, soothed, fed and finally exhausted me" (CE II, 235). The image of nurturance is even more explicit in "Pictures," where Woolf describes viewing another still life of flowers: "We nestle into its color, feed and fill ourselves with yellow and red and gold till we drop off, nourished and content" (TM, 143). In the nurturing galleries of "Walter Sickert" and "Pictures," she envelops herself in the maternal, represented by the flower. The emphasis on sensory and sensual experience does its part in re-creating the pre-Oedipal world, as it does in "A Sketch of the Past." The regressive impulse, fatal in The Voyage Out and carefully guarded against in Night and Day, lends these engagements with art their special flavor and intensity, moving the viewer beyond an abstract appreciation to an almost palpable interaction with the work.

In addition to these primarily visual experiences, Woolf sees writing itself and the texts which it produces as restoring a nurturant and protective environment. In two important essays, she describes writing as enclosing the reader, with imagery which recalls the panoply of her mother's presence: "[Proust's novels form] an envelope, thin but elastic, which stretches wider and wider and serves not to enforce a view but to enclose a world" ("Phases of Fiction," CE II, 82); "[An essay] must draw its curtain around us, but it must be a curtain that shuts us in, not out" ("The Modern Essay," CE II, 43). The shelter which these forms offer, making a world whole, is especially striking in the last passage, where Woolf's rather gratuitous qualification that the writer should shut the reader in—what writer (at least before World War II) would wish to shut the reader out?—emphasizes how strongly she turns to art for a sense of almost physical security. Interestingly enough, these values, which find a parallel in her mother's special gifts, form the basis of her explicitly feminist aesthetics: the "sentence of the feminine gender" which is "capable . . . of enveloping the vaguest shapes" ("Romance and the Heart," Contemporary Writers, 123) and the self-effacing narrative stance of the woman writer who "envelops all these odds and ends in the flow of her own personality" ("Dorothy Osborne's Letters," CE III, 62). But whether employed by men or women, the form which strives for wholeness and enclosure appeals to Woolf's imagination. She attempts the same effect in her own essays and fiction: writing The Common Reader, First Series, she aspires "to envelop each essay in its own atmosphere" (Diary II, 261); over a decade later, she formulates an almost identical plan for The Years, "to envelop the whole in a medium" (Diary V, 25).

Woolf's narrative stance also partakes of this desire for wholeness. Rejecting a single, controlling consciousness, "the damned egotistical self" which she dislikes in the works of James Joyce and Dorothy Richardson (Diary II, 14), she seeks instead to pass a "wet brush" over her writing (p. 323), creating a seamless verbal texture in which no element dominates or subordinates the others. In the second half of her career, Woolf seems to reject the central, dominating character (except, of course, for Orlando). The Waves, The Years, and Between the Acts focus on a group of equally important characters, unlike, for instance, Mrs. Dalloway or Jacob's Room, whose titles assert their special interest in a single character. While writing The Years, Woolf splits her protagonist Elvira into Eleanor and Sara to diffuse the center of attention (Diary IV, 152). The fusing of narrator and character has often been noted as the hallmark of her style. James Naremore offers perhaps the most telling description of this technique in relation to my interests: distinguishing Woolf's self-effacement from that of other modern writers such as Joyce, Ford, and James, he says, "In fact, Woolf does not withdraw; she is pulled into the fiction by the intensity of her emotions"—as if she were actually fusing with her characters.[13] One is tempted to say that she finds a way of exploiting the diffuse ego boundaries which Chodorow describes as part of feminine psychology, turning what would be a lia-

13. James Naremore, The World Without a Self (New Haven, 1973), 28.

bility in Freudian theory, which considers autonomy the desired end of human development, into a distinctive technical achievement. In "Evening Over Sussex: Reflections in a Motor-car," an essay which describes a creative mind confronting its environment, Woolf begins with a sense of inadequacy at not being able to "master" the scene (CE II, 290) or to take it all in; her solution is not to further exert her will but "to sit and soak; to be passive" (p. 291). Rather than strengthening her ego, she disperses it into several selves, like the diffusion of Clarissa Dalloway, "laid out like a mist between the people she knew best" (MD, 12), and of Mrs. Ramsay, traveling as a disembodied "wedge-shaped core of darkness" to India and Rome (TTL, 95–96). Like the six-sided flower which constitutes characterization in The Waves, in which an individual self is simply an emanation from an original unified whole, this narrative stance is a strategy for evading autonomy and egotism, allowing Woolf a closer and more complete connection with the world around her.

The most explicit instances of art as a means of recapturing the mother appear in The Voyage Out and The Waves. The idea of regression which informs these works also structures their descriptions of the creative process; both Rachel Vinrace, amateur pianist, and Bernard, the androgynous writer, experience art as a way back to the mother. Rachel's interest in music clearly fills the void left by her mother's death. Shut out of a discussion of motherhood between her aunt Helen Ambrose and Clarissa Dalloway, two women who might provide her with emotional support, feeling "outside their world and motherless," she retreats into her cabin to play the piano: "Over her face came a queer remote impersonal expression of complete absorption and anxious satisfaction . . . an indivisible line seemed to string the notes together, from which rose a shape, a building. She was . . . absorbed in this work, for it was really difficult to find how all these sounds should stand together" (TVO, 57). These aspirations echo Woolf's own description of the pleasures of writing—"discovering what goes with what . . . making a character come together" (MB, 72–73)—and Rhoda's description of deploying squares and oblongs to make a "dwelling-place" (TW, 288). These echoes suggest that Rachel's music does not merely distract her from her exclusion but also consoles: it provides some measure of the wholeness associated with the mother, covering the space left by her death.

In a similar passage, Rachel's music transports her even more explicitly into the realm of pre-Oedipal experience, the "oceanic consciousness" of infancy: "Her mind seemed to enter into communion, to be delightfully expanded and combined, with the spirit of the sea, with the spirit of Beethoven Op. 111, even with the spirit of poor William Cowper there at Olney. Like a ball of thistledown it kissed the sea, rose, kissed it again, and thus rising and kissing passed finally out of sight. The rising and falling of the ball of thistledown was represented by the sudden droop forward of her own head, and when it passed out of sight she was asleep" (*TVO*, 37). Like the previous passage, this one implies a yearning for the mother as a motivation for art while it also reveals the inadequacies and dangers of such a quest. It almost parodies Woolf's serious assertion "we are the music," as Rachel's communion with the spirit of Beethoven Op. 111 produces sleep rather than aesthetic rapture. Artistically self-defeating, Rachel's Orphic creativity trails off into silence. Its goal is to recapture the dreamy, somnambulent state of union, beside which the music itself seems incidental. In her fusion with the external world, with Op. 111, with the spirit of William Cowper, Rachel acts out a regressive urge whose ultimate desire is complete dissolution. Her sleep prefigures her death at the end of the novel, as the recurrence of water imagery to describe her fatal illness makes clear. At first a thistledown kissing the surface of a pond and dropping off to sleep, Rachel actually enters the pond in her delirium, curling up under the water like a fetus in the womb.

Not surprisingly, this early, often autobiographical work reveals the dangers of regression as an impetus for art. In *The Waves*, written at the height of her career, Woolf offers a more successful and productive version of the same paradigm in the experience of Bernard, the androgynous artist. Like Rachel, Bernard links the ideas of creativity and human closeness, but what for Rachel is a confusion of motives—music as a means of regressing—is in Bernard's hands a fruitful interdependence. Bernard's friendships are constantly taking the shape of art; as Neville observes, "Bernard says there is always a story. I am a story. Louis is a story" (*TW*, 200). By the same token, Bernard's art depends on human interaction: "I need an audience . . . I need eyes on me to draw out these frills and furbelows [of narration]" (p. 255). Like the female self which is formed in relation to the mother, Bernard's artistic self is relational. Yet, unlike Rachel, Bernard consciously controls the motifs of regressive desire. In the first episode, he carefully orchestrates a childhood game which seems to recapitulate Rachel's journey into the Amazon: he crawls into the bushes which he calls "the malarial jungle" (p. 198), urging his companions to "curl up" under the canopy of leaves and experiencing the retreat as a descent into the ocean as "waves close over us, the beech leaves meet above our heads" (p. 185). But for Bernard, the jungle is merely the exotic setting for his fictions: "Let us . . . tell stories," he proposes (p. 189). Rachel's direct experience has become Bernard's self-conscious drama. Thus, this first scene establishes the essence of Bernard's creativity, both its genesis in the search for wholeness and the superior strength of its ability to formalize, to represent, to make use of that search.

The clearest example of this ability occurs when, as an adult, Bernard enters London by train. Bernard personifies London as the mother and describes his arrival as a return to nurturance and protection. "Fold[ed]" and "enveloped" by the city's "maternal somnolence" (TW, 252), "like a child [at] the breast," Bernard feels united with London and with his fellow passengers in "this omnipresence, this general life" (p. 253), phrases which recall Woolf's memories of her mother's "general presence" (MB, 83). As his train enters the station, he imagines rejoining "the body of our mother": "We are about to explode in the flanks of the city like a shell in the side of some ponderous, maternal, majestic animal. She hums and murmurs; she awaits us" (TW, 252). In this passage, the mother-infant relationship is already in the service of art, as Bernard uses the imaginative reconstruction of fusion to shape a highly rhetorical, self-consciously "artistic" description; the above passage begins, "How fair, how strange . . . glittering, many-pointed and many-domed London lies before me under mist" (p. 252). The recurrence of common maternal motifs in this passage also marks experience transformed into art. The sounds of humming and murmuring, for instance, are consistent evocations of the mother; they appear in "A Sketch of the Past" (MB, 66), Letters III (p. 275, describing a meeting with Vita Sackville-West), and—most interesting, in connection with this passage—in To the Lighthouse (p. 80). Lily's desire to merge with Mrs. Ramsay, to become "inextricably the same, one with the object one adored" (TTL, 79) leaves her with a mysterious sense of Mrs. Ramsay's essence as "the sound of murmuring . . . and the shape of a dome" (p. 80), a phrase which almost duplicates Bernard's description of "many-domed London" which "hums and murmurs." Having laid to rest her "obsession" with her mother by writing *To the Lighthouse,* Woolf seems to have revised one of the central experiences of that obsession for *The Waves,* presenting it not as an unfulfilled emotional longing but as a means of artistry, under the conscious control of the artist.

Bernard's use of pre-Oedipal memories to structure his art is even more apparent a moment later, when, sitting in a restaurant, he describes creativity in a series of metaphors drawn from his arrival in London: "Images breed instantly. I am embarrassed at my own fertility . . . My mind hums hither and thither with its veil of words for everything. To speak about wine even to the waiter is to bring about an explosion. Up goes the rocket. Its golden grain falls, fertilising, upon the rich soil of my imagination. The entirely unexpected nature of this explosion—that is the joy of intercourse. I [am] . . . mixed with an unknown Italian waiter" (*TW,* 256). The humming of Bernard's mind recalls the mother's presence, while the notion of mixing with other human beings is part of the communion which both Rachel and her creator experience; as in Bernard's childhood Elvedon fantasies, human relationships and creativity intermingle. Not only infantile experience but the mother herself contributes to this model of creativity in the (admittedly commonplace) metaphors of breeding and fertility. In addition, both passages contain a strong element of sexuality—in the exploding shell, the soaring rockets, and, most obviously, the phrase "the joy of intercourse." This potency counterbalances the potential for dissolution; Bernard creates rather than simply entering a trance of desire as Rachel does.[14]

Although Bernard follows Rachel in joining regression and art, he inverts the relationship which she experiences: instead of using art to regress, he harnesses his desire for the mother as a component of his art. *The Voyage Out* and *The Waves* seem to me companion pieces, sharing the defining motif of water expressed in their titles, which points to the importance of pre-Oedipal states of experience, and interweaving the ideas of regression and art. Their dichotomous endings, Rachel's

14. This potency may be part of the masculine side of Bernard's androgynous nature, but Woolf also grants it to her most feminine heroines, Clarissa Dalloway and Mrs. Ramsay, both of whom enjoy an orgasmic moment which symbolizes their special and explicitly female power (*MD,* 47; *TTL,* 58–61). Woolf's sexual experience with Vita Sackville-West, whom she saw as offering "maternal protection" as well as sensuality, may have something to do with this representation of re-entering the mother as a sexual act (*Diary* III, 52).

half-desired death and Bernard's defiant assertion, "Against you I will fling myself, unvanquished and unyielding, O Death!" (*TW*, 383), mark different uses of the raw material of experience. They offer opposing possibilities: succumbing to regressive psychological urges or transforming those urges into something positive and creative. Bernard's triumph is Woolf's own, of course; it is she who has transformed the dynamics of regression into a model of creativity in *The Waves*, endowing Bernard with her own characteristic gifts. Like him, she uses her desire for the mother, a potentially crippling obsession, as food for her imagination; as process, motive, and subject matter it shapes Woolf's long and prolific career.

3

The Maternal Legacy

STATES OF FUSION and the process of art reunite mother and daughter across space; the idea of inheritance does so across time. By following her mother's model and re-enacting her values, the daughter symbolically achieves the closeness and continuity of the mother-daughter relationship. Woolf's feeling of having been "bound . . . from the first moment of consciousness to other people" (*MB*, 80) has its counterpart in her sense of connection with her precursors, of having been formed from "instincts already acquired by thousands of ancestresses in the past" (p. 69). Like the responsive mother of the mirror phase, an ancestress can confirm a metaphorical daughter's sense of identity, providing a reassuring model of femininity. As inheritors, Woolf and the daughters she creates in fiction attempt to carry on the mother's values: her gift for unifying and soothing, for providing an atmosphere of wholeness and community. Woolf identifies herself as her mother's inheritor when she announces her desire to "think back through our mothers," for thinking back is itself a way of making connections among people, the sort of unifying act which the mother herself performs. Woolf likens it to sewing, the female task which recurs as a unifying act throughout her novels. "Memory is the seamstress . . . Memory runs her needle in and out, up and down, hither and thither" (*O*, 78), as Clarissa Dalloway stitches together her party dress in an act of making whole which anticipates the work of the party itself: "Her needle, drawing the silk smoothly to its gentle pause, collected the green folds together and attached them, very lightly, to the belt. So on a summer's day waves collect, overbalance and fall" (*MD*, 58). Yet all true inheritance, as opposed to mere mimicry, involves some departure. Ideally, it is a process of renewal rather than imitation. Like the

45

regressive urge, this process is dangerous if it succeeds too literally. Although not as dramatically as in "successful" regression, the daughter can lose her identity in reproducing her mother too exactly. She must strike a balance between loss of connection and loss of self, between identification and integrity.[1]

Three Guineas offers a highly successful version of female inheritance in the context of feminism. Woolf insists that women retain traditional "feminine" values but create a new understanding of their meaning; her feminism is revisionist rather than revolutionary as she attempts to make use of past female experience, however shaped by oppression. Thus, she reviews women's disenfranchisement and finds that it has freed them from complicity in war. Having named "poverty, chastity, [and] derision" as symptoms of women's social inferiority, Woolf urges women to maintain these conditions as guarantees against male egotism (*TG*, 21). She redefines the terms, of course: poverty means just enough money to live on; chastity means intellectual integrity (that is, the refusal to sell one's mind as one would refuse to sell one's body); derision, the rejection of the fame and praise which corrupt disinterested virtue (p. 80). While acknowledging the inadequacy of an old vocabulary for these new interpretations, Woolf nevertheless retains it, ensuring continuity with the experience of her mothers.

Her endorsement of institutional change also seeks a connection with past experience rather than repudiating it. Urging the headmistress of a women's college to reject the exclusive, snobbish hierarchies of male schools, Woolf recommends building a "new house," a public version of a room of one's own: "And let the daughters of uneducated women dance round the new house . . . and let them sing, 'We have done with war! We have done with tyranny!' And their mothers will laugh from their graves. 'It was for this that we suffered obloquy and contempt! Light up the windows of the new house, daughters! Let them blaze!'" (*TG*, 83). In calling the new women's college a house—it is quite explicitly a "poor house . . . in a narrow street," not a monumental institution—Woolf implies a continuity with the purely domestic space which women historically occupied. In transforming that imprisonment into the site of distinctly female achievement, she

1. D. W. Winnicott connects the idea of cultural inheritance with the issues of object-relations psychology in "The Location of Cultural Experience," *Playing and Reality*, 99.

also validates the experience of her mothers. Yet the transformation is essential: the daughter cannot liberate herself until the old space is put to new uses. The passage suggests the double impulse of inheritance: the desire to carry on the mother's values and the need to break fresh ground, to find a new house which the mother might approve of and even envy but which she did not herself inhabit.

The revisionist attitude of *Three Guineas* represents a healthy balance between change and continuity, but Woolf elsewhere explores pathological varieties of inheritance from the mother. In *The Voyage Out*, for instance, Rachel is tyrannized by the maternal model; the spectre of the dead mother hangs over her, especially in the early part of the novel, coloring the judgments others make of her and undermining her individuality. Over and over again, she is compared—often unfavorably—to her mother. "Ah! She's not like her mother," Ridley Ambrose observes when Rachel fails to distinguish herself as a hostess (*TVO*, 15). "She's a good girl . . . There is a likeness?" her father inquires of Helen, pointing to Theresa's portrait and adding, "I want to bring her up as her mother would have wished" (p. 85). Her aunts assure her that they love her because "you're your mother's daughter, if for no other reason" (p. 36). Rachel possesses a purely contingent identity, valued only insofar as she resembles her mother and performs effectively the unifying role of hostess.

As Rachel's plight suggests, the mother's influence may be so pervasive that her daughters cannot find their own voices but can only contemplate their separate identities covertly. In this way, even Woolf's most celebrated mother, Mrs. Ramsay, inhibits her daughters in *To the Lighthouse*: "She was now formidable to behold, and it was only in silence, looking up from their plates, after she had spoken so severely about Charles Tansley, that her daughters, Prue, Nancy, Rose—could sport with infidel ideas which they had brewed for themselves of a life different from hers; not always taking care of some man or other; for there was in all their minds a mute question of deference and chivalry" (p. 14). The passage touches on two ways in which the mother can silence her daughters. First, her authority as a compelling model of femininity discourages any divergence, so that the daughters must be silent in her presence and stifle their differences into "mute questions," objections which cannot be spoken aloud. Second, the particular role which she represents, "always serving some man or other," enforces the daughter's subordination within a social structure and reduces her to a merely peripheral object of the mother's attention, which focuses first of all on men (as Mrs. Ramsay consistently attends to James before Cam). The daughters neither build a new house nor occupy an important place in the old one. Paradoxically, then, the mother can be both symbolically compelling and emotionally distant, a powerful influence but a remote presence, because of the model of femininity which she enacts.

The Years explores the possibilities of the daughter's inheritance most comprehensively, following the lives of several daughters in two branches of the same family to trace the various ways in which the maternal legacy can be embraced, rejected, or modified. The novel opens with the death of one mother, Rose Pargiter, implicitly questioning whether and how the daughters will carry on her legacy. We have some intimation that she provided a unifying presence in health; even in her semi-delirious state, she remembers birthdays, instructing her daughter Delia to send best wishes to Uncle Digby and recalling the idyllic days spent with her sister in the familiar female space of the garden (p. 24). One of her functions is to recall a happier past, symbolized by the portrait of her as a girl in white standing by a flower. Her sister Eugenie, who also dies early in the novel, provides a slightly more glamorous and potent version of the maternal legacy: like Woolf's hostess figures, beautiful, feminine, charming, she is associated with the unifying magic of the party. When she tucks her daughters, Maggie and Sara, into bed after a celebration next door, she exudes the woman's special atmosphere, "beaming, glowing, as if she were still under the influence of the party" (p. 140).

As Rose remains a continuing presence through her portrait, Eugenie lives on through the Italian mirror which her daughters inherit upon her death, an implicit suggestion that they emulate her, seeing their own images reflected where hers once was. As the mothers' possessions, these inherited gifts symbolize the maternal ideal of community. When their daughters, Rose, Sara and Maggie, attempt a reunion, they begin by remembering these maternal symbols as if the heirlooms themselves could create a feeling of communion and help the luncheon succeed:

> "And that glass," said Rose, looking at the old Italian glass blurred with spots that hung between the windows, "wasn't that there too [in Sara and Maggie's family home]?"
> "Yes," said Maggie, "in my mother's bedroom." (*TY,* 165)

"I remember Abercorn Terrance," said Maggie. She paused. "There was a long room; and a tree at the end; and a picture over the fireplace, of a girl with red hair?"
Rose nodded. "Mama when she was young," she said. (*TY*, 166)

As tokens of an ideal of community and as aids to the seamstress memory, the mirror and the portrait serve positive functions, but in other ways they can be destructive. Both maternal symbols emphasize motherhood as a role by framing the woman's image. They fix her as the mirror fixes life in Woolf's short story "The Lady in the Looking-Glass," turning "a handful of casual letters" into "tablets graven with eternal truth" (*HH*, 90). The daughters have inherited not simply the memory and possessions of an individual woman but authorized images of womanhood, of conventional sociability and family ties. The power of such images lies in their generalized and symbolic quality; they are both coherent and potentially oppressive. In a sense, both portrait and mirror act as Winnicott's mirror, offering the daughter a place to confirm her identity, but insofar as both symbols already presume an approved image, they are also coercive and threaten the daughter's sense of self, urging her into mere imitation. Milly, displaying her conventional grief under the mother's portrait (*TY*, 37), simply apes the maternal tradition without capturing any of its power. She mimics her mother at the beginning of the novel as if to take her place: "'Mama wouldn't like you to use language like that!'" Milly tells her brother Martin, "as if in imitation of an older person" (p. 11), and she repeats this mimicry throughout the episode. As an adult, she appears in tedious conformity to the female social role, wearing "draperies proper to her sex and class" and dragging Delia's guests down in a stupefying semblance of familial unity: "Everything . . . became dulled. She cast a net over them; she made them all feel one family" (p. 373). The image of the net suggests the same entrapment and coercion of the "diamond-glittering web" with which Mrs. Hilbery prevents her guests from leaving and her daughter from growing up (*N&D*, 22). Milly's life follows a formulaic female path in which "the women broke off into innumerable babies. And babies had other babies" (*TY*, 375).

In contrast, her sister Delia openly rebels against the oppression of her mother's influence. She interprets the portrait's unchanging representation of Rose Pargiter's youth as a "smiling indifference" (*TY*, 45) and "simpering malice" (p. 39) which mock her desire for her mother's death and the freedom it implies: "'So you're not going to die,' she said, looking at the girl balanced on the trunk of the tree. . . . 'You're not going to die—never, never'" (p. 39). Even at the moment of death, she can scarcely believe that her mother will relinquish her hold: "You're not going to die—you're not going to die," Delia repeats "bitterly," glaring at the portrait, which is illuminated by candles like the shrine of a saint (p. 45). Delia's obsession with maternal omnipotence, her resentment of the mother as icon, and her anesthetized reaction to the death (modeled on Woolf's own numbness at Julia's, which she recalls in a contemporary diary entry, *Diary* IV, 242, and in *Moments of Being*, 92) hint at the psychological complexities of *To the Lighthouse*, but Delia's emotion expresses itself as a desire to reject tradition, "to do away with the absurd conventions of English life" (*TY*, 398).

Yet Delia does not entirely abandon convention, despite her carefully cultivated image as a spontaneous Irish hoyden. Her own marriage recreates her mother's, attaching her to a scion of the empire like her father, Colonel Pargiter: "Thinking to marry a wild rebel, she had married the most King-respecting, Empire-admiring of country gentlemen" (*TY*, 398). And, although she imagines herself radically extending the inclusiveness of the mother's art of the party, her actual achievement is doubtful. Delia looks with some complacency on her social world: "All sorts of people were there, she noted. That had always been her aim; to mix people. . . . And she had done it tonight, she thought. There were nobles and commoners; people dressed and people not dressed; people drinking out of mugs, and people waiting with their soup getting cold for a spoon to be brought to them" (p. 398). This last group of guests, with their cooling soup, suggests that Delia has not quite perfected her casual social arrangements; moreover, her nephew North sees her restructuring of convention as severely limited: "For all Delia's pride in her promiscuity, he thought, glancing at the people, there were only Dons and Duchesses, and what other words begin with D? he asked himself, as he scrutinized the placard again—Drabs and Drones?" (p. 404). Desiring to escape the tyranny of her mother's image, Delia has erected her own in its place, inviting only guests whose identities share the initial of her own name.

Delia's failed rebellion only begins to suggest the complexities of inheritance. Sara's role in the novel explores them even more fully. Like Milly, Sara is an imitator, and she uses her gift for mimicry to win her mother Eugenie's attention: "She took her mother's hand and stroked the bare arm. She imitated her mother's manner so exactly that Maggie smiled. They were the very opposite of each other—Lady Pargiter so sumptuous, Sally so angular. But it's worked, she thought to herself, as Lady Pargiter allowed herself to be pulled down onto the bed. The imitation had been perfect" (*TY*, 141).

Imitating her mother, Sara achieves not only resemblance but the actual physical closeness of the mother-child relationship as Eugenie lies down on the bed with her; a moment before, she asks Woolf's characteristic question about fusion and autonomy: "Am I that, or am I this? Are we one, or are we separate" (*TY*, 140). Yet Sara's participation in the feminine mode of reflexiveness becomes increasingly disquieting as the novel progresses. Imitation seems to encroach on much of her conversation: she imitates Renny (p. 238) and Nicholas (p. 323), repeats to North the contents of his letters to her (pp. 319–20), and frequently falls into the mirror-talk practiced by Rachel and Terence in *The Voyage Out*. Like Rachel, Sara may be stalled in a purely contingent identity. She is marked by a childish quality throughout the novel: perched on the edge of a chair "with a smudge on her face, swinging her foot" (p. 324), clinging to her sister Maggie when they expect guests (pp. 64–65), skipping down the street (p. 239), and falling asleep with Maggie's baby "enclos[ed] . . . in a circle of privacy" (p. 245).

Despite this childishness, which implies a desire to remain tied to the mother, Sara departs from tradition as well. Like Delia, she experiments with new social arrangements, forming her closest relationship with a foreign homosexual, an attachment which her cousin Eleanor sees as a sincere and fulfilling "love" (*TY*, 370). She also criticizes patriarchal culture in terms which bear at least a family resemblance to Woolf's own feminism: she mocks North's military aspirations and, more subtly, Martin's conventional and money-conscious behavior in the male-club atmosphere of a restaurant.[2] In these scenes, she might be the familiar political daughter of a social mother—one of the daughters of *Three Guineas*, perhaps—and hence a reviser of the tradition. But along with Sara's new attitudes come chaos and confusion. She lives in a flat where the plumbing works only intermittently and the bell not at all; she serves North a meal which is an unpalatable parody of feminine nurturance, Boeuf en Daube degenerating into undercooked mutton. Sara's

2. Joanna Lipking, "Looking at Monuments: Woolf's Satiric Eye," *Bulletin of the New York Public Library*, LXXX (1977), 141–45.

status is ambiguous throughout. It is unclear whether she has found a new way of living or merely sullied the old. Her bizarre conversation, full of trance-like mimicry, passionate outbursts, and sudden gaps, seems alternately incoherent and visionary. She responds to Maggie's question about the purpose of a public meeting with poetic gibberish from their childhood: "'There were pigeons cooing . . . Take two coos, Taffy. Take two coos'" (*TY*, 187). Yet it is she who sets in motion Eleanor's meditation on her life (p. 366) and who captures Rose's character in a flight of the imagination (p. 169). Her deformity might be the sign of degeneracy or a paradoxical mark of specialness—her mother loves her "perhaps because of her shoulder" (p. 141)—like the naïveté of the third and youngest son in fairy tales, who triumphs where his more smug and calculating brothers fail. Embodying the central ambiguity of the novel, Sara is the direct antecedent of "the younger generation," the two children who sing their incomprehensible song at the close of Delia's party, signaling either the complete collapse of order and meaning or the advent of a new message which, like the Orator's nonsense syllables at the end of Ionesco's *The Chairs*, is so novel as to be inaccessible to the present age.

The implication of Sara's disquieting character, that new forms have not provided the security of the old, appears most clearly in the social occasions which recur throughout the novel. Sara's unappetizing dinner is an extremely unsuccessful but by no means unrepresentative example. The party is the mother's domain, the kingdom of the unifying hostess, and her absence is felt there most painfully, however much her daughters chafe at the restrictions of her role. Maggie's dinner party during the war, for instance, demonstrates the vulnerability of social life in the mother's absence, once her omnipotent presence no longer offers protection. Like the earlier luncheon among the three women, this event begins with reminiscences about the mother as Sara and Maggie recall Eugenie waltzing in their bedroom after a party. The charm of this idyllic past cannot protect the present, however, as an air raid interrupts their conversation. Maggie continues her dinner party in a way which reveals both the desire to restore an earlier sense of peace and the extreme difficulty of doing so. They retreat to the womb-like environment of the wine cellar, which, "with its cryptlike ceiling and [damp] stone walls" (*TY*, 289), resembles the regressive cave of Rachel's dream in *The Voyage Out*. Maggie and her guests wrap themselves in dressing gowns and quilts as if to recreate the bedroom scene which

Sara and Maggie have just recalled (p. 290). But this attempt to recapture past harmony is at best a temporary retreat, threatened not only by the general attrition of custom through the passage of time but by the specific evils of a particular age, the German planes of World War I, which render earlier modes of response obsolete. The spider web, one of Woolf's common symbols of female order, quivers precariously in the cellar as bombs shake the house, testifying to the fragility of the past ideal.

Delia's party, which closes the novel, offers the fullest exploration of this transitional society. By having Delia, the daughter who wishes most violently for the mother's death, preside over this final chapter, Woolf implicitly asks what a party without a mother can make of itself. Certainly, it lacks the coherence of celebrations in earlier novels. The "woman's atmosphere" is so far from being in evidence that one of the guests wonders who her hostess is, and Peggy wanders through the house "looking for the hostess, who was not there" (*TY*, 293). The party takes place in a "new house" of sorts, that of a real estate agent and not the family home, and opens "with an empty space in the middle of the room" (p. 351) as if to emphasize the mother's absence. The desire for new social arrangements, reiterated throughout the evening, suggests a resolution to make do without her. Peggy voices the desire of many of the Pargiters when she recommends "living differently, differently" (p. 391). Both Delia and Martin concur in having found family life at Abercorn Terrace unbearable (p. 417), Kitty is delighted to have escaped the tyranny of her youth, and North finds that he agrees with Peggy's challenge, directed against him. But much of the party reveals the inability of new forms to adequately replace the old. Peggy's own life is a clear example: she has found the sort of career that was unavailable to women of earlier generations, but her "living differently" is in some ways a dehumanizing distortion of the maternal ideal. Her only contact with motherhood comes as a professional obligation, "sitting up late with a woman in childbirth" (p. 354), an experience which leaves her fatigued and without emotional satisfaction. This detachment pervades and chills her interactions at the party: she finds herself "hard; cold; in a groove already; merely a doctor" (p. 354). With bitterness, Peggy regards a modern image of femininity, the statue of Nurse Clavell, which reminds her of "an advertisement for sanitary towels" (p. 336). In contrast to Rose Pargiter's portrait, the statue parodies maternal care and fertility, especially because the statue is a war monument of sorts, representing the misuse of female nurturance to patch up a hostile masculine culture.

As Delia's party and Peggy's experience suggest, *The Years* treats the loss of the maternal legacy as more dangerous than its slavish imitation. Begun as an indictment of Victorian mores, it develops into a recognition of the dislocations which accompany the loss of tradition. The most fulfilling moments at the party grow from the efforts of Eleanor, one of Rose Pargiter's daughters, to reanimate the maternal legacy. From the first, she comes closest to carrying out the mother's role, not as an imitator like Milly but as a genuinely unifying force: she is "the soother, the maker-up of quarrels, the buffer" (p. 14). As if to signal the mother's resurgent influence, she cleans Rose's portrait, which had become obscured with grime, before Delia's party (p. 325). Eleanor offers the most hopeful version of inheritance, insisting that life is a process, not a product, and implying that transitional forms are the only ones possible. At the same time, she acknowledges her debt to the past and her own role as inheritor by seeing herself as a "knot" like the knots which she ties in her handkerchiefs to aid her memory: "Oughtn't a life to be something you could handle and produce?—a life of seventy odd years . . . Atoms danced apart and massed themselves. But how did they compose what people called a life? . . . Perhaps there's an 'I' at the middle of it, she thought; a knot; a centre; and again she saw herself sitting at her table drawing on blotter paper, digging little holes from which spokes radiated" (p. 367). Eleanor herself steps into the emptiness left by the mother's death, seeing herself as a "centre" and picturing herself at the table she inherited from her mother, along with the portrait (p. 34).

Eleanor renews not only herself with her vision—she feels eighteen again (*TY*, 387)—but also her embittered niece Peggy, in an imperfect but indisputably new version of mother-daughter inheritance between two single women. Sitting against Eleanor's "sheltering" knee (p. 392), an image which recalls Lilly sitting with Mrs. Ramsay in *To the Lighthouse*, with Eleanor's encouragement Peggy voices her own vision of "a world in which people were whole, in which people were free" (p. 390), the basis of her insistence on "living differently." Neither Eleanor nor Peggy succeeds in communicating her vision; each attempts to "grasp something that just evaded her" (p. 427), but by the end of the novel Peggy's vision is more accessible than she thinks. Her brother North, against whom she directed her speech, catches her meaning despite the failure of language: "It was what she meant that was true . . . her feeling, not her words" (p. 422). In grasping her meaning, he also sees a new version of the cool, modern professional woman as a descendant of Rose Pargiter: "Now she was smiling; her face was gay; it reminded him of his grandmother's face in the picture" (p. 422). But he mentally superimposes another expression on her face, frustration at not being able to communicate her vision of the future. These two expressions capture the alternatives inherent in Peggy's "living differently": the happy security of convention and the insecurity of more adventurous but troublesome arrangements.

The complicated, even contradictory threads of inheritance traced by *The Years* also inform Woolf's own attempts to recover the mother through art. Although the mother's talents are primarily social, Woolf the artist seeks her as a direct precursor and a role model, re-evaluating conventional "woman's work." She celebrates the role of the hostess in Clarissa Dalloway, the "magician" who creates an "enchanted garden" with her party (*MD*, 291), and in Mrs. Ramsay, who creates a harmonious social world "like a work of art" (*TTL*, 240). Drawn from the mother's unifying gifts, the aesthetic values of "atmosphere" and "envelope" indicate Woolf's interest in the mother as a source of artistic tradition as well as her more personal desire to identify herself as her mother's true daughter. Even her choice of a pen reflects the desire to establish a connection with the maternal past: "Here I am experimenting with the parent of all pens—the black J., *the* pen, as I used to think it, along with other objects, as a child, because mother used it; and therefore all other pens were varieties and eccentricities" (*Diary* I, 208). A double metonymy invests the passage with meaning: first, the pen stands for the mother, thus recalling a childhood filled with her presence; second, the two pens—remembered and actual—stand for the relationship between mother and daughter, the reincarnation of the "parent" pen in Woolf's own suggesting continuity and inheritance. What is striking, apart from the content of the passage itself, is that Woolf takes up the pen of her mother rather than that of her father, the professional writer and most obvious model. Sometimes, too, she draws an analogy between aesthetic production and procreation, seeing writing as an expression of the maternal instinct. The spinster-scholar of "The Journal of Mistress Joan Martyn" feels a "maternal passion" for her manuscripts.[3] Mrs. Gaskell, in a similar vein, begins writing novels to compensate for the death of a child ("Mrs. Gaskell," *Books and Portraits*, 138) and fulfills herself by mothering her readers ("Indiscretions," *Women and Writing*, 75). Woolf describes her own writing as a process of giving birth (*Letters* I, 348; *Diary* V, 31, 148)—certainly not an unusual trope but a significant one in light of her consistent preoccupation with the maternal and her relationship to it.

Indeed, in *The Waves* Woolf seems to move beyond the desire of the daughter and actually becomes the mother, creating the fictional waves which give birth to the characters and reuniting the six friends in a novel which, in its unifying narrative technique, is the verbal analogue to the mother's body. In *The Waves*, the creativity of art and nature, including human procreation, are metaphorically linked as Woolf embeds the notion of literary production in a matriarchal creation myth.[4] The dawn goddess who opens the novel seems to author the natural world as she illuminates it with "bars" and "strokes" like the strokes of the pen; her human counterparts, the gardeners who sweep and the lady who writes, reiterate her motions in acts which likewise order and articulate, but they take the process one step further by shaping the natural world into human designs. As nature becomes artifice, procreation and artistic creativity are seen as complementary aspects of the same impulse. This continuum of articulation not only tames nature, mitigating the horror of its inhuman strangeness (its inarticulateness in *The Voyage Out* and its blank objectivity in the "Time Passes" section of *To the Lighthouse*), but also secures for the writer the mother's power: "I am the thing in which all this exists. Certainly without me it would perish . . . I am capable of disposing of these innumerable children—at least mine is the power of drawing conclusions. Here I am in the centre of the room & they come flocking around me" (*TW/DI*, 39; I have omitted cancelled passages). Her "extraordinary omnipotence" (p. 39) is that of the writer as mother, the "centre" who draws her children together and then draws conclusions, the woman who can create "innumerable" children who depend on her absolutely for their continued existence.

3. Virginia Woolf, "The Journal of Mistress Joan Martyn," ed. Susan Squier and Louise DeSalvo, *Twentieth Century Literature*, XXV (1979), 240.
4. Joseph Allen Boone, "The Meaning of Elvedon in *The Waves*: A Key to Bernard's Experience and Woolf's Vision," *Modern Fiction Studies*, XXVII (1981–82), 629–37.

While these observations suggest a neat congruence between mother-hood and art, the two are not always so happily attuned. Just as often, Woolf sees writing and maternity as competing accomplishments, mea-suring her work against her sister Vanessa's family as if motherhood were the only true standard of female achievement. Comparisons with Van-essa, sometimes envious and sometimes self-approving, abound in her letters and diaries. Jealous of her sister's children (*Letters* II, 108, 276, 305), Woolf nevertheless remarks while writing *The Waves*, "I had a day of intoxication when I said 'Children are nothing to this'" (*Diary* III, 298). Following *Orlando's* success, she writes, "So I have something, in-stead of children" (p. 217). Indeed, Woolf is particularly discomfited when Vanessa's art is praised, for Woolf considers aesthetics her own domain and artistic achievement her special badge of self-affirmation: "As you have the children, the fame by rights belongs to me" (*Letters* III, 271), and "I will not be jealous, but isn't it odd—thinking of gifts in her? I mean when she has everything else" (*Diary* IV, 322). These re-marks imply that Woolf relied on art to compensate for not being a mother—not that this compensation was her motive or primary reward (indeed, she had been writing reviews long before her marriage and was well along in her first novel before she and Leonard decided not to have children), but that, with her writing, she could assert herself in the face of what she felt to be personal inadequacy: not having chil-dren, not having the female gift for creating social harmony, not being, in her own words, "a real woman" (*Diary* III, 52). These entries also suggest that Woolf saw Vanessa, not herself, as her mother's true daugh-ter; from her childhood, Vanessa was a motherly presence, whose care of her younger brother makes Julia's "heart leap" with joy in a scene which Woolf imagines in "Reminiscences" (*MB*, 28).

If Woolf feels a stepchild of the maternal tradition within her own family, she encounters other sources of estrangement in less personal contexts. In her efforts to celebrate female values and activities, Woolf inevitably contends with the female stereotypes of her society; any at-tempt to clear for the mother a central space in art and culture neces-sarily confronts traditional—and often unflattering—views of women. These stereotypes take two main forms which, not surprisingly, con-flict with the necessities of art. First, women are creatures of their bodies, closely allied with nature and incapable of transcending the physical as art requires. In this view procreation and creation are mutually exclusive categories; as women already occupy the first, they cannot hope for access to the second. The other stereotype holds that women are creatures of the spirit, self-effacing and dedicated to serving others selflessly, and therefore could not possibly wish to assert themselves by creating a work of art.[5]

This cultural schizophrenia was probably reinforced by Woolf's own experience. She watched her half-sister Stella die newly pregnant shortly after her honeymoon, a combination of circumstances which, according to Phyllis Rose, "must have confirmed the yoking of the ideas of death and sex"—that is, how closely women's bodies tie them to the natural cycle.[6] On the other hand, her mother's saintly self-effacement (along with *The Mausoleum Book*) told her that motherhood was a spiritual state as well. Both versions of motherhood left an imprint on Woolf's imagination. Her novels do not simply exalt the hostess-artist but offer complicated images of women derived from culture and her own difficult, ambivalent childhood; they do not advance monolithic, utopian visions of motherhood and femininity but rather attempt to explore the problems and resolve the contradictions embedded in the figure of the mother.

The first stereotype divorces the mother from the artist because of her family responsibilities. Adrienne Rich writes, "Not only have women been told to stick to motherhood, but we have been told that our intellectual or aesthetic creations were inappropriate, inconsequential, or scandalous, an attempt to become 'like men,' or to escape from the 'real' tasks of adult womanhood: marriage and childbearing." In an extreme form of the argument, such ambition is not merely an undesirable distraction from motherhood but actually incompatible with it. Regarded in a male-dominated culture as "a passive function occurring without violation," procreation becomes, paradoxically, inherently uncreative. Simone de Beauvoir argues, "The woman who gave birth . . . did not know the pride of creation . . . giving birth and suckling are not *activities*; they are natural functions . . . [which] imprisoned her in repetition and immanence."[7] In other words, woman is

5. See, for example, Simone de Beauvoir, *The Second Sex*, ed. and trans. H. M. Parshley (New York, 1952); Dorothy Dinnerstein, *The Mermaid and the Minotaur: Sexual Arrangements and Human Malaise* (New York, 1976); Adrienne Rich, *Of Woman Born: Motherhood as Experience and Institution* (New York, 1976).

6. Rose, *Woman of Letters*, 15.

7. Rich, *Of Woman Born*, 40, 101; de Beauvoir, *The Second Sex*, 57–58.

at the mercy of her body, ruled by processes which she contains or enacts but does not control. Like Susan in *The Waves*, women *are* nature, passive and fecund: "I shall lie like a field bearing crops in rotation," Susan says, thinking of motherhood, "heat and cold will follow each other naturally without my willing or unwilling" (*TW*, 266). Once these formulations about childbirth are generalized to the whole woman, it is only a short step to the position that biological fertility disqualifies a woman from artistic fertility, that the body drowns the brain.

Woolf's attitudes here are not entirely consistent, but her difficult relationship to her own body is clear. Molestation by her half-brothers left her with a sense of "shame," "guilt," and even "ancestral dread" centered on her identity as a female sexual being (*MB*, 68). As she announces, "We were famous for our beauty—my mother's beauty," which Woolf identifies as "femininity," she recalls those shameful, damaging incidents which "check[ed]" her pride in her physical appearance (p. 68). This intense ambivalence about the female body, which represents both a part of her own identity ("our beauty") and her inheritance from her mother ("my mother's beauty"), is a central problem in Woolf's self-image as a woman writer; her estrangement from her physical self is a recurring theme in her life.[8] In fact, many of her comments insist upon the incompatibility of female biology and creativity: "I had thought to write the quickest most brilliant pages in Orlando yesterday—not a drop came, all, forsooth, for the usual physical reasons [menstruation], which delivered themselves today. It is the oddest feeling: as if a finger stopped the flow of the ideas in the brain: it is unsealed, & the blood rushes all over the place" (*Diary* III, 175; see also 59). Woolf describes her menstruation as sapping and appropriating her creativity in a Dr. Strangelove economy of precious bodily fluids. Her biological identity as a woman literally prevents her from writing.

More metaphorically, she perceives the womb as the source of a glib, gushing style; when she assesses the work of Vita Sackville-West, her motherly lover who is also a writer, she finds Vita's influence pernicious on that ground: "Vita's prose is too fluent. I've been reading it, & it makes my pen run. When I've read a classic, I am curbed &—not castrated; no, the opposite, I can't think of the word at the moment" (*Diary* III, 126). Apart from Woolf's periphrasis, which at the very least suggests the significance of the general subject, the passage asserts the

8. Frances Partidge, *Love in Bloomsbury: Memories* (Boston, 1981), 80.

need to reject the biology of womanhood and, by implication, what a female writer might inherit from the mother. Woolf imagines a hysterectomy which will free her from the womb's too-fluent effusions—despite the fact that "fertility and fluency" of style are precisely the virtues which she develops during her association with Vita (p. 59), whose charms as a lover become "mixed up" with Woolf's plans for a novel (p. 57). Given the long history of pen-as-penis, it is unthinkable that a male artist would wish to be castrated so he could write.[9] Femininity, particularly the potential for motherhood, clearly emerges as an impediment to art, revealing one problematic aspect of the maternal legacy. In implying that she is an artist because she is *not* a mother, Woolf has obviously assimilated a cultural stereotype; she also redresses her sense of being on the wrong side of the life-art distinction. Woolf has outstripped the mother: however gorgeous, "full-breasted," and "pearl hung" Vita is (p. 52; see also p. 144), she will never be the writer Woolf is because of the very maternity and sensual opulence which make her so attractive.

Woolf's virginal or non-heterosexual female artists—Clarissa Dalloway, Lily Briscoe, and Miss La Trobe—are created partly in response to these difficulties of motherhood. Certainly Lily's intertwined anxieties about her role as an artist and her relationship to the mother-figure, Mrs. Ramsay, derive from the same assumptions about maternity. Lily's desire to be like Mrs. Ramsay—in fact, to merge with her "like waters poured into one jar" (*TTL*, 79)—interferes with her art because it represents a desperate, clinging dependency and because it ties her to an inappropriate role model. Both aspects of Lily's self-defeating attachment to Mrs. Ramsay—emotional effusion and the incompatibility of motherhood and art—are suggested by the description of Lily laughing "hysterically" while she sits deferentially at Mrs. Ramsay's knee (p. 78); the Greek root of the word means "womb." Judith Shakespeare in *A Room of One's Own* acts out another, more straightforward version of this conflict between female biology and aesthetic achievement. In her tragedy, biology is destiny; she comes to London to develop her artistic gifts, but the inevitable happens instead: "At last Nick Greene the actor-manager took pity on her; she found herself with child by that gentleman and so—*who shall measure the heat and violence of the poet's heart*

9. For a useful survey of the history of this metaphor, see Sandra Gilbert and Susan Gubar, *The Madwoman in the Attic: The Woman Writer and the Nineteenth-Century Literary Imagination* (New Haven, 1979), 5–7.

when caught and tangled by a woman's body—killed herself one winter's night and lies buried at some cross-roads where the omnibuses now stop outside the Elephant and Castle" (*AROOO*, 50; my italics). Woman's body, then, is as much the enemy as patriarchal oppression. The hope of transcendence has been wrenched back into the cycle of immanence, ensnared by female biology.

The connection between childbirth or pregnancy and death makes the final case against the woman as artist: birth and death go together—as they did in the life of her half-sister Stella and as they must in the organic world. Women are involved in these processes much more obviously than men; they seem to enact them in their procreative abilities and their menstruation, governed by the cycles of the moon. Woman's body is a constant reminder that humans are merely mortal; how can it serve an art which seeks to overcome, to transcend death? The speaker of Yeats's "Sailing to Byzantium" is not alone; he speaks for many poets in his wish to trade the "dying animal" of his body for a place in "the artifice of eternity"—the realm of pure art into which the natural does not intrude. How can a woman participate in this tradition if she not only experiences but actually embodies the natural world? Even if she is not perceived or does not perceive herself as memento mori, she finds it hard to disclaim her tie to nature. Although this tie may confer a kind of mystical power as scholars of myth such as Campbell and Neumann have noted in their respective studies of human and divine heroic figures, it does not make her a poet.[10] In fact, Margaret Homans argues that the nineteenth-century woman poet's greatest difficulty was overcoming the sense of self as object (rather than subject), the Mother Nature whom the English Romantics addressed in a specifically male voice.[11] In the cultural tradition, woman is nature, as surely as Mother Nature is female.

The second, more moderate version of female immanence which informs Woolf's diary entry about female "castration" concerns itself with involuntary emotional rather than biological behavior. In place of the inevitability of death, we find the inevitability of woman saying whatever enters her head. In the hierarchy of functions which dates at least back to Plato, women are stalled at the emotional, the intuitive, the

10. Joseph Campbell, *The Hero with a Thousand Faces* (Princeton, 1949), 116; Neumann, *The Great Mother*, 89–210.

11. Margaret Homans, *Women Writers and Poetic Identity: Dorothy Wordsworth, Emily Brontë, Emily Dickinson* (Princeton, 1980).

instinctive, unable to attain the higher reaches of reason and intellect.[12] Although Woolf often employs this stereotype to the advantage of women, contrasting the richness of intuition to the aridity of logic, she suspects that female impulsiveness is inimical to the control required by art. In an admittedly coy and nervous letter to Clive Bell (the first she ever wrote to him), she comments on the letter-writer's formulaic insistence that his letter would have been better "had he had time or temper, and so on." She continues, "And I put 'he' because a woman, dear Creature, is always naked of artifice; and that is why she generally lives so well, and writes so badly" (*Letters* I, 289). The archness of the tone suggests either extreme self-consciousness or the deliberate parody of a male posture ("dear Creature" hardly seems an epithet which a woman would apply to her own sex with a straight face), but Woolf repeats the accusation more seriously in other places. She chides women for writing impulsively or from a strong sense of personal grievance and reminds them that, for her, art requires an impersonality, a detachment incompatible with immediately felt emotion.

The implications of this emotional impulsiveness are spelled out clearly in the aesthetic doctrine of significant form, first put forward by Roger Fry and expanded by Clive Bell—both, of course, close friends of Woolf. Fry begins his argument by distinguishing our emotional responses in life—running away from a charging bull, for example—from our more detached responses to art, claiming that instinctive emotion inhibits aesthetic performance and appreciation: "The more poignant emotions of actual life have, I think, a kind of numbing effect. . . the motives we actually experience are too close to us to enable us to feel them clearly. They are in a sense unintelligible."[13] Bell is even more explicit in judging the emotions aesthetically incompetent. They are, in fact, symptomatic of the failure to produce or understand art: "A painter too feeble to create forms that provoke more than a little aesthetic emotion [as distinct from life emotion] will try to eke that little out by suggesting the emotions of life. . . . If the artist's inclination to play upon the emotions of life is often the sign of a flickering

12. *The Republic of Plato*, trans. Alan Bloom (New York, 1968), books VI–VII. For a discussion of Plato's consistent association of women and the body, and his use of women to symbolize the inferior, appetitive part of the soul, see Elizabeth V. Spelman, "Woman as Body: Ancient and Contemporary Views," *Feminist Studies*, VIII (1982), 115–16.

13. Roger Fry, *Vision and Design* (New York, 1956), 26.

inspiration, in the spectator the tendency to seek, behind form, the emotions of life is a sign of defective sensibility always."[14]

This distinction between the emotions of life and those of art recapitulates Woolf's arch assessment that woman "lives so well and writes so badly." Both Fry and Bell emphasize the contrast between the demands of life and the demands of art—Bell, in fact, goes as far as to say that "art owe[s] nothing to life."[15] In divorcing life from art, the doctrine of significant form also tends to repudiate the body, returning us to the original form of the stereotyped association of woman as nature. Fry implies that emotion and bodily experience are both corruptions of the "higher" functions of intellect when he says, "All art depends upon cutting off the practical responses to a situation of ordinary life [here Fry uses the example of the charging bull, tying together instinctive emotion and physical response under the heading of the "practical"], thereby setting free a pure and as it were *disembodied* functioning of the spirit" (my italics).[16] In intent a refutation of representation as a primary criterion of art, significant form also asserts that the emotional and the physical are impediments to artistic achievement.

The intersection of this aesthetic theory and female stereotypes does not encourage the woman writer. Given Woolf's own anxieties about womanhood and writing, and given her close association with Fry and Bell, it is not surprising that she frequently criticizes women according to the standards of significant form. Using the image of the singing bird, she chastises women writers for the emotional impulsiveness which has kept the development of female art stalled at the stage of "sheer self-expression": "In the past, the virtue of women's writing often lay in its divine spontaneity, like that of the blackbird's song or the thrush. It was untaught; it was from the heart. But it was also, and much more often, chattering and garrulous—mere talk spilt over paper. . . . The novel [should] cease to be the dumping-ground for personal emotions" ("Women and Fiction," *CE* II, 148). In *Night and Day*, Woolf portrays such ineffectual spontaneity in the character of Mrs. Hilbery, who is entirely unable to complete the book she has started: "She had no difficulty in writing and covering a page every morning as instinctively as a thrush sings, but nevertheless, with all this to urge

14. Clive Bell, *Art* (London, 1913), 29.
15. *Ibid.*, 59.
16. Fry, *Vision and Design*, 242.

and inspire, and the most devout intention to accomplish the work, the book still remains unwritten. . . . Where did the difficulty lie? Not in their materials, alas, nor in their ambitions, but in something more profound, in her [Katharine's] own ineptitude, and, above all, in her mother's temperament" (p. 40).

Mrs. Hilbery's characterization, based on Woolf's Aunt Anne Ritchie (née Thackeray), depends heavily on stereotypes of femininity. She is "delightfully" scatter-brained and impractical, chattering along about the first—and fiftieth—thing which comes into her head, scribbling furiously when inspiration strikes, producing insights which are "lightning-like in their illumination" but lacking the power to arrange events coherently (N&D, 40–41). In short, her feminine mind is capable of fitful intuitions but does not possess the reason and application which produce a sustained achievement. When Woolf writes that Mrs. Hilbery "gave them [words] the substance of flesh" (p. 40), she may be toying with the old dichotomy between life and art, for Mrs. Hilbery's writing is as chaotic and confusing as life itself. The female "temperament" expressed in Mrs. Hilbery's giddiness and lack of discipline either disfigures art with personal grievance or prevents it from taking shape altogether. Great novelists, according to Woolf, have "mastered their perceptions, hardened them, and changed them into art" ("Life and the Novelist," CE II, 131), but impulsive women have not. Moreover, the image of the thrush not only suggests that woman's emotion is incompatible with art but also returns her to the realm of nature where biology first placed her.

Another mother, Mrs. Flanders in Jacob's Room, acts out this stereotype in an even more dramatic way as her feeling literally spills onto the page. Crying while she composes a letter, she makes a "horrid blot" which blurs and then erases what she has written (JR, 7). Florinda, another female letter-writer, also covers her pages with tears; this demonstration of "the fact that she cared" is the only value in her letters, which are otherwise "rambling" and "infantile" (p. 94). Like Mrs. Hilbery, these women write artlessly. No discipline shapes or structures their feelings, and their attempts at this formal, symbolic mode of communication devolve ultimately into bodily processes. Woolf pictures Florinda's efforts at writing as almost grotesque; again like Mrs. Hilbery, she is described as an animal, but she writes without any of the charms of the singing thrush: "The impediment between Florinda and her pen was something impassable. Fancy a butterfly, gnat, or other winged insect, attached to a twig which, clogged with mud, it rolls across the page" (p. 94). Florinda's writing is distinctly untranscendent. By casting the passage in metaphors of nature—the gnat, the twig, the mud—Woolf emphasizes the notion that women occupy the lowest rung in the ladder of abstraction, that they are more a part of the natural world than of rational society. Thus in Florinda's hands, the act of writing is reduced to a bizarre, mindless insect ritual.

Throughout *Jacob's Room*, Florinda is a particularly clear example of immanent womanhood. Her name ties her to the flowers of nature, and her face is described as "flowering out of her body" as if she were a plant (p. 80). She participates in many unsavory aspects of the stereotype as the passage above suggests: physically beautiful, she is also "horribly brainless" (p. 80). Nor is she the only woman in the novel touched by this characterization. Rose Shaw in her "dumb beauty" (p. 96) is representative of all women who are merely physical vessels for this more abstract quality: "Thus if you talk of a beautiful woman you mean only something flying fast which for a second uses the eyes, lips, or cheeks of Fanny Elmer, for example, to glow through" (p. 115). Even Clara Durrant, who evades the stigma of the body with her purity, is imprisoned in her emotions: she is "one . . . who loves, or refrains from loving" as if these are the only possible responses to Jacob (p. 71). With the assertion that "women are always, always, always talking about what one feels," the picture is complete (p. 144). These women are sunk in nature and emotion, able to embody and feel but not to think, like the archetypal earth mother Susan in *The Waves*, who can only understand the simplest encoding of basic emotion: "The only sayings I understand are cries of love, hate, rage and pain" (p. 266). They can barely understand the written products of what is ostensibly their culture. With the exception of Clara, with her "flawless mind" (*JR*, 123), they are all egregious philistines, Fanny slogging her bewildered way through *Tom Jones*; Sandra Wentworth Williams garnering a superficial show of intelligence from her book collection (used mainly to impress people and provide accessories for her outfits); Florinda "horribly bored" by Shelley (p. 79).

A second problematic version of the mother is the Angel in the House, the heroine of Coventry Patmore's poem of the same name, who came to symbolize the ideal of Victorian womanhood.[17] When we envisage this

17. Coventry Patmore, *Poems* (London, 1928).

ideal today, we generally think of the Angel in the House as pure, virtuous, and nearly incorporeal. She abhors sex, faints at the slightest provocation, has limbs instead of legs, glows rather than perspires. But in Patmore's poem, her most conspicuous attribute is not, finally, her spirituality, but her malleability, her passivity, her subordination:

> Her virtues please my virtuous mood
> But what at all times I admire
> Is not that she is wise or good
> But just the thing that I desire. (Canto VIII, I, ll. 5–8)

She is completely responsive to the wishes of her husband, the poet. Once taken in marriage, she embraces her destiny as a function of her husband's will, abandoning her own desires in the process:

> Her soul, which once with pleasure shook,
> Did any eyes her beauty own,
> Now wonders how they dare to look
> On what belongs to him alone;
> The indignity of taking gifts
> Exhilarates her loving breast;
> A rapture of submission lifts
> Her life into celestial rest. (Canto VIII, I, ll. 9–16)

Her supreme virtue lies in her ability to be so wholly possessed; asked why he mourns so for his wife when other women seem equally beautiful and good, an unnamed character sobs, "She was mine" (Canto VII, I, l. 12). Lest any reader mistakenly locate the source of the poet's satisfaction in his own uncritical adoration, Patmore informs us: "I praised her, but no praise could fill / The depth of her desire to please" (Canto VIII, I, l. 3).

Woolf acknowledges Patmore's poem as her source in "Professions for Women," naming the Angel in the House specifically as a major threat to female art. Woolf emphasizes in particular this final point, the insatiable desire to please. Precisely this trait, which Woolf defines as the willingness to lie, makes her the enemy of the female artist. Writing a review of a man's novel, Woolf is admonished: "'My dear, you are a young woman. You are writing about a book that has been written by a man. Be sympathetic; be tender; flatter; deceive; use all the arts and wiles of your sex. Never let anybody guess that you have a mind of your own'" (CE II, 285). For this advice, Woolf throttles her, saying, "Killing the Angel in the House was part of the occupation of a woman writer" (p. 286). Charged with murder, she would have pleaded self-defense.

The trait of flattery in particular recurs in the mother-figures of Woolf's most autobiographical novels, Helen Ambrose in *The Voyage Out* and Mrs. Ramsay in *To the Lighthouse,* apparently incongruous in a strong and honest personality. The trait seems merely grafted onto Helen, but in *To the Lighthouse* it reveals the central irony in Mrs. Ramsay's character: her admirable willingness to care for others enslaves her in the role of placater; superior to men in many ways, she is nevertheless dependent on them. If nurturance is her art, her selflessness forbids her to create anything that she can leave behind aside from mourners and marriages. As Woolf says of her own mother, "What reality can remain real of a person who died forty-four years ago at the age of forty-nine, without leaving a book, or a picture, or any piece of work—apart from the three children who now survive and the memory of her that remains in their minds?" (*MB*, 85).[18] It remains for the reserved, standoffish Lily Briscoe to create something permanent of Mrs. Ramsay's experience, just as Woolf preserves her own mother through memory and art.

Seen in light of the Angel in the House, the mother's possibilities as an artist are problematic. Even in the realm of private letters, for instance, Mrs. Flanders in *Jacob's Room* feels the need to censor her writing for fear of offending a man. She begins her letter rejecting Mr. Floyd's proposal of marriage by saying, "'I am much surprised' . . . but the letter which Mr. Floyd found on the table when he got up early the next morning did not begin 'I am much surprised'": Mrs. Flanders has evidently found a more acceptable response. The final version is "motherly, respectful, inconsequent, regretful" (*JR*, 21)—all terms which describe socially approved stances of women toward men, whereas surprise might imply either criticism or indifference—that Mr. Floyd had transgressed the bounds of the appropriate or that Mrs. Flanders had never really considered him an attractive prospect.

On a larger and more public scale but in a similar vein, Mrs. Hilbery's feminine subservience eliminates any possibility of her own achieve-

18. In fact, Julia did publish a book entitled *Notes from Sick Rooms* (1883), but she was no champion of female self-assertion; see Jane Marcus, "Liberty, Sorority, Misogyny," in Carolyn G. Heilbrun and Margaret R. Higonnet (eds.), *The Representation of Women in Fiction* (Baltimore, 1983), 69.

ment in *Night and Day.* She is engaged in an endless biography of her father Richard Allardyce, a famous poet, respectfully enshrining in prose "the irreproachable literary character that the world knows" (*N&D*, 102). "Living . . . in his shade" as she did in her youth (p. 304), she carries on his tradition by writing herself but not in any way which would compete with his accomplishments. Biography is a dependent form, coming into existence because of its subject's greatness; Mrs. Hilbery uses her talents to advance her father's reputation rather than her own. Even as she appears to be creating, she remains dependent and subservient. A helper and supporter rather than an achiever, she casts herself in the role of handmaiden to the true, male, artist. Mrs. Hilbery passes on this role to her daughter Katharine, insisting that she, too, devote her labor to the interminable biography. Katharine wishes to build a "new house"—which means, in her mind, to pursue a profession—but instead she follows her mother's footsteps. Asked what she does, Katharine identifies her amateur occupation with chagrin: "I only help my mother, I don't write myself" (p. 20; see also p. 59), suggesting both the marginal nature of her accomplishments and her general subordination to her mother's wishes. In this instance, embracing the mother's legacy yields a contingent status rather than the female integrity of *Three Guineas.* The weight of Katharine's inheritance acts on her like Rachel's regressive urges in *The Voyage Out,* as a tendency toward annihilation. Thinking of her ancestors, "she very nearly lost consciousness that she was a separate being, with a future of her own" (*N&D*, 114).

Woolf recognizes that such perfect self-effacement can be not only dishonest or constricting but fatal; her mother died, in essence, of the same disease, obsessed with a compulsion to serve others which one biographer has called "suicidal."[19] It is not preposterous to conjecture that Woolf's uncharacteristic violence in "Professions for Women" might be rage against her mother for self-destructing so early in life. In her memoirs, Woolf quietly remarks, "It might have been better, as it certainly would have tired her less, had she allowed some of those duties [doing charity work, responding to private appeals for help, teaching her children] to be discharged for her" (*MB*, 39). And, despite the comedy of Julia's regularly and transparently flattering either Sir Leslie or the male guest whom he offended—"Kitty wants to tell you how much

19. Love, *Sources of Madness and Art,* 68.

she loved your lecture" (p. 143)—Woolf may well have resented the neglect she suffered in favor of her father and brothers, particularly Adrian, whom, she remembers, Julia "cherished separately" and called "My Joy" (p. 83). According to Woolf, her mother believed that "all men required an infinity of care" (p. 143). Quentin Bell's re-creation of the family certainly bears out this judgment: "Julia lived chiefly for her husband . . . his health and happiness had to be secured; she had to listen to and to partake in his worries about money, about his work and his reputation, about the management of the household; he had to be fortified and protected from the world. He was, as he himself said, a skinless man, so nothing was to touch him save her soothing and healing hand."[20] The suggestion that Woolf unconsciously directs her anger against her mother in "Professions for Women" is unprovable, of course. Nevertheless, Woolf's insistence on the "fictitious nature" of the Angel in the House—she is dismissed as a "phantom"—seems surprising, even ingenuous, given the perfection to which Julia Stephen fit the stereotype.

The stereotype is not yet exhausted; it has even more dangerous implications for Woolf as a woman writer. Ostensibly, it is the opposite of Mother Earth; far from being mired in biology, the Angel in the House seems to have risen above it into a realm of pure spirituality. Patmore describes her as

> a woman deck'd
> With saintly honors, chaste and good,
> Whose thought celestial things affect
> Whose eyes express her heavenly mood!   (Canto IV, II, ll. 9–12)

She does not simply perform good deeds, she embodies virtue, with heaven in her eyes. As Mrs. Hilbery says of her female ancestors, "They *were*, and that's better than doing" (*N&D*, 116). Thus, the Angel in the House represents the idealization, not the opposite, of Mother Nature; they are linked by the quality of immanence. In both cases, the woman embodies rather than creates; she is not an agent but a vessel. While an object may simply "be," an artist must do.

Of course, the Angel in the House serves as an object for Victorian poets and painters as much as her counterpart, Mother Nature, does for the Romantics. Patmore's poem has comparatively little to do with the

20. Quentin Bell, *Virginia Woolf*, I, 38.

woman, who is as passive in the poem as the husband says she is in life, but a great deal to do with the poet's emotional progress through love. "The Angel in the House" is really another version of *The Prelude*, tracing the development of the poet's character, with the angel Honoria playing the part of Mount Snowden, although with more flattering attentiveness to the poet's expectations. Increasingly as her career progresses, Woolf discards the mother as artist and takes her up as object. *To the Lighthouse* is obviously the pivotal point in this line of development, as it includes both the mother and the artist who paints her, a figure who seems both sexless and aloof. This novel signals Woolf's recognition of the difficulties involved in being both womanly and an artist.

Despite this tactic, female immanence poses an almost insoluble problem for Woolf as a writer. If meaning is inscribed in woman, what need has she to speak? If she is Logos, what use has she for words? Clearly, the question is not merely theoretical but is embedded in Woolf's memories of her own mother as the source of all beauty and meaning in life. For Julia Stephen's beauty always resolved itself in silence. Woolf comes to the brink of saying that her mother was not merely beautiful but was Beauty: "But apart from her beauty, if the two can be separated, what was she herself like?" (*MB*, 82) and tells us that Julia "shed a certain silence round her by her very beauty" (p. 88). Again and again, Woolf describes her mother as "silent" (pp. 83, 87), until she says in frustration, "If I turn to imagine my mother, how difficult it is to single her out as she really was; to imagine what she was thinking; *to put a single sentence in her mouth!* I dream, I make up pictures on a summer's afternoon" (p. 87; my italics). Ardent and tenacious, Woolf's attempts to create the mother in her own image, as an artist, do not always succeed. Her mother's enigmatic silence and inaccessibility foil the writer's attempts to embrace the maternal legacy. Deified as the Madonna in Burne-Jones's *Annunciation*, Julia is both an unlikely artist and a remote ancestress, indifferent to her daughter-inheritor.

In the idealized mother-daughter myth of Demeter and Kore, Mother and Maid are seen as complementary rather than conflicting aspects of womanhood.[21] In the ideal mother-daughter relationship of object-relations theory, the daughter looks to her mother for confirmation of

21. Neumann, *The Great Mother*, 307; Robert Graves, *The Greek Myths* (2 vols.; 1955; rpr. New York, 1980), I, 92; Harrison, *Mythology*, 83.

her own gestures and expressions, drawing on the model of her mother for her own identity. But in much of Woolf's writing, cultural stereotypes, prevailing theories of art, and her actual daughterhood complicate the task of "thinking back through our mothers." After Woolf's radical attempt to define the hostess as artist in Mrs. Dalloway, frustration and divergence increasingly define the mother-daughter relationship. The conflicts between life and art, and between self-effacement and self-expression, drive a wedge between two women whom Woolf would in many ways prefer to unite. In To the Lighthouse and Between the Acts, one of the central questions of inheritance becomes how to manage estrangement. Like the mirror and portrait in The Years, symbol-making frames capture the mother-figures in these novels: Mrs. Ramsay the Madonna, whose status as cultural icon is confirmed as she stands outlined by the gilt frame of a painting (TTL, 48), and the lady in yellow, unofficial ancestress of the Olivers, who appears only in a portrait. Thus fixed, both her power and her distance are increased. Yet Woolf never discards the mother as a potent influence, desirable even when she is not attainable, compelling even when she is not wholly desirable. Although Woolf ultimately fails to play Kore to Julia Stephen's Demeter, her mother's "burning torch" (MB, 40) illuminates conflicts and desires at the heart of her identity as woman and writer.

II

THE WOMAN
ARTIST

4

Mrs. Dalloway

MRS. DALLOWAY is at once the most conventional and the most radical of Woolf's formulations of femininity: conventional, because it assumes many cultural stereotypes about women, particularly the problematic nature of female biology; radical, because it completely reinterprets the lightly regarded sphere of women's social life as the realm of legitimate art. Clarissa Dalloway brings together disparate strands of life and fashions them into the harmonious whole of the party. In *Mrs. Dalloway,* the hostess is an artist, just as the artist is a kind of hostess in "Mr. Bennett and Mrs. Brown," written at the same time. In that essay, Woolf argues that "in life and in literature it is necessary to have some means of bridging the gulf between the hostess and her unknown guest on the one hand, the writer and his unknown reader on the other" (*CE* I, 330); Woolf notes the importance of a "common meeting-place" of convention, either social or literary, in facilitating "the difficult business of intimacy" for hostess and artist (p. 331). Stressing unity and human relationships as essential to art, she links the party and the novel as comparable endeavors, exalting the hostess' role as a profoundly creative one.

Moreover, although she is often criticized for her shallowness and prudery—even by Woolf, who feared she might be too "tinselly" to appeal to readers (*Diary* II, 272)—Clarissa is nevertheless an authentically female heroine.[1] As hostess, she is a kind of social mother, nur-

---

1. For such criticism, see Frank Baldanza, "Clarissa Dalloway's Party Consciousness," *Modern Fiction Studies,* II (1956), 27; Jeremy Hawthorne, *Virginia Woolf's Mrs. Dalloway: A Study in Alienation* (Sussex, 1975), 92; Jean M. Wyatt, "Mrs. Dalloway: Literary Allusion as Structural Metaphor," *Publications of the Modern Language Association,*

turing and protecting her guests; her party-giving impulse emanates from a consciousness which is distinctly feminine in its capacity for empathy, its sense of communion with other people and the outside world, and its origin in relationships with other women. Embodied in Clarissa's diffuse consciousness and in her self-conscious identity as a hostess is a myth of femininity possessing its own coherence and integrity. Yet the emphasis of *Mrs. Dalloway* falls on symbolic versions of motherhood and the mother-daughter relationship, not the thing itself. Alongside the celebration of the feminine stands an intense anxiety about motherhood and a need to reconstitute femininity to exclude its dangerous emotional and biological contingencies. Clarissa's relationship to her mother is largely implicit, her relationship to her daughter vexing, her relationship to female sexuality an outright problem. All of these actual relationships are translated into more distant or disembodied forms; ironically, the myth of femininity is secured only by transforming, evading, or repudiating several central experiences of womanhood. T S

Clarissa's identity as a hostess originates in her daughterhood, for she sees herself as having inherited from her parents the responsibility to use life creatively: "For she was a child, throwing bread to the ducks, between her parents, and at the same time a grown woman coming to her parents who stood by the lake, holding her life in her arms which, as she neared them, grew larger and larger in her arms, until it became a whole life, a complete life, which she put down by them and said, 'This is what I have made of it! This!'" (pp. 63–64). When she gives her party, Clarissa remembers her inherited responsibility—"one's parents giving it into one's hands, this life"—with special vividness (p. 281). The party itself is Clarissa's gesture of giving, a way of doing justice to "this thing she called life" (p. 184) by bringing people together: "And it was an offering; to combine, to create, but to whom? An offering for the sake of offering, perhaps. Anyhow, it was her gift" (p. 185). Clarissa's question "to whom?" has two answers: her party is an offering both to her guests and to her parents, her proof that she has used their gift of life wisely. And, although Clarissa does not say so, it seems clear from the feminine nature of her accomplishment that hers is a female inheritance: her knack for creating social harmony is a "woman's gift"

LXXXVIII (1973), 445; Kenneth J. Ames, "Elements of Mock-Heroic in Virginia Woolf's *Mrs. Dalloway*," *Modern Fiction Studies*, XVII (1972), 368.

(p. 115), an exclusively feminine attribute. Neither Peter nor Richard understands her party-giving, as if it were entirely beyond the grasp of men.[2]

Indeed, Woolf carefully separates Clarissa's efforts from what she defines as masculine culture, emphasizing the femininity of the hostess role and valuing it precisely because it departs from masculine models. Clarissa's disengagement from public, political culture frees her from complicity in its imperialistic and death-dealing ways. As Woolf observes in *Three Guineas*, "Those also serve who remain outside" (p. 119), preserving the integrity of their life-affirming femininity without compromise. Woolf's bifurcation of the world of Mrs. *Dalloway* into masculine and feminine is clear and well documented; of all Woolf's novels, this one bears out most clearly Elaine Showalter's charge that Woolf projects all hostility and evil onto men while idealizing women.[3] Masculinity is associated with authority, abstraction, and hierarchical forms of organization; with the numbing of emotion; and with the destruction of individuality and spontaneity. Femininity, its opposite, is associated with accommodation, empathy, intuition, feeling, individuality, and spontaneity.[4] Masculine destructiveness has its domestic and international versions: the coercive authority of Bradshaw's Proportion and Conversion is simply another expression of the actual military exploits of the empire; the way in which the two conspire so effectively in Septimus' madness and death makes their connection clear.[5] (While most women in *Mrs. Dalloway* are feminine and most men masculine, these are gender categories, not sexual ones; that is, they are social constructs rather than biological properties. Peter Walsh, "not altogether masculine," enjoys a feminine quickness of feeling which endears him to Clarissa, while Miss Kilman, as masculine as her name suggests, is rigid and antagonistic.)

2. See also Suzette Henke, "*Mrs. Dalloway*: The Communion of Saints," in Marcus (ed.), *New Feminist Essays*, 127.

3. Elaine Showalter, *A Literature of Their Own: British Women Novelists from Brontë to Lessing* (Princeton, 1977), 264.

4. Lee R. Edwards, "War and Roses: The Politics of Mrs. *Dalloway*," in Arlyn Diamond and Lee R. Edwards (eds.), *The Authority of Experience* (Amherst, 1977), 162, 166; Alex Zwerdling, "*Mrs. Dalloway* and the Social System," *Publications of the Modern Language Association*, XCII (1977), 72; Shalom Rachman, "Clarissa's Attic: Virginia Woolf's Mrs. *Dalloway* Reconsidered," *Twentieth Century Literature*, XVIII (1972), 6; Barbara Hill Rigney, *Madness and Sexual Politics in the Feminist Novel* (Madison, 1978), 46.

5. Naremore, *World Without a Self*, 108; Zwerdling, "*Mrs. Dalloway*," 75.

Underlying these external manifestations is a masculine state of consciousness, a general conception of the relationship between Self and Other. Its interpersonal imperialism dehumanizes and objectifies the Other to block out any disturbing sympathy or sense of likeness which might impede conquest. Thus Bradshaw constructs a binary, hierarchical structure—"doctor" and "patient" modulate easily into "master" (p. 154) and "victim" (p. 155)—which allows no freedom, no integrity, no equality to the Other. This distribution of power permits him two related stances: an absolute separation from the inferior Other-object and a total consuming of it: conversion aims "to stamp indelibly on the sanctuaries of others the image of herself. Naked, defenceless, the exhausted, the friendless received the impress of Sir William's will. He swooped; he devoured" (p. 154). Miss Kilman, pointedly denied femininity, is Bradshaw's counterpart. Her appetite is insatiable, her obsession with food simply the body acting out the soul, which wishes to "grasp . . . clasp . . . [and] make her [Elizabeth] hers absolutely and forever" (p. 200). Taking Elizabeth to Communion (p. 16) embodies all the tendencies of imperialism: the capital letter of dogma, the objectification of a human being (certainly an atheist's view of transubstantiation), and the literal consumption of the Other-object.

Clarissa's lower-case communion, on the other hand, her sense of being close to and even part of other people and the environment, offers an alternative set of values and relationships. Clarissa's stance revises the extreme tendencies of imperialism: instead of the opposite poles of separating and devouring, Clarissa permits difference and closeness. She wants "only that people be themselves," yet she frequently feels a part of those selves. She experiences a telepathic relationship with her husband (p. 179) and especially with Peter as the two move "in and out of each other's minds without any effort" (p. 94; see also p. 90). Even strangers are part of her consciousness: "Odd affinities she had with people she had never spoken to" (p. 231); she feels "part of people she never met" (p. 14). In Clarissa, empathy broadens into diffusion; her elastic consciousness unifies separate egos and experiences by filling the isolating space between them. Clarissa possesses what object-relations theory would call the diffuse ego boundaries of a specifically feminine consciousness formed by the relationship of mother and daughter.

Woolf identifies Clarissa's special talent in words which recapitulate her own mother's magic: "that woman's gift of making a world of her own

wherever she happened to be" (p. 115). Woolf records a similar observation in her diary at the time of *Mrs. Dalloway's* publication: "A woman
is much more warmly sympathetic. She carries her atmosphere with
her" (*Diary* III, 38). These quotations suggest something beyond setting a pleasant emotional tone; they describe the creation of an almost
physical world made coherent and whole by the woman's presence.
Thus Clarissa "felt herself everywhere," not simply establishing an
atmosphere but almost literally becoming one. Her intangible self
"spreads wide" (*MD*, 232), "being laid out like a mist between the
people she knew best" (p. 12). In more tangible, everyday interactions,
this sense of connection expresses itself as "that network of visiting,
leaving cards, being kind to people . . . that women of her sort keep
up" (p. 117).

In Woolf's imagination, parties are a quintessential expression of this
"woman's gift," as Clarissa's gatherings can accommodate not only im-
promptu visits from old friends such as Peter and Sally Seton but other
"odd, unexpected people . . . an artist sometimes; sometimes a writer,
queer fish in that atmosphere" (p. 115). In her diary, Woolf calls this
harmony "the party consciousness": "people secrete an envelope which
connects them and protects them from others" (*Diary* III, 12–13). In
Mrs. Dalloway, this envelope appears as Clarissa's "panoply" (p. 17), the
unusual word which Woolf uses, along with "atmosphere," to describe
her mother's protective aura in "A Sketch of the Past" (*MB*, p. 83). Feminine atmosphere, envelope, and panoply subvert the masculine grammar
of subject and object, unifying and protecting both in a single field.[6]

This sense of unity is also embodied in what Clarissa calls "the moment." Clarissa first describes "the moment" while walking down a London street: "In the swing, tramp, and trudge; in the bellow and the
uproar; the carriages, motor cars, omnibuses, vans, sandwich men shuffling and swinging; brass bands; barrel organs; in the triumph and the
jungle and the strange high singing of some aeroplane overhead was
what she loved; life; London; this moment of June" (*MD*, p. 5). "Life;
London; this moment of June," a phrase whose components are strung

6. French feminist critics have formulated the same kind of subject-object relationship as essentially feminine; see Luce Irigaray, "Ce sexe qui n'en est pas un," trans.
Claudia Reeder, in Isabelle de Courtivron and Elaine Marks (eds.), *New French Feminisms:
An Anthology* (Amherst, 1980), 104–105; Hélène Cixous, "Poetry is/and (the) political," Thirty Years After: Feminism Since *The Second Sex* (conference), New York University, October, 1977.

together without grammatical subordination, suggests not a hierarchy but the elasticity of the moment, capable of enveloping carriages, sandwich men, and barrel organs—all the diverse vitality of the London street.

The moment breaks down the rigid, uniform compartments of time, the official, standardized hours and minutes "ratified by Greenwich" (p. 155); "divid[ed] and subdivid[ed] by the clocks in Harley Street" (where Bradshaw's office is, not coincidentally, located; p. 155); pronounced "irrevocably" by the temporal patriarch Big Ben. The feminine clock, St. Margaret's, custodian of "the moment," strikes with "the voice of the hostess" and "wants to confide itself, to disperse itself . . . like Clarissa" (p. 74). Always striking after Big Ben, St. Margaret's is evidently at leisure to include whatever it wishes in its intervals of time: "It came shuffling in with its lap full of odds and ends, which it dumped down as if Big Ben were all very well with his majesty laying down the law, so solemn, so just, but she must remember all sorts of little things besides—Mrs. Marsham, Ellie Henderson, glasses for ices—all sorts of little things came flooding and lapping and dancing in on the wake of that solemn stroke which lay flat like a bar of gold across the sea. Mrs. Marsham, Ellie Henderson, glasses for ices. She must telephone now at once" (pp. 193–94). Opposed to Big Ben, timekeeper for masculine culture who speaks for "majesty" and "law," St. Margaret's is in league with Clarissa, encouraging the hostess' duties with its own hostess-like accommodation.

With a clock as its spokeswoman, "the moment" does not transcend time but revises it, mocking mechanical precision with a *rubato*. Woolf's description in her diary shows the moment swelling out of time and daily experience, then subsiding back into them: "Life—say 4 days out of 7—becomes automatic; but on the 5th day a bead of sensation (between husband and wife) forms, wh. is all the fuller and more sensitive because of the automatic customary unconscious days on either side. This is to say the year is marked by moments of great intensity. Hardy's 'moment of vision'" (*Diary* III, 105). The moment is not, strictly speaking, an epiphany, a sudden illumination which takes one out of time. It is, literally, a "movement in time," stretching the boundaries of an hour to achieve more commodious proportions, admitting more time, more life. In its female time, St. Margaret's includes its "odds and ends," just as Clarissa's parties and her consciousness include past and present, friends, strangers, and odd fish.

Yet, in an apparent paradox, Clarissa's feminine gifts are in some ways at odds with her identity as a mother. Certainly, Clarissa's more metaphorical femininity, her "woman's gift" and diffuse consciousness, overshadows her actual motherhood. Indeed, her relationship with Elizabeth threatens rather than reinforces her female consciousness. "My Elizabeth," she calls her daughter (p. 71), displaying a proprietary tendency at odds with her usual accommodating posture. Actual mother-hood tempts Clarissa into an unfeminine possessiveness as she competes with Miss Kilman for Elizabeth's affections, thinking, "This woman had taken her daughter from her" (p. 190). But in a movement central to *Mrs. Dalloway*, the actual is translated into the symbolic: Clarissa abandons her emotional preoccupation with her daughter for a symbolic relationship with the old woman next door, to whom she turns her attention when Elizabeth departs for the Army and Navy Stores with Miss Kilman. Going about her business "quite unconscious of being watched," the old woman in her detachment reminds Clarissa of "the privacy of the soul" (p. 192), a corrective not only to Miss Kilman's devouring intimacy but to Clarissa's own. The old woman walks to her upstairs bedroom and sits at her dressing table (pp. 190–93) just as Clarissa withdrew to her attic room and sat at her dressing table earlier in the day, seeking a time of peace and solitude. The woman acts as a kind of mirror-model, showing Clarissa the image of "the privacy of the soul" so that Clarissa may re-form her identity after the intrusion of dangerously intense emotions. Under the woman's influence, Clarissa calls Miss Kilman's attachment to Elizabeth a "degrading passion"—implying that she will not degrade herself by matching it. Thus, this more distant and less obsessive female bond replaces the mother-daughter relationship. It forms and consolidates female identity, offering the sense of likeness and empathy which is part of femininity without the dangerous emotionality of motherhood itself.

Indeed, Woolf sets out consciously to save Clarissa's femininity from actual womanhood, particularly the biological functions which express her tie with nature and comprise the stereotype of the immanent female. Woolf's attempt to convert biology, particularly sexuality and motherhood, into symbolic values is central to the myth of femininity, for through it the vulnerable becomes inviolate. "The problem is insoluble, the body is harnessed to the brain," says the narrator of *Jacob's Room* (p. 81), but Woolf sets out to solve it here. "Mrs. Dalloway in Bond Street," the short story which grew into *Mrs. Dalloway*, reveals the degree to which the problem of the body preoccupied Woolf and the extent to which she imagines women as particularly vulnerable to the aging and death which haunt nearly every page of the novel.[7] In "Mrs. Dalloway in Bond Street," the health problems of both Clarissa and Hugh Whitbread's wife, named Millie here, are clearly menopausal. Hugh reports delicately that Millie is "out of sorts . . . That sort of thing" and Clarissa reflects "Of course . . . Millie is about my age—fifty—fifty-two. So it is probably *that*" (*HH*, 20; Woolf's italics). Thinking of the effects of menopause, Clarissa wonders, "How then could women sit in Parliament? How could they do things with men?" (p. 20), voicing the assumption of *Jacob's Room* that female biology estranges women from public culture. Woman's body runs as an undercurrent throughout the story: Clarissa regrets taking so long with a saleswoman on "perhaps the one day in the month . . . when it's agony to stand" (*HH*, 26), alluding to menstruation. Both menopause and menstruation are liabilities, illnesses, as female biology intensifies the weakness, the vulnerability, of the body. The maternal legacy is one of decay and death. Although men die, too, the organic cycle is not inscribed in the male body as it is in the female.

In *Mrs. Dalloway*, however, all this has changed. Clarissa is the victim not of menopause but of heart disease, an illness whose chief significance is metaphorical: the pain at having refused Peter ("an arrow sticking in her heart," p. 10), the moment of dread in the midst of her party ("these triumphs . . . had a hollowness; at arm's length they were, not in the heart," p. 265), and her essential coldness. Woolf clearly intends to distinguish Clarissa from other, earthier women. At Bourton, Sally Seton wanders through the vegetable garden, a place consciously dedicated to organic growth (pp. 110, 114, 285); on one of these occasions, she and Peter discuss his love for Clarissa while Clarissa herself, retreating from sexuality, lies in bed with a headache (p. 110). As an adult, with her insistent motherhood ("I have five enormous boys," pp. 261, 284), Sally grows beds of flowers. Clarissa, "unmaternal as she was," cultivates instead the "enchanted garden" of her party, using "a few fairy lamps" to cast a spell over her backyard (p. 291). Sally, gardener and mother, participates in the processes of organic growth; Clarissa,

7. For this discussion, I am greatly indebted to Judith P. Saunders, "Mortal Stain: Literary Allusion and Female Sexuality in 'Mrs. Dalloway in Bond Street,'" *Studies in Short Fiction*, XV (1978), 139–44.

with "a virginity preserved through childhood" (p. 46), is a "magician" (p. 291) working the miraculous transformations of art. Her dress shines only in artificial light (p. 55).

The death of Clarissa's sister continues this preoccupation with biological vulnerability. The incident is mentioned only in passing, but it is evidently the source of Clarissa's defiant fatalism, "her notion being that the Gods, who never lost a chance of hurting, thwarting and spoiling human lives were seriously put out if, all the same, you behaved like a lady. That phase came directly after Sylvia's death—that horrible affair. To see your own sister killed by a falling tree" (p. 117).[8] Sylvia is not simply the victim of vegetative nature, the realm of trees and grass which is different from the realm of human beings. Her name, which means "forest," suggests that she is symbolically the victim of her own immanence, doomed to die because she is herself a part of nature. With the names "Sylvia" and "Clarissa," Woolf continues to exploit the contrast of names she established in *Jacob's Room*, where "Florinda" and "Clara" suggested organic nature and inorganic light (these contrasting versions of womanhood evolve into the roles of artist and mother in her next novel, *To the Lighthouse*). Clarissa stands at a distance from biology as if to diminish the body's vulnerability.

As an arena for both male imperialism and female immanence, sexuality represents the most obvious and dramatic version of this vulnerability. Clarissa's frigidity is a response to that threat and not simply a character flaw. Clarissa denies her actual sexuality only to participate in it imaginatively; having "failed" her husband with her coldness (p. 46), she nevertheless experiences an orgasm of consciousness alone in her bedroom:

> It was a sudden revelation, a tinge like a blush which one tried to check and then, as it spread, one yielded to its expansion, and rushed to the farthest verge and there quivered and felt the world come closer, swollen with some astonishing significance, some pressure of rapture, which split its thin skin and gushed and poured with an extraordinary alleviation over the cracks and sores! Then, for that moment, she had seen an illumination; a match burning in a crocus; an inner meaning almost expressed.

8. Woolf may have adapted this incident from D. H. Lawrence's novella *The Fox*, which she was reading in 1923 or 1924, perhaps drawing on the combination of lesbian love and the dangers of sexuality; see Brenda R. Silver (ed.), *Virginia Woolf's Reading Notebooks* (Princeton, 1983), 131.

But the close withdrew; the hard softened. It was over—the moment. (p. 47)

This transformation, from the "contraction" of sexual coldness (p. 46) to the "expansion" of illumination, assures the integrity of femininity in two ways. First, it excludes the male Other and admits the female, for this rapture grows from "falling in love with women" (p. 48) and specifically Clarissa's remembered love for Sally Seton. While Clarissa imagines feeling passion "like" a man's, "the charm of women," not the masculine role, draws her into these moments (p. 46). Second, it converts sexuality into another form of energy: physical prudery becomes imaginative potency. Sexual metaphors shape and drive this moment of illumination as consciousness appropriates all the vitality of corporeal life. Sexuality and its implied procreative function give way to self-contained mental fertility, akin to what Woolf conceives as the parthenogenesis of art: "for children are not enough after all; one wants something to be made out of one's self alone" (Diary III, 20). In Clarissa's mind, the "horrible passion" of sexual love is linked to the "degrading passion" of maternal possessiveness (MD, 192); both must be translated into symbolic forms to preserve the myth of femininity.

In Mrs. Dalloway, the female body does have a value, but it is derived from, not part of, organic reality. Along with the party, it provides the chief occasion for art. Peter sees "design, art, everywhere" in women's fashions and make-up (p. 108). Clarissa's perfect guest is Nancy Blow, beautified "with an apricot bloom of powder and paint, . . . dressed at enormous expense by the greatest artists in Paris, . . . looking as if her body had merely put forth, of its own accord, a green frill" (pp. 269–70; likewise, in The Waves, Jenny, another social artificer whose "imagination is the body's," blossoms forth when she attracts a flattering gaze: "My body instantly of its own accord puts forth a frill," pp. 264, 218). In Mrs. Dalloway, under the party's magical auspices, the processes of the body produce not death and decay but an imperishable artificial leaf, the green frill. In the apricot bloom of powder and paint, nature, stripped of its fatal power, becomes a metaphor for the artifice of feminine beauty.

Presiding over the party is Clarissa's hostess self, the public embodiment of the myth of femininity. It is the product of Clarissa's experiences and values: the "atmosphere" of consciousness, the empathic Self-Other relationships, the experience of "the moment," and the principle of transformation. Three incidents structure this social identity: Sally Seton's kiss, Clarissa's construction of her "dartlike" self before the mirror, and her withdrawal from the party to contemplate the old woman next door. Each scene marks a coming into selfhood; each involves some loose equivalent of self-contemplation, calling attention to the self-conscious nature of this identity, to its artifice. These scenes chart the development, the testing, and the affirmation of the hostess. They are versions of the mother-daughter paradigm, structured by motifs of reflexiveness and mutuality; in a sense, one might say, they are standing in for the actual relationship, carrying on its central values without invoking any of its dangers, part of the displacements from the actual to the symbolic which govern much of *Mrs. Dalloway*.

Clarissa's youthful infatuation with Sally Seton is the raw material on which the two later moments are built. Like the old woman next door who restores Clarissa's detachment, Sally is an avatar of the mother, helping to create Clarissa's self; she is a central, magical female presence, "all light, glowing, like some bird or air ball that has flown in" (p. 51); of Bourton itself and her other guests, Clarissa thinks, "All this was only a background for Sally. . . . The others disappeared; there she was alone with Sally" (p. 52). Sally provides the perfect Other for Clarissa's feminine consciousness: their relationship is based on their likeness, with "a quality which could only exist between women" (p. 50) drawing them "in league together" (p. 49) in their attic retreat. Yet Sally is a foil as well, so different in beauty and temperament that Clarissa "could not take her eyes off" her (p. 48). Their difference, then, is a complementarity which brings them together, encircled by shared femininity.

Sally's kiss crystallizes their relationship; face to face, each one's femininity is reflected in the other (in contrast, coming face to face with Peter immediately after the kiss is like "running . . . against a granite wall," a feeling of obdurate difference; p. 53). The two share what Ellen Hawkes calls "the gift of self in friendships between two women."[9] Clarissa's "cross[ing] the hall . . . to meet Sally" (p. 51) prefigures this transaction: an active moving outward of consciousness, with the double suggestion of stepping beyond a boundary and entering into an exchange with the self-reflecting Other who lies on the other side.

9. Ellen Hawkes, "Woolf's 'Magical Garden of Women,'" in Marcus (ed.), *New Feminist Essays*, 54–55.

Clarissa crosses another boundary as well: she has been deflowered, as Sally's plucking of a flower the instant before makes clear, and initiated into a new knowledge, although it is spiritual rather than sexual, in keeping with the myth of femininity.[10] Clarissa feels she has received from the moment a "radiance," a "revelation," or a "diamond" (p. 53). The gem aptly represents the qualities of feminine interaction and the new identity it engenders: the reflexive likeness of the two women is figured in the diamond's facets, which reflect light among themselves to create its radiance.

This diamond is, to Clarissa, "a present, wrapped up" (p. 52)—a version of the gift of life which she received from her parents (and particularly her mother) off-stage, as it were. In this way, Sally's kiss contributes directly to the "offering" of the party. Perhaps it also transmits Sally's own special "gift" (p. 49), her talent for arranging flowers—the party preparation which Clarissa takes on as the novel opens when she decides to buy the flowers herself (p. 3). More generally, of course, her relationship with Sally gives Clarissa the diamond-present of feminine consciousness which is at the core of Clarissa's hostess-identity, the "woman's gift" for empathy which makes the party possible. The double meaning of the word "gift" expresses the nature of this consciousness: it is both a personal attribute, the talent of an individual, and a way of connecting to another person, a gesture of communion.

On the afternoon of her party, Clarissa remembers the infatuation with Sally as she sits before her mirror, trying half-heartedly to conjure up the emotions of the past by sympathetic magic: retreating to the attic, site of the earlier intimacy; brushing her hair as she did before meeting Sally at dinner. But Clarissa does not recreate the moment; instead, she transforms the motifs of purity, crossing, reflection, revelation, and the symbol of the diamond into a paradigm of self-creation, a ritual for focusing her identity as hostess. DiBattista argues convincingly that Clarissa's air of virginity, repeatedly stressed in this scene, must be judged in two ways: although a sexual failure seen in relation to the bed, it represents "an exclusively female symbol of freedom and integrity . . . [a] spiritual inviolability" in relation to the mirror.[11] The integrity of the kiss between women is maintained here as Clarissa

10. Wyatt, "Mrs. Dalloway," 441.

11. Maria DiBattista, Virginia Woolf's Major Novels: The Fables of Anon (New Haven, 1980), 38; Henke, "Mrs. Dalloway," in Marcus (ed.), New Feminist Essays, 131; Elizabeth Abel, "Narrative Structure(s) and Female Development: The Case of Mrs. Dalloway," in

faces her feminine reflection in the mirror. Patterned on her relationship with Sally, this moment involves "crossing" to meet a reflection; it
yields a sense of revelation, of "seeing . . . afresh" (p. 54); of "radiance"
(p. 55); and of a new self which is like a "diamond" (p. 55).

The original encounter, already desexualized by its exclusive femininity, moves one step further from the organic here. Clarissa's great
achievement, as she sits before the mirror surveying the cosmetic
bottles which assist the artifice of feminine beauty, is to transform herself from a natural thing into an artifact, a kind of art:

> Laying her brooch upon the table, she had a sudden spasm, as if, while
> she mused, the icy claws had the chance to fix in her. She was not old
> yet. She had just broken into her fifty-second year. Months and months
> of it were still untouched. June, July, August! Each still remained almost
> whole, and, as if to catch the falling drop, Clarissa (crossing to the
> dressing-table) plunged into the very heart of the moment, transfixed it,
> there—the moment of this June morning, on which was the pressure of
> all other mornings, seeing the glass, the dressing-table, and all the
> bottles afresh, collecting the whole of her at one point (as she looked
> into the glass), seeing the delicate pink face of the woman who was that
> very night to give a party; of Clarissa Dalloway; of herself. (p. 54)

A chain of metaphors marks Clarissa's progress: the "icy claws" of death,
the inevitable conclusion of the natural cycle, thaw into a "drop," losing
their rigidity. They are reconstructed as the "glass," the man- (or
woman-) made mirror which focuses, confirms, and frames the self like
a picture, casting over it the "trance of immortality," as Woolf says in a
short story, "The Lady in the Looking-Glass." In that story, Isabelle,
the protagonist, is finally "fixed" by the mirror into a kind of death-
mask, this being the cost of the order which the mirror imposes on its
living subject. *Mrs. Dalloway* emphasizes much more the positive, liber-
ating effects of the mirror. Through it, Clarissa "transfixes" nature and
time, the icy claws which would "fix in her" and fix her into mortality;
she takes them across the boundary which confines them to their deterministic function. The "icy claws" become the mirror's artifice; "June,
July, August," the inexorable march of months leading toward death,
becomes "the moment."

The word "there" also has a double image. It suggests on one hand

---

Elizabeth Abel, Marianne Hirsch, and Elizabeth Langland (eds.), *The Voyage In: Fictions
of Female Development* (Hanover, N.H., 1983), 161–85.

Clarissa's identity as object, the perfectly composed image in the glass—"there" as "*là.*" But it is also an utterance by Clarissa as subject, an exclamation of accomplishment, a seal of creativity—"there" as "*voilà.*" Clarissa both creates and is herself as she both gives her parties and fills them with her feminine atmosphere, connecting mist, and protecting panoply. The traditional distinction between subject and object does an injustice to the amplitude of Clarissa's consciousness. Sitting before the mirror—as subject and object, original and image, artist and art—she merely intensifies the mutuality and reflexiveness of her relationship with the world. This moment is the purest, most absolute version of feminine consciousness.

Despite Clarissa's careful preparations, the party does not, at first, fulfill its promise. Symbol of feminine culture, it is, paradoxically, the crisis through which all the latent fears of inefficacy and death assert themselves, testing the myth of the feminine. Clarissa's party-self does not take hold; her guests may "go much deeper," but she cannot "for now; not yet, anyhow" (p. 260). Instead, time's determinism clouds the party with the sense that life is running out, that one might not be able to arrest the process of decay. Dressed in her "silver-green mermaid's dress," a costume of virginity and, by implication, immortality (a mermaid is not a woman below the waist), Clarissa nevertheless feels that "age had brushed her; even as a mermaid might behold in her glass the setting sun on some very clear evenings over the waves" (p. 264).[12] The inviolability of feminine reflexiveness has apparently failed; the glass reflects not purity and integrity but mortality.

Mrs. Hilbery, one of the guests, reminds Clarissa of her literal female inheritance: "She [Clarissa] looked tonight, she said, so like her mother as she first saw her walking in a garden." Mother and garden, symbols of immanence, have lodged in Clarissa's artifice; the reference to Clarissa's mother, long since dead, reinforces what Mrs. Hilbery thinks a moment before: "how it is certain we must die" (p. 267). "That wandering will-o'the wisp" Mrs. Hilbery, the "magician" of *Night and Day*, seems to have stepped into *Mrs. Dalloway* with her characterization intact (p. 267). Described also as a "phosphorescence" and thus linked to Clarissa through the idea of light, she acts as a kind of tutelary spirit, signaling the source of Clarissa's malaise. Later, after Clar-

12. Rachel Vinrace also identifies herself as a mermaid to evade sexuality in *The Voyage Out*, 298.

issa renews herself by watching the woman next door, Mrs. Hilbery assures her that the spell of artifice has been restored by praising the "enchanted garden" fashioned from the organic one (p. 291). If Clarissa's actual mother leaves a legacy of death, Mrs. Hilbery is a symbolic mother passing on the myth of femininity, as one magician to another.

It is Septimus, Clarissa's suicidal double, who acts out the latent fear which weighs down Clarissa's party: "in the middle of my party, here's death," Clarissa thinks (p. 279). When Clarissa confronts Septimus' fate, she faces the paradox of mortality—the inevitability of death insists that she do life justice, that she achieve "the moment" and fill it with her atmosphere. Faced with the necessity of doing something which is commensurate with life itself, Clarissa finds her efforts inadequate; only Septimus' suicide seems an act of absolute integrity: "Somehow it was her disaster—her disgrace. It was her punishment to see sink and disappear here a man, there a woman, in this profound darkness, and she forced to stand here in her evening dress. She had schemed, she had pilfered. She was never wholly admirable" (p. 282). Once her consolation, parties are now her "punishment": sorry compromises, self-deluding excuses for a tepid acceptance of living. Septimus' death momentarily strips images, reflections, and artifice of their power; his act is the absolute which renders all approximations and equivalences meaningless. Clarissa's parties, and the decorative, accommodating femininity which they express, seem impotent.

Yet the myth rescues and restores her when she contemplates the old woman next door. The woman, we recall, has helped Clarissa in another crisis, restoring her equilibrium after Elizabeth leaves for the Army and Navy Stores with Miss Kilman. In that earlier scene, the purely symbolic pairing of Clarissa and her neighbor preserves that "disinterested" quality between women which Clarissa prizes so highly but which actual motherhood undermines (p. 50). Thus, she is precisely the person to render death symbolic rather than actual when it appears in the midst of Clarissa's party.

The scene in which Clarissa retreats from her party to watch this woman next door recapitulates the earlier moments of reflected femininity: the old woman, "crossing the room . . . stared straight at her!" (p. 283). With "the clock's striking the hour, one, two, three" echoing the "June, July, August" of deterministic time before the mirror, and the old woman turning out the light so that "the whole house was dark," the scene also represents death, a vision of darkness and stillness in contrast to the activity of the party, where "people [are] still laughing and shouting" (p. 283). In effect, Clarissa sees her own image extinguished, a vicarious experience of death signified by the exclamation "there" as the woman turns out her light. As in the mirror scene, "there" has a double meaning: a movement has been completed ("there" as "*voilà*"), but it is there, not here, a symbolic death, not death itself. The woman merely goes to bed, she does not die, and she is not Clarissa. The scene enacts a pattern of renewal through loss initiated by Septimus' death; it is only "like" death, allowing the heroine to return from the abyss to bring her sense of rebirth—"it was new to her"—back to the world (p. 283).

More broadly, this regeneration goes to the heart of Mrs. *Dalloway's* conception. Like the transitional object of psychoanalytic theory, the old woman represents the power of the symbolic and its ability to lend a measure of control in arenas where human agency is otherwise impotent. In this way, she not only allows Clarissa to experience the ritual death and rebirth of the mythic heroine but also protects her against the temptation to follow Septimus' suit, to undo her metaphorical transformations and return to the realm of the literal, "the thing itself." As Clarissa's double, Septimus acts out in exaggerated form her sense of unity and fusion, bringing to the surface the hidden subtext of fatal regression which, like the problem of female immanence, has been carefully displaced. The delicate balance of Clarissa's female consciousness, preserved by the transformations of artifice and imagination, becomes clear in light of Septimus' exaggerated enactment of its qualities. He crashes through the window as Rachel breaks through the water's surface in The *Voyage Out*, seeking an absolute communion with the external world, but Clarissa's plunges are always metaphorical, beginning with her famous opening memory of how "she had burst open the French windows and plunged at Bourton into the open air," exclaiming with joy, "What a lark! What a plunge!" (p. 3). Clarissa's vivid memories and telepathic intuition become Septimus' hallucinations, returning his dead companion Evans to life, just as Woolf hallucinated her mother's presence in her most serious episode of madness. His suicide simultaneously calls into question and affirms Clarissa's symbolic mode, revealing both the literal reality which it evades and the necessity for doing so. Clarissa's appearance at the end of the novel confirms the survival of her femininity, for it touches both on Woolf's characteristic phrase for praising the mother's magic and on Clarissa's own experience of self-creation marked by the word "there": seeing her enter the room, Peter says, "For there she was" (p. 296).

The act of looking which structures the three scenes—always an act of the imagination as well as sight—assists in this renewal. Regarded by an empathic consciousness, the external world yields the same sense of revelation which Clarissa experiences when she looks at Sally, at her own reflection in the mirror, and at the old woman next door. In *Mrs. Dalloway*, an obliging reality offers itself up to the inventiveness of the human mind: "For heaven only knows why one loves it so, how one sees it so, making it up, building it round one, creating it every moment afresh" (p. 5).

A similar passage from *Jacob's Room* reveals the different, more pessimistic assessment of looking and seeing which underlies that novel:

> In any case life is but a procession of shadows, and God knows why it is that we embrace them so eagerly, and see them depart with such anguish, being shadows. And why, if this and much more than this is true, why are we yet surprised in the window corner by a sudden vision that the young man in the chair is of all things in the world the most real, the most solid, the best known to us—why indeed? For the moment after we know nothing about him.
>
> Such is the manner of our seeing. Such the conditions of our love.
> (p. 72)

In *Jacob's Room*, seeing is poignantly untrustworthy, for it holds out a glimpse of knowledge which quickly evaporates. Seeing and loving are the most unstable of experiences, dependent on unpredictable contact with the objects of an evanescent reality, at one moment "the most real, the most solid," the next, utterly inaccessible. In *Mrs. Dalloway*, this slippery reality is an invitation to create, each fading image an opportunity for creating "every moment afresh" rather than an occasion for mourning. Just as Clarissa's consciousness flowers with memories and meditations at the touch of reality, so reality responds to Clarissa's gaze. Simply by looking, the self can transform the outside world. Thus, Daisy and her children "become more and more lovely as Clarissa looked at them" (p. 68), as if the gracious and graceful hostess burnishes what she beholds with her own charm, like a benign Medusa.

The old woman herself, distant, anonymous, and finally invisible in the dark, evokes this potential of the outside world to be made into art, the negative capability of reality itself. In this capacity, she bears an intriguing relationship to the Mrs. Brown of Woolf's famous essay "Mr.

Bennett and Mrs. Brown," the essay in which Woolf compares the
writer to the hostess. "I believe that all novels begin with the old lady
in the corner opposite," Woolf asserts (*CE* I, 324), and continues: "She
is an old lady of unlimited capacity and infinite variety; capable of ap-
pearing in any place; wearing any dress; saying anything and doing
heaven knows what. But the things she says and the things she does and
her eyes and her nose and her speech and her silence have an over-
whelming fascination, for she is, of course, the spirit we live by, life
itself" (pp. 336–67). While the potential symbolized by Mrs. Brown
resides in "life itself," *Mrs. Dalloway* suggests that women may be a special inspiration to the female consciousness. Woolf's statement, "women
alone stir my imagination" (*Letters* IV, 203), may exaggerate, but it does
not entirely falsify Clarissa's imaginative responses—or Woolf's own. In
Jacob's Room the narrator found her male object inaccessible and sometimes alienating, explaining that a "difference of sex" makes it difficult
to know "what was in his mind" (*JR*, 94). Here, the narrator's voice
blends imperceptibly with Clarissa's thoughts, and the novel as a whole
reflects the qualities of Clarissa's unifying consciousness: characters
and narrator intermingle, experiences overlap, chapter divisions are
done away with.

In fact, Clarissa acts out in her fictional world what Woolf planned
for the novel itself and for *The Common Reader, First Series*, undertaken at
the same time:

> One works with a wet brush over the whole, & joins parts separately
> composed and gone dry. (*Diary* II, 323)

> I should mitigate the pomposity & sweep in all sorts of trifles. . . . The
> thing would be to envelop each essay in its own atmosphere. To get them
> into a current of life, & so to shape the book. (p. 261)

The unifying field of consciousness, the atmosphere and envelope, the
embracing of odds and ends as St. Margaret's feminine time and Clarissa's parties do, are all part of Woolf's aesthetic aspirations. Clarissa is
Woolf's own reflection, the artist translated into the figure of the hostess, a set of aesthetic values transfixed into a myth of femininity. Thus
Woolf redeems the hostess from the realm of the trivial and at the same
time places her own creativity within the maternal tradition, writing
novels and essays which embody the same values as the social art of the
party.

5

To the Lighthouse

WHEN WOOLF TURNS to more autobiographical material in *To the Lighthouse*, she reopens questions about the mother-daughter relationship and female art which *Mrs. Dalloway* apparently resolved. In Mrs. Ramsay, Woolf creates a portrait of her mother which her sister Vanessa found "almost painful" in its acuity (*Letters* III, 572); in Lily Briscoe, a portrait of herself—modified and fictionalized, of course, but with deliberate and important resemblances. Lily is forty-four in Part 3, when she finishes her painting of Mrs. Ramsay; Woolf is forty-four when she finishes *To the Lighthouse*. The author seems to insist on her presence in the novel by placing a shadow-writer discreetly beside the painter, sharing her insecurities and achievements: "Women can't paint, *women can't write*" (*TTL*, 75; my italics) and "the sight, *the phrase* had its power to console" (p. 270; my italics); "all changes; *but not words*, not paint" (p. 267; my italics). Woolf's complicated feelings about her own mother shape the fictional relationship between Lily and Mrs. Ramsay, and Lily's need to assert herself as an artist, bound up in her ambivalent attachment to the mother-figure, reflects the struggles of her creator.

Throughout *To the Lighthouse*, psychological tensions between mother and daughter make themselves felt as issues in feminist aesthetics. Although their creative projects are alike in important respects, the two women are also antagonists. The contrast between the maternal, marriage-minded Mrs. Ramsay and the virginal Lily again raises the bogey of female biology and implicitly questions whether womanhood and art are compatible. Whereas in *Mrs. Dalloway* Woolf expanded the domain of art to include parties, clothing, and cosmetics, here female culture and art proper occupy distinct, if in some ways analogous realms. In the process, anxieties about female creativity, assuaged by Clarissa's magical transformations, reappear, most conspicuously in the dilution of the hostess-artist's powers. With these changes come two of the central questions of *To the Lighthouse* and of Woolf's career: what can the daughter-artist inherit from her mother, and what must she avoid inheriting?

At first glance, the hostess-artist apparently lives on unchanged in Mrs. Ramsay. Her dinner party achieves the "merging and flowing and creating" of Clarissa's (p. 126). Like Clarissa's, Mrs. Ramsay's party envelops her guests, protecting them from the threat of violence or chaos; she unites them "into a party round a table, for the night was now shut off by panes of glass, which, far from giving any accurate view of the outside world, rippled it so strangely that here, inside the room, seemed to be order and dry land; there, outside, a reflection in which things wavered and vanished, waterily" (pp. 146–47). Mrs. Ramsay is the hub, the center of life at the vacation house, soothing wounded feelings, making guests feel welcome, possessing like Clarissa "that woman's gift" for creating social harmony.

Yet the passage just quoted suggests points of difference as well. From *Mrs. Dalloway's* myth of inviolable femininity, *To the Lighthouse* turns to a more realistic portrayal of woman and mother. Mrs. Ramsay's party only "*seemed* to be order and dry land" (my italics); its harmonious safety is in some way at odds with "any accurate view of the outside world." Femininity is no longer magical. The moment of unity succeeds, but it never promises the actual protection against death and decay which Clarissa undertook. Mrs. Ramsay's powers of transformation are limited: the green frill which flowers out of Nancy Blow's body, wresting artifice from the organic, is replaced here by the green shawl which conceals but cannot deny the skull, symbol of death, which it eventually drops away to reveal.

Emphatically a mother, Mrs. Ramsay is at the mercy of her own organic processes. The protective spaces over which she presides reflect her own vulnerability; the apparent security of the dinner party takes place in the midst of a general deterioration. She is associated not only with the lighthouse but also with the greenhouse (another of Woolf's light/nature contrasts, along with Clara/Florinda and Clarissa/Sylvia); unlike the lighthouse, largely unchanged after ten years in Part 3, the greenhouse has already begun to decay in Part 1, like the nature which it contains. Mrs. Ramsay repeatedly frets over the cost of that decay, considering it side by side with her own aging: "She made herself look in her glass a little resentful that she had grown old, perhaps by her own fault. (The bill for the greenhouse and all the rest of it.)" (p. 149). As the greenhouse mirrors her physical aging, the main house mirrors her emotional exhaustion: the home grows shabbier as "every door . . . is left perpetually open" (p. 44), just as Mrs. Ramsay's constant accessibility drains her: "They came to her, naturally, since she was a woman, all day long with this and that; one wanting this, another that" (p. 51). After her death, Lily thinks, "Giving, giving, giving, she had died" (p. 223). Phyllis Rose calls her "the pelican woman, feeding her brood with her own vital substance."[1] The celebrated woman's gift becomes a fatal profligacy.

At the heart of her vulnerability as a mother and nurturer is her allegiance to heterosexuality, "the love of man for woman . . . bearing in its bosom the seeds of death" (p. 151). The threat of death resides not only in the immanence of the female body but in the economy of heterosexual relationships. Although, as in *Mrs. Dalloway*, sexuality provides a set of defining metaphors for female identity and the feminine role, its dynamics are not so much transformed as re-enacted in emotional life. Clarissa uses her sexuality in a paradigm of self-creation; the orgasmic "rapture" which she experiences in her attic bedroom is a ritual of renewal. For Mrs. Ramsay, sexuality shapes a ritual of depletion. The potential threat of male difference is realized here as Mrs. Ramsay pours her "delicious fecundity" into her husband's "sterility." While her sexuality is still potentially a source of power as well as vulnerability, Mrs. Ramsay ultimately places it in the service of masculine needs, in direct contrast to Clarissa, who carefully retreats from the masculine sphere.

The ritual begins as Mr. Ramsay interrupts his wife, who is reading Grimm's fairy tale "The Fisherman and his Wife" to James, and demands her sympathetic attention. As Mrs. Ramsay responds, the woman's gift of comfort reveals itself as a power, a strength, rather than a passive acquiescence to another's demands. Mrs. Ramsay feels "animated and alive as if all her energies were being fused into one force"; like Clarissa, she experiences a sense of revelation, "burning and illuminating" (p. 58) in this moment of "successful creation" (p. 61), the emotional accomplishment which constitutes female art. The power is also an erotic one, "a delicious fecundity, this fountain and spray of life" (p. 58). As Mrs. Ramsay proceeds, the erotic imagery continues: she seems to "rise in a

1. Rose, *Woman of Letters*, 157.

rosy-flowered fruit tree laid with leaves and dancing boughs" (p. 60); when Mr. Ramsay is finally satisfied, she drifts into a post-coital relaxation: "She had only the strength to move her finger, in exquisite abandonment to exhaustion, across the page of Grimm's fairy story, while there throbbed through her, like a pulse in a spring which has expanded to its full width and now gently ceases to beat, the rapture of successful creation" (p. 61). Yet the translated orgasm, symbol of female inviolability in *Mrs. Dalloway*, is here the property of the male. Mrs. Ramsay's "rapture" is a response to what seems in the passage a metaphorical rape at the hands of her husband: "Into this delicious fecundity . . . the fatal sterility of the male plunged itself, like a beak of brass" (p. 58); "her strength flaring up to be drunk and quenched by the beak of brass, the arid scimitar of the male, which smote mercilessly" (p. 59); "the arid scimitar of [the] father, the egotistical man, plunged and smote" (p. 60). The phallic beak and scimitar, assaulting Mrs. Ramsay with demands for sympathy, reveal the masochistic pleasure of being the Angel in the House. Sexuality and maternity intersect in the stereotype of nurturant, giving womanhood, for Mrs. Ramsay also acts as a mother to her husband, who departs "filled with her words, like a child who drops off satisfied" (p. 60). The shift from sexual to maternal imagery reinforces the economy of the transaction. It is not a mutual giving but the appropriation of the female by the male: he is "restored, renewed" (p. 60); she sinks "in exhaustion" (p. 61). Female power spends itself—willingly—in the service of another, not in self-preservation, as it invites ravishment and ends in exhaustion.

Mrs. Ramsay's power is ultimately self-devouring, its expression a cycle of self-assertion and self-abnegation. Seeing her "proper function" (p. 63) as nurturance and submission, especially in relation to her husband, Mrs. Ramsay denies her power because it implies a need or weakness on her husband's part. The moment of successful creation reveals a hidden paradox in marriage: the husband may have the power to demand, but he is under his wife's power when he receives. Mrs. Ramsay denies this meaning, refusing to "let herself put into words her dissatisfaction" (p. 61), her uneasiness about her husband's needs. She repudiates her potency with thoughts of extreme, even melodramatic self-abnegation: "She did not like, even for a second, to feel finer than her husband" (p. 61). Similar thoughts run throughout Part 1: "She was not good enough to tie his shoe strings, she felt" (p. 51); "That was what she wanted—the asperity in his voice reproving her" (p. 184). This self-flagellation is her penance for having the power to heal.

Significantly, Mrs. Ramsay covers her dissatisfaction with her husband by reading "The Fisherman and his Wife," a cautionary tale which neatly mimics her own situation. In this story, a poor fisherman is undone by a wife who "wills not as I'd have her will" (p. 87). The fisherman catches a magic flounder which can grant wishes; in defiance of her husband's sensible reticence, the wife asks to be made king (and finally God in the original tale). Predictably, the wish has consequences which leave the couple poorer and more obscure than ever. The moral of the story is clearly that a woman should have no will of her own and should not seek to appropriate male power, represented by kingship. "Ilsabil" in the ongoing action, a woman with her own name, she is reduced to her proper contingent role by the frame of the narrative as a whole, which identifies her as the wife of the fisherman. Her power is subsumed and defused by the moral teleology of the narrative, which allows her to assert herself only so that she can be put in her place, just as Mrs. Ramsay's "delicious fecundity" leads to her exhaustion and self-abnegation.

Stifling her words with a patriarchal fairy tale, denying her power, Mrs. Ramsay is not a true artist, but she is an object of art. She resembles Susan in *The Waves*, "wholly woman, purely feminine . . . born to be the adored of poets" but no poet herself (*TW*, 348). Susan represents an extreme version of immanent womanhood, vessel rather than agent; her aspirations unite nature, maternity, and silence: "I shall lie like a field bearing crops in rotation" (p. 266), "I shall be like my mother. Silent in a blue apron" (p. 243). Mrs. Ramsay and Susan are far from identical, but both represent embodiment: Susan as the earth mother, Mrs. Ramsay as her spiritual counterpart, the Angel in the House and, more specifically, the cultural icon of the Madonna. Regarding her image in Lily's abstract painting, William Bankes thinks, "Mother and child . . . objects of universal veneration, and in this case the mother was famous for her beauty," wondering how a purple shadow can represent such profundity "without irreverence" (*TTL*, 81). The symbol of the window, which lends this first section its title, contains the dual aspect of Mrs. Ramsay's significance: as the protective barrier of her party, enclosing her guests in her feminine atmosphere, it represents her actual nurturance; as a frame which surrounds her, it confirms her status as icon. Mr. Ramsay turns to this image for solace: he looks "at his wife and son in the window" and returns to his work "fortified" and "satisfied" by this appropriate and meaningful configuration (p. 53). "With her head absurdly outlined by the gilt frame," Mrs. Ramsay, the perfect Madonna, comforts her son (p. 48).

All that remains of feminine inviolability is Mrs. Ramsay's image of herself as a "wedge-shaped core of darkness" (p. 95). It represents a sense of privacy and integrity in contrast to her self-destructive altruism in the male-dominated family structure. Whereas Woolf unified orgasm and retreat in *Mrs. Dalloway,* she splits them here, emphasizing Mrs. Ramsay's biological vulnerability and possession by the male. Mrs. Ramsay's private moments replenish the self "so lavished and spent" in the service of others. Her reveries are a mixture of Katharine Hilbery's and Clarissa's. Like Katharine, Mrs. Ramsay occasionally chafes in her role as hostess and seeks relief from other people, "the fret, the hurry, the stir" (p. 96), turning instead to "inanimate things" (p. 97) as Katharine turns to the impersonal stars and mathematics. Like Clarissa's, Mrs. Ramsay's act of looking is one of empathy to the point of merging: Mrs. Ramsay "became the thing she looked at—that light" (p. 97) when she sees the beam of the lighthouse. She decides that the third stroke of light is hers: "It seemed to her like her eyes meeting her own eyes, searching as she alone could search into her mind and her heart, purifying out of existence that lie ["we are in the hands of the Lord"], any lie" (p. 97). As Clarissa created herself from her reflected image in the mirror, Mrs. Ramsay's sense of herself is reflected back from the outside world; the "lies" of patriarchy—the Lord's omnipotence and the flattery demanded by her husband—fall away, leaving her with the purity of the exclusively feminine moment. The three strokes of the lighthouse's beam may actually define Mrs. Ramsay's wedge-shaped core of darkness, outlining its dark triangle. These "strokes" tinge the scene with the erotic but not with the aggressive sexuality of Mr. Ramsay's scimitar. The stroking of the beam which is like Mrs. Ramsay seems a vaguely maternal caress in its soothing gentleness.

This moment is all that remains of Clarissa's inviolability. In other respects, the hostess figure is greatly changed, returned to the arms of the husband and to male culture. These changes present significant problems for Lily, the daughter-artist who rejects marriage and, like Rachel Vinrace in *The Voyage Out,* "loathe[s]" sexuality (p. 261), although Lily is also sensible—at a distance—of its "glory" (p. 262). To begin with, Mrs. Ramsay's identity as a Madonna-icon is a product of masculine culture; as a female artist, Lily must find a different Mrs. Ramsay and establish a different relationship to her. Underlying this difficulty is a more serious and impacted one: Lily must come to terms with the way in which the icon and the mother herself exclude and devalue her.[2] The iconography of the Madonna and Jesus leaves no room for a daughter, and, in enshrining motherhood, it repudiates the spinster. Mrs. Ramsay dismisses the single woman, saying she "has missed the best of life" (p. 77); she values instead the closeness of the family and social intercourse, "that community of feeling with other people which emotion gives . . . it was all one stream, and chairs, tables, maps, were hers, were theirs, it did not matter whose, and Paul and Minta would carry it on when she was dead" (pp. 170–71). Mrs. Ramsay clearly identifies herself with the tradition of female emotion and sees Paul and Minta, the heterosexual married couple, as her inheritors. The spinster-artist has no place in this line of descent.

Detaching Mrs. Ramsay from patriarchal perspectives seems, at first, the simplest problem to solve. Lily's painting brings to the fore shadow-values and characteristics which elude the demands of marriage and role of the Angel in the House. Unlike Minta Doyle, who loses her grandmother's brooch when she decides to marry Paul Rayley, Lily retains her allegiance to a purely female line uncontaminated by male involvements. Emulating the friends of Mrs. Ramsay's grandmother who "mixed their own colors" (p. 24), she replaces Mr. Pauncefort's sentimental pastels and "shapes etherealised" with her own vivid palette (p. 75). Likewise, while she admires William Bankes's reverence for Mrs. Ramsay, Lily does not share it: "No woman would worship another woman in the way he worshipped. . . . Looking along his beam she added to it her different ray, thinking that she [Mrs. Ramsay] was unquestionably the loveliest of people (bowed over her book); the best perhaps; but also, different too from the perfect shape which one saw there" (pp. 75–76). Rather than seeking an icon, Lily approaches Mrs. Ramsay's individuality, "the spirit in her, the essential thing, by which, had you found a crumpled glove in the corner of a sofa,

2. For further discussions of mother-daughter ambivalence in *To the Lighthouse*, see Rose, *Woman of Letters*, for a biographical approach, and Jane Lilienfeld, "'The Deceptiveness of Beauty': Mother Love and Mother Hate in *To the Lighthouse*," *Twentieth Century Literature*, XXIII (1977), 345–76, for an archetypal one.

you would have known it, from its twisted finger, hers indisputably" (p. 76). She searches for the idiosyncrasy which mars the "perfect shape" of the Madonna.

Lily seeks Mrs. Ramsay's essence in "her relations with women" (p. 76). These less conventionalized, less scrutinized relations yield precisely that aspect of Mrs. Ramsay which is most problematic, most disguised in the context of heterosexuality: female power, "highhandedness" (p. 75), and a will to command (p. 76), qualities better captured by Lily's bright colors than Mr. Pauncefort's pastels. Mrs. Ramsay's rather autocratic match-making antagonizes Lily, a reaction which distinguishes her from the reverential men and which Lily holds onto as a source of insight. "All this she would adroitly shape; even maliciously *twist*" (pp. 76–77; my italics), thinks Lily, finding in the struggle of wills between women a glimmer of Mrs. Ramsay's essence, like the twisted finger of her glove.[3] Lily's abstract art further undermines the icon. William Bankes wonders if mother and child can be represented as a purple triangle "without irreverence," but Lily has apparently captured Mrs. Ramsay's private self, the "wedge-shaped core of darkness" into which she retreats from her role as Angel in the House.

Lily's relationship to Mrs. Ramsay seems likely to yield other insights as well, giving the female artist a kind of access to her female subject different from the reverence and rape of men. Gazing at Mrs. Ramsay, Lily wonders:

> What device for becoming, like waters poured into one jar, inextricably the same, one with the object one adored? Could the body achieve, or the mind, subtly mingling in the intricate passages of the brain? or the heart? Could loving, as people called it, make her and Mrs. Ramsay one? for it was not knowledge but unity that she desired, not inscriptions on tablets, nothing that could be written in any language known to men, but intimacy itself, which is knowledge, she had thought, leaning her head on Mrs. Ramsay's knee. (p. 79)

3. An incident recorded in Woolf's diary reveals an interesting autobiographical parallel to Lily's experience. Receiving the Femina Prize for fiction written by women, Woolf encountered a friend of her mother who recalled Julia as "the most perfect Madonna and at the same time the most complete woman of the world," but whose occasional acerbity was so incongruous that it seemed "vicious"—an observation which delighted Woolf as the twist in Julia's glove. A moment later, Woolf makes herself pay for her eagerness to de-idealize the mother: she becomes depressed by her shabby clothes, implicitly berating herself for not living up to her mother's feminine ideal (*Diary* III, 183).

In her desire to become one with Mrs. Ramsay, Lily recapitulates not only the feminine motifs of selfhood and interaction established in *Mrs. Dalloway* but also Mrs. Ramsay's own moment of communion with the lighthouse, in which she "became the thing she looked at."

This passage is central to Lily's emotional and artistic identity, suggesting both the strengths and the dangers of the mother-daughter relationship.[4] The regression implied here is a central and recurrent motif in Woolf's writing, where it is represented not only as a psychological state but as a component of creativity. In *Mrs. Dalloway* it shapes Clarissa's diffuse consciousness as well as her parties; in *The Voyage Out* it inspires Rachel to play the piano (although her slide into dissolution and death reveals the dangerous, self-destructive aspects of such desires); in *The Waves* it underlies Bernard's sense of union with the other characters which is also part of his art. However, Lily is still too entangled in her need for Mrs. Ramsay to make use of it. Her "plea for sympathy" has not yet become a "source of insight," to borrow a phrase from Suzanne Langer.[5] The double meaning of Lily's desire—as both a potentially fruitful aesthetic relationship and a dangerous emotional dependency—is hinted at by Lily's alternation of the terms "knowledge" and "intimacy," as if she wanted to understand how her confusion of impulses might make sense: "It was not knowledge but unity that she desired . . . intimacy itself, which is knowledge" (p. 79). It is also contained in the ambiguous phrase describing the intimate knowledge she seeks: "nothing that could be written in any language known to men" (p. 79). The phrase might refer to a special language among women which substitutes love and intuition for the authority and intellect engraved on the stone tablets of masculine law. But it also evokes the preverbal, infantile union of *The Voyage Out*, the silence which is more soothing than the divisiveness of language. Like Rachel, whose "I want—" is the clue of "things she had never told any one—things she had never realized until this moment"—that is, her loneliness without her mother (*TVO*, 60)—Lily has a silent secret which she inscribes in her canvas, bound up in the image of Mrs. Ramsay: "something more

4. For other views of Lily's desired union with Mrs. Ramsay in relation to her painting, see Helen Storm Corsa, "*To the Lighthouse*: Death, Mourning and Transfiguration," *Literature and Psychology*, XXI (1971), 122–24; and Elizabeth Abel, "(E)merging Identities: The Dynamics of Female Friendship in Contemporary Fiction by Women," *Signs*, VI (1981), 416.

5. Suzanne Langer, *Philosophy in a New Key* (Cambridge, Mass., 1942), 188.

secret than she had ever spoken or shown in the course of all those days" (*TTL*, 81).

Furthermore, as in *The Voyage Out*, the strength of the longing for fusion seems proportional to the impossibility of achieving it. The passage ends on a note of frustrated desire: "Nothing happened. Nothing! Nothing! as she leant her head against Mrs. Ramsay's knee" (p. 79). Mrs. Ramsay's physical proximity offers the same unfulfilled promise as the mirror in *The Voyage Out*, an enticing approximation of the actual fusion which eludes Lily. Lily's relationship to the Ramsays reflects the impossibility of the intimacy which she desires; she is, after all, only a friend of the family, staying in a local hotel rather than in the family home, and is more frequently the object of Mrs. Ramsay's affectionate condescension than her outpourings of sympathy, which are reserved for men.

The knowledge of Mrs. Ramsay which Lily does acquire through her yearning is the knowledge of desire, the kind of paradoxically unshared intimacy which Woolf encounters when she dreams of a friend: "my dream giving me, as my dreams often do, the essence of a relationship which in real life will never find expression" (*Diary* IV, 175). Lily gains the shadowy sense of something wished for so intensely that it takes on an almost sensual reality. Echoing one of the central images in the mother-daughter myth of Demeter and Kore,[6] Lily thinks of Mrs. Ramsay as a dome-shaped bee hive and has a sense of having been inside the hive—an obvious version of the regressive urge—and having participated in or experienced, in some almost inexpressible way, Mrs. Ramsay's interior self: "For days there hung about her [Mrs. Ramsay], as after a dream some subtle change is felt in the person one has dreamt of, more vividly than anything she said, the sound of murmuring and . . . the shape of a dome" (p. 80). The passage is extremely suggestive, for it recalls Woolf's memories of the sensual Eden of St. Ives, where "the gardens gave off a murmur of bees . . . The buzz, the croon, the smell, all seemed to press voluptuously against some membrane; not to burst it, but to hum round one" (*MB*, 66). Woolf consistently uses this imagery to describe nurturant/erotic experiences. She announces the arrival of her lover/mother-figure Vita Sackville-West by saying, "The garden is full of lust and bees" (*Letters* III, 275); according to Bernard, mother-London "hums and murmurs" (*TW*, 252). The mem-

6. Neumann, *The Great Mother*, 267.

brane, part of the family of female images which includes atmosphere and panoply, implies the memory of Julia Stephen and the infant's world of sensual protection over which she presides.

Moreover, Woolf's recollections of her own mother are, in their own way, as distant as Lily's relationship to Mrs. Ramsay, her knowledge as dream-like as Lily's own. Both Woolf and Lily are at the mercy of what Lily calls "the deceptiveness of beauty" with regard to the mother, "so that all one's perceptions, half-way to truth, were tangled in a golden mesh" (p. 78). The idealization which pervades *Moments of Being* is a symptom of actual distance, and Woolf clearly found her mother—rather aloof in life and heavily encrusted with the varnish of sainthood in memory—impenetrable as a human being. Her memoirs impress the reader not only with Julia's magical aura as a "general presence" and "panoply" but also with Woolf's frustrating lack of knowledge and intimacy:

> But apart from her beauty, if the two can be separated, what was she herself like? (*MB*, 82)
>
> But how can I get any closer to her? (p. 83)
>
> [With the knowledge of more facts Julia might not seem] so rubbed out and featureless, not so dominated by the beauty of her own face, as she has since become. (p. 85)

The iconic quality of the mother is precisely what distances her from her daughter, in Woolf's life as in *To the Lighthouse.*

Moreover, the specific conditions of Julia's sainthood involved neglecting her daughter Virginia in favor of other claims: "She had not the time, nor the strength, to concentrate, except for a moment if one were ill or in some child's crisis, upon me or upon anyone—unless it were Adrian. Him she cherished separately; she called him 'My Joy'. . . . I see now that a woman who had to keep all this in being and under control must have been a general presence rather than a particular person to a child of seven or eight. Can I remember being alone with her for more than a few minutes? Someone was always interrupting" (*MB*, 83). In *To the Lighthouse*, inaccessibility is also a condition of Mrs. Ramsay's general presence: Lily finds herself neglected by Mrs. Ramsay because of her "giving, giving, giving"—mainly to her son and husband—and it is not too farfetched to say that she wishes to destroy the icon, not only in the disinterested pursuit of truth or of a feminist aesthetic, but also to turn the mother from other preoccupations and win attention for herself.

The obsessive desire to merge with the mother—predicated on a painful sense of actual distance and even exclusion—makes any sense of individuality problematic. Lily's understanding of the ways in which she is different from Mrs. Ramsay is a highly charged and threatening one: "She would urge her own exemption from the universal law [Mrs. Ramsay's insistence that everyone must marry]; plead for it; she liked to be alone; she liked to be herself . . . Then, she remembered, she had laid her head on Mrs. Ramsay's lap and laughed and laughed and laughed almost hysterically at the thought of Mrs. Ramsay presiding with immutable calm over destinies which she completely failed to understand" (pp. 77–78). This passage reveals the symbolic daughter's ambivalent relationship with her mother. Lily wishes to insist on her own difference, her unsuitability for Mrs. Ramsay's program of universal marriage, but this thought propels her back into a position of extreme dependence, head on Mrs. Ramsay's lap, as Katharine Hilbery's rebellion against her mother led back to mutual dependence in *Night and Day*. Lily's hysterical laughter suggests both the intensity and the inexpressibility of her response: her warring needs to be different and dependent, thoughts of Mrs. Ramsay's lack of understanding and the desire to hold fast to her, and Lily's anxiety about wishing to reject the mother's legacy of child-bearing suggested by the word "hysterical."

Although Lily formulates her individuality as a resistance to marriage—"she liked to be herself"—she compares her solitary life unfavorably to Mrs. Ramsay's nurturance. At the dinner party, "Lily contrasted that abundance with her own poverty of spirit" (p. 152). Looking through the eyes of men, Mrs. Ramsay passes a similar judgment, describing Lily in negative constructions as if to characterize her by what she lacks: "Only Lily Briscoe [had overheard her husband's histrionics], she was glad to find; and that did *not* matter. . . . With her little Chinese eyes and her puckered-up face, she would *never* marry; one could *not* take her painting very seriously" (p. 29; my italics). In "The Window," the daughter is devalued and dispossessed. Although the section may evoke a childhood which Woolf attempts to represent as idyllic in "A Sketch of the Past," for Lily it is a fallen world, distorted not only by the mother's complicity in patriarchial values but also by Lily's paralyzing needs to become "one with the object one adored" and to separate from her. Neither merging nor difference provides her with a useful stance as an artist.

It is only after the death of the mother in Part 2 that Lily completes her painting. Death deconstructs the maternal icon and in doing so removes the lynch pin which secures the destructive relationship of male culture, mother, and daughter so that new relationships may be formed. Although Mrs. Ramsay's death ostensibly testifies to and completes her transcendently self-sacrificing nature (whether by apotheosis or suicide depends on one's point of view), it actually calls into question the mother's power. Death reveals Mrs. Ramsay's art for the illusion it was; biological vulnerability, hinted at by the deterioration of the houses and her own subtle aging, emerges full-face. In Part 1, Mrs. Ramsay civilizes the forces of nature into the figure of the Madonna, but here nature overcomes her, breaking its vessel and becoming inhuman, terrifying, fatal, as the green shawl drops away to reveal the skull beneath. Procreation produces not the civilized structures of family and garden; it issues in the death of Prue in childbirth and the chaos of a promiscuous nature as "poppies sowed themselves among dahlias . . . giant artichokes towered among roses; a fringed carnation flowered among the cabbages" (p. 207).

The myth of inviolable femininity no longer transforms or protects. The icon is here reduced to a trio of ineffectual symbols in an old woman's dream: "What power could now prevent the fertility, the insensibility of nature? Mrs. McNab's dream of a lady, of a child, of a plate of milk soup?" (p. 207). And while the almost-complete deterioration of the house suggests Mrs. Ramsay's power in life—for she managed to stave off such total decay—the damage is finally reversed by the "witless" Mrs. McNab (p. 196), a figure of unheroic proportions. At first a parody of Mrs. Ramsay, watching herself in Mrs. Ramsay's mirror (perhaps mimicking the moment of self-reflecting communion with the lighthouse; pp. 196, 207), the commonplace Mrs. McNab performs her own uncelebrated, comic motherhood, effecting "some rusty laborious birth" (p. 210) as she retrieves the house from ruin.

While Part 2 represents an ending to Mrs. Ramsay's career and the spell of her motherhood, it is also a new beginning, a vacancy into which her daughter can step and assert herself. Mrs. Ramsay's natural daughter, Cam, profits from this change: banished by Mrs. Ramsay during the reading of "The Fisherman and his Wife," Cam joins her father and brother on the boat in Part 3, and the Oedipal triangle weakens with her presence. Although familiar tensions assert themselves at the beginning of the trip, they are resolved at least in part because the daughter does not elicit the intense, conflicted emotions which the mother did (Mr. Ramsay's bid for her loyalty consists of offering her a gingernut; p. 305), so that Cam can love father and brother. Cam seems to find a new role for herself as well as a new structure for the family. In Part 1, Mrs. Ramsay arrests her hoyden energy and puts it in the service of a domestic errand, the relaying of a message about dinner which Cam delivers "in a colorless singsong" (p. 85), but here Cam uses the voyage to construct her own fantasy of "adventure and escape" (p. 280), trying on a new kind of experience which departs significantly from her mother's. Nevertheless, Cam makes no dramatic gestures toward self-actualization. She remains a shadowy figure, a person in potential. Her vagueness seems to reflect how completely Woolf identifies with Lily as the daughter-figure.

The most important changes come to Lily, who becomes the daughter ascendent: once relegated to a nearby hotel, she now stays at the family house, accompanied by Mr. Carmichael, himself an artist and the only guest not susceptible to Mrs. Ramsay's charms. Moreover, the mother's death offers the daughter the occasion for art: it leaves a void which must be filled, providing the impetus to create. It is a specific version of what Hartman calls the "'space' or apparent discontinuity . . . [into which] the general inventor can project his mind"; thus, Woolf's "art becomes interpolation rather than mimesis."[7] In Mrs. Dalloway, the old woman next door who turns out her light and goes to bed serves the same function, symbolizing for Clarissa "the center which mystically evaded them" by presenting the image of death. To the Lighthouse traces that space to its psychological origin, the death of the mother, whose absence—"ghost, air, nothingness" as she is to Lily after death—creates "a centre of complete emptiness" (p. 266). The desire to recover the mother, to fill the center, informs artistic efforts throughout Woolf's works—Rachel Vinrace playing Bach, Delia giving her dinner party in The Years, Miss La Trobe struggling with her pageant in Between the Acts—as well as Woolf's own aesthetic experience, as I have tried to show in

7. Hartman, "Virginia's Web," in Vogler (ed.), Twentieth Century Interpretations of "To the Lighthouse," 78.

Chapter 1, and the private imaginings with which she kept her mother alive in memory for decades after death (*MB*, 80).

In Part 3, as she paints, Lily relives her relationship with Mrs. Ramsay in stages which call up and resolve the conflicts and ambivalences of Part 1. Woolf claims to have achieved the same end in writing *To the Lighthouse:* "I suppose I did for myself what psychoanalysts do for their patients. I expressed some very long felt and deep felt emotion. And in expressing it I explained it and then laid it to rest" (*MB*, 81). Lily begins with an evocation of Mrs. Ramsay's private self, meeting the blankness of the canvas with three strokes of her brush (*TTL*, 235) like the three strokes of the lighthouse beam by which Mrs. Ramsay defined herself in Part 1. With this beginning, Lily establishes both her subject matter and the purpose of her art. The strokes might be said to form a shape, but to Lily "they enclosed (she felt it looming out at her) a space" (p. 236). The distinction between presence and absence reveals the program of Lily's painting: to recover the dead mother and to control the "looming" emotions which she evokes.

In an obvious way, Lily's painting is a mutually creative feminine act like the literary history which Woolf describes in *A Room of One's Own* and in her essays. Lily recovers and celebrates the mother by painting her, and Mrs. Ramsay "makes" Lily an artist by providing her with subject matter and, to some extent, a model for creativity. Lily does compare her art to Mrs. Ramsay's social accomplishments as she paints, remembering "Mrs. Ramsay making of this moment something permanent (as in another sphere Lily herself tried to make of this moment something permanent)" (p. 241). But this identification is suspect; it is not quite an ideal complementarity of life and art. The passage is a device for identifying the daughter as the mother's legitimate heir, implying an anxiety that the daughter might not occupy such a privileged position, that she might be simply a deviant spinster who prefers painting to marriage and children. Woolf herself sometimes assessed her own childless life in the same way: "Nessa and her children . . . My own gifts and shares seemed so moderate in comparison" (*Diary* III, 107). The passage represents only a tentative step in a process by which the daughter finds a proper image of Mrs. Ramsay and a proper relationship to her.

Lily makes one unsuccessful attempt to recover Mrs. Ramsay in her iconic identity. As if she has forgotten her earlier recognition of how she differs from William Bankes, she tries to see Mrs. Ramsay through his eyes, the image of Beauty in a deer-stalker's hat (p. 264). The exercise in male impersonation quickly takes her "half out of the picture" (p. 265) as the alien vision breaks her concentration. But the greater danger lies as Lily works her way *into* the picture, "tunnelling her way into the picture, into the past" (p. 258) to "model her way into the hollow" of her painting (p. 255). These are metaphors which Woolf uses to describe her own creative process, but they also recall the tunnel and vault imagery of Rachel's dreams in *The Voyage Out* and the cycle of regression and frustration which accompanies her loneliness. The conclusion which Lily draws from her resemblance to Mrs. Ramsay—"She owed it all to her" (p. 241)—clarifies the implications of the imagery by stressing Lily's dependence.

In these early stages, Lily uses her painting to recover her sense of the mother's atmosphere, the "hollow" of her party, and to be nurtured in the mother's enfolding space, to lay her head on the maternal lap. Her memories of Mrs. Ramsay reflect her dependent status: Lily plays the child's game of ducks and drakes at the beach, "highly conscious" of Mrs. Ramsay's watchful eye, feeling that "the whole scene . . . seemed to depend somehow upon Mrs. Ramsay" (p. 239). Yet the memory, with its improbable happy family of Lily, Charles Tansley, and Mrs. Ramsay, idealizes a reality of neglect and coercion: Mrs. Ramsay achieves the harmony of her party by insisting that Lily participate in a self-destructive tradition of femininity, flattering Charles Tansley, who belittles her. In the hollow of the omnipotent mother's protective space is a "hollowness" (p. 266), the estrangement which underlies Lily's idealizations and her desire to resemble Mrs. Ramsay, as well as the space left by her death. Lily must resolve both her sense of loss and her sense of exclusion before she can complete her painting.

Lily returns to the ground of her initial emotional obsession, the frustrating problem of intimacy and knowledge which she faced at Mrs. Ramsay's knee, and recognizes the impossibility of her wish: "Who knows even at the moment of intimacy, This is knowledge?" (p. 256). Grasping this insight, Lily "rammed a little hole in the sand and covered it up, by way of burying it." The image of burial suggests that she is not preserving the insight so much as leaving it behind, abandoning the quest for union. The emotional hinge of this resolution is mysterious and ultimately inaccessible. Appropriate to Lily's abstract art, it is marked by a purely formal device, a symbolic rather than mimetic gesture, the mutilation of the fish in Section VI. Like the death of Mrs.

Ramsay and the other deaths recorded in Part 2, it is enclosed by brackets, and it suggests the nature of Lily's loss and frustration: the division of a single body into two pieces, that is, the separation of mother and child. We do not see the mental or emotional process by which Lily masters her grief, but her feelings build to a climax before this section—"'Mrs. Ramsay!' she said aloud, 'Mrs. Ramsay!' The tears ran down her face" (p. 268)—and subside immediately thereafter—"the pain of the want, and the bitter anger . . . lessened" (p. 269). With her new detachment, Lily discovers the "twist" of Mrs. Ramsay, the individuality embodied in the characteristic twist of a glove, which she sought in Part 1. Lily identifies this twist as the gift for instinctive action, which she contrasts to her own preference for contemplation (p. 292). Ironically, Lily first approached this "twist" by detaching Mrs. Ramsay from patriarchal perspectives in Part 1 and finds it in Part 3 by detaching Mrs. Ramsay from her own emotional needs.

Lily's private catharsis is matched by more public, visible resolutions achieved by the imagination. She begins to assert her autonomy with "the story of the Rayleys" (p. 259), significant not only because it departs from Mrs. Ramsay's scenario of happy marriage but because, as a story, it is under Lily's control. She makes it up herself, assembling "a whole structure of imagination" from a phrase of Paul's (p. 258), deliberately asserting an interpretation which runs counter to Mrs. Ramsay's expectations. We know the story of the Rayleys' marriage not as their experience but as Lily's art. It forms a counterpart to the novel's other story, "The Fisherman and his Wife," the authorized version of heterosexual relations which Mrs. Ramsay passes on to her son in a moment of intimacy. Significantly, she deliberately banishes her daughter from the reading: "'Come in or go out, Cam,' she said . . . Cam shot off. Mrs. Ramsay went on reading, relieved, for she and James shared the same tastes and were comfortable together" (p. 86). When Lily "imagine[s] telling it to Mrs. Ramsay" (p. 259), she changes both the meaning and the lines of communication as woman tells woman a revisionist tale about marriage. In "summing up the Rayleys," Lily takes on the authority of the story-teller, feeling she has "triumphed over Mrs. Ramsay" (p. 260).

Implied by this triumph is a reassessment of the virgin-artist against the maternal hostess. Mrs. Ramsay dies by "giving, giving, giving" in the economy of heterosexuality, but Lily, withholding her sympathy from Mr. Ramsay and keeping her effusions to herself, is "saved from that dilution" (p. 154) and survives to paint, like Roger Fry, who, according to Woolf, "preserves his own vital juices entirely by keeping them banked in" (*Diary* III, 45). A virgin-artist like Clarissa, Lily maintains an emotional privacy comparable to Clarissa's physical self-protection. Her difference from Mrs. Ramsay, seen in Part 1 as inadequacy or lack, becomes her means of survival and creativity, turning on the hinge of Part 2 which transforms negativity into a necessary space.

Lily's painting finally secures her freedom from the mother's obsessive attraction, purging Mrs. Ramsay of her overpowering emotional significance. Having buried her thoughts about knowledge and intimacy, Lily turns, significantly, to her painting: "Lily stepped back to get her canvas—so—into perspective" (p. 256). This single line contains the central aspects of Lily's undertaking. She must "step back"—that is, distance herself emotionally from Mrs. Ramsay—and move from feeling to art; she must also put her art "into perspective"—both re-evaluate it in relation to the mother's talents and adopt a new, more objective vantage point from which to regard the mother. We have seen how Roger Fry's theory of significant form divorces art from emotion. Lily's painting follows Fry's model, seeking not to create the illusion of an actual woman but to balance abstract forms and masses, thus reducing Mrs. Ramsay to an object in the context of her art. Sharon Proudfit observes: "Lily is painting a picture in which Mrs. Ramsay is one of the objects being painted. For the picture to be completed along Post-Impressionist lines, Mrs. Ramsay must become merely a part of the system of formal relations; and in order to accomplish this, Lily must overcome Mrs. Ramsay's ability to dominate her emotionally."[8] The painting, of course, is the means by which Lily secures her detachment, the "extraordinary power" of "distance" (p. 292). With her artist's sense of balanced composition, Lily tames the "looming emotions" evoked by Mrs. Ramsay, subordinating this single element in the interests of the overall design. The overlapping language of art and emotion, form and feeling—words such as "distance," "relationship," and "perspective"—emphasizes the metamorphosis which the mother undergoes in Lily's painting from emotional obsession to neutral form. It also marks the shift in control represented by Lily's painting, as Part 3 vests the principle of order in the painter's eye rather than the woman's gift.

8. Sharon Proudfit, "Lily Briscoe's Painting: A Key to Personal Relationships in *To the Lighthouse*," *Criticism*, XIII (1971), 32–33.

Finally, Lily's sense of herself as Mrs. Ramsay's heir comes full circle. Again, she imagines herself as carrying out the mother's unifying values, but within the superior sphere of art: "It was some such feeling of completeness perhaps which, ten years ago, standing almost where she stood now, made her say that she must be in love with the place. Love had a thousand shapes. There might be lovers whose gift it was to choose out the elements of things and place them together and so, giving them a wholeness not theirs in life, making some scene, or meeting of people (all now gone and separate), one of those globed compacted things over which thought lingers, and love plays" (p. 286). The completeness and the globe are part of the woman's gift, but the power of granting a "wholeness not theirs in life" belongs to the artist alone, who recovers and preserves the mother and her accomplishments as Lily does in her "vision." The painting itself, destined for obscurity in someone's attic, may not be a perfect work of art, but the imagination—in the specialized exercise of the painter's eye and in the more general act of remembering—perceives the "globed compacted thing," the coherent wholeness which experience alone cannot offer.

As if by magic, the painting achieves its goal of recovery. By a "stroke of luck . . . an odd-shaped triangular shadow" appears on the step (p. 299). This shadow is the complex embodiment of Lily's emotional and artistic experience: it recalls the triangular shape on Lily's original canvas and so brings back the past; it also fills the empty space marked by the three brushstrokes with which Lily began the painting, fulfilling art's implicit promise to find understanding in loss. Lily is rewarded for her efforts by Mrs. Ramsay's mystical appearance, announced by the phrase which Woolf uses repeatedly to evoke the unifying security of the mother's presence: "There she sat" (p. 300). This triumph is more Lily's than Mrs. Ramsay's, for the mother is not actually there; her image has been summoned by the daughter's imagination, which grants a permanence she could not win for herself. As the narrator of *To the Lighthouse*, Woolf performs the same labor of love and power. "Life stand still here," Mrs. Ramsay says, but the novelist says "no" and writes the section "Time Passes," asserting the power of art to resurrect the mother who was distant in life and irrevocably gone in death.

Paradoxically, only the daughter who resigns the maternal legacy of self-sacrifice can celebrate it in art, yet the desire to celebrate and to model her gifts on her mother's suggests attachment as well. *To the Light-*

house is sometimes compared to "Professions for Women," an essay in which Woolf kills the Angel in the House to become an artist, to prove that Lily must reject Mrs. Ramsay—"Had I not killed her she would have killed me. She would have plucked the heart out of my writing" (*CE* II, 286). However, this conclusion must be balanced by another version of the daughter's inheritance, "Moment of Being: 'Slater's Pins Have No Points.'" This short story, conceived while Woolf was writing *To the Lighthouse*, atones for that act of matricide and claims the mother as an artistic precursor. It describes a relationship between an older woman musician and her favorite woman pupil: the older mentor, who provides not only artistic encouragement but a "moment of being," an illuminating kiss like the one between Clarissa and Sally Seton, is named Julia, the name of Woolf's own mother.

In *To the Lighthouse*, Julia/Mrs. Ramsay is a much more problematic mentor, which perhaps explains why Woolf's greatest triumph comes in the act of recovery rather than emulation. Woolf emphasizes her power as narrator with the appearance of the triangular shadow. She completes Lily's painting with this miraculous instance of wish-fulfillment, a striking event in a narrative which offers many examples of the reality principle and the limits of human control: Mr. Ramsay's inability to move from Q to R, Lily's frustrated longings to be counted a privileged daughter, Mrs. Ramsay's death. Woolf hints that this phenomenon belongs to another kind of story, the world of fairy tales and magical flounders, by attributing it to a presence, never identified or revealed, who might "come floundering out" of the house (p. 299). The "stroke of luck" to Lily is really the magic stroke of the writer's omnipotent pen.

But no magician believes her own illusions. This rather showy display of the narrator's control—a bit too felicitous, a bit too convenient—seems to imply that all narrative is mere contrivance. The narrator is not, of course, omniscient to herself, for she sees all the Wizard of Oz machinery by which she asserts her power. To complete her vision, Woolf needs Lily Briscoe as a double, just as Lily needs Woolf the narrator's magical intervention to complete her painting. Woolf's status as Lily's secret sharer achieves its full significance here. The shadow-writer who whispers words when Lily says paint—"all changes; but not words, not paint"—seems to speak the last words of the novel along with Lily: "It was done; it was finished . . . I have had my vision" (p. 310).

Jane Lilienfeld suggests the degree to which Woolf identifies herself with Lily at this final moment by describing the manuscript version of the novel:

> On the last page of the rough draft of the novel, there are three paragraphs, each separated from the other by a horizontal line. Thus the page is cut into three blocks, even as there are three blocks of material in the three sections of the novel. Connecting each paragraph to each, connecting each block to one another, down the center of the manuscript is drawn one slashing line. Virginia Woolf herself drew that one line down her own white paper even as Lily affixed her firm stroke. Author and character, each had completed "her vision."[9]

Through Lily, blessed artist in a perfectly responsive world if only for a moment, Woolf can see her own illusion through eyes to which it is reality; she can be the credulous audience at her own magic show. In the double role of omnipotent narrator and artist-daughter, Woolf approaches the impossible desire which lies behind her elegaic impulse, not simply to console but to restore.

9. Jane Lilienfeld, "The Necessary Journey: Virginia Woolf's Voyage to the Lighthouse" (Ph.D. dissertation, Brandeis University, 1975), 242.

6

Between the Acts

IN ITS INTEREST in the broader patterns of society and culture, *Between the Acts* represents a new phase of "thinking back through our mothers." The relationship which it examines between the mother-figure, the lady in yellow, and her unlikely daughter-artist, Miss La Trobe, is not a personal one but involves a line of descent in the context of cultural history. Defining the self-effacing communal art of ritual and pageant as essentially feminine, Woolf presents the lady in yellow as a distant originator and Miss La Trobe as an inheritor who attempts to recover the lost tradition in her play at Pointz Hall. Placing the issues of mother-daughter inheritance in this broader context follows the conviction of *Three Guineas* that feminine values—self-effacement, empathy, and the desire to unify—must be used to renew the culture as a whole. While in *Mrs. Dalloway* Clarissa maintains her integrity by drawing a magic circle around her home, *Between the Acts* posits no special retreat for the feminine. It belongs to the more radical feminism of Woolf's later life and reflects her belief that "public and private worlds are inseparably connected" (*TG*, 142) and that the values of one inevitably infuse the other. With this understanding, the question of whether the daughter can carry on the maternal legacy becomes a matter of importance for the entire culture.

The pageant at Pointz Hall, a collaboration of mother and daughter, represents an attempt to give one's "vision"—purely private in *To the Lighthouse*, jealously guarded from any audience and quickly stored away in an attic—to the outside world. Like *The Waste Land*, a work to which it is often compared, *Between the Acts* explores a crisis of confidence within a culture, as Elizabeth Hardwick eloquently observes: "This novel and *The Waste Land* are the most powerful literary images we have

114

of the movement of life and cultures, the dying of the past in the dying of a day, the shift from one order to another in an overheard conversation."[1] Woolf shares a fear and hope with two of her contemporaries in the modernist pantheon, Eliot and Joyce: a recognition of civilization threatened—although Woolf locates the threat in the rise of fascism rather than in a general cultural decadence—and an attempt to turn to older, mythic forms of order as models. She thinks back through her mothers as Eliot and Joyce think back through their fathers, the Fisher King and Ulysses, for a source of renewal.

The portrait of the woman in yellow presides over *Between the Acts*, symbolizing an older, more harmonious order which awaits restoration. The mother herself is no longer actually "there," to use Woolf's charged vocabulary, but has become a purely symbolic presence. She represents a tradition which extends long before the Olivers' tenure at Pointz Hall (p. 7) and which departs significantly from that of the direct ancestor, the bluff, matter-of-fact gentleman whose portrait flanks hers and who exclaims, "dang it, sir," and insists on being painted with his famous hounds, Colin and Buster. The woman, in contrast, is silent; she is also anonymous, unlike the man, who "had a name" (p. 36): "'Who was she? . . . Who painted her?'" wonders Lucy Swithin (p. 68). The picture itself has an air of peaceful mystery: "In her yellow robe, leaning, with a pillar to support her, a silver arrow in her hand, and a feather in her hair, she led the eye up, down from the curve to the straight, through glades of greenery and shades of silver, dun and rose into silence" (p. 36). As she leads the eye through her landscape, the woman in yellow establishes a special kinship: "We claim her because we've known her—O, ever so many years," says Lucy (p. 68), a secret, obscure sorority behind the official line of descent.

Exciting interest while remaining enigmatic, an ancient ancestress who will not declare herself, the lady in yellow is an inaccessible or absent mother, receding in her mystery from the idiosyncrasy and clutter of ongoing, present-day life. Leading the viewer's eye "into silence," she is a locus of absence and negativity, casting a similar spell over the room she inhabits: "Empty, empty, empty; silent, silent, silent. The room was a shell, singing of what was before time was; a vase stood in the heart of the house, alabaster, smooth, cold, holding the still, dis-

1. Elizabeth Hardwick, *Seduction and Betrayal: Women and Literature* (New York, 1970), 149.

tilled essence of emptiness, silence" (pp. 36–37). The female portrait of silence and emptiness, enclosed in the feminine space of the shell- and vase-like room "in the heart of the house," is the familiar empty center in Woolf's work. As in *Mrs. Dalloway* and *To the Lighthouse*, it is the arena for a potentially renewing experience, one which, in *Between the Acts*, might extend beyond an individual to the whole community.

For the woman in yellow is a specific cultural version of the absent mother: she represents the lost communal art which preoccupied Woolf in the last years of her life.[2] In fact, she has two identities and partici- pates in two traditions, Greek and English, which Woolf explored. The portrait's iconography—the yellow gown, the arrow, the bird feather, and the pillar—identifies the woman as Artemis, goddess of the Greek matriarchal rituals which Woolf encountered in the writings of Jane Harrison, the contemporary classical scholar.[3] According to Harrison, Artemis was an important figure in a matrilineal culture later supplanted by male-centered inheritance. Although best-known today as a virgin goddess, she is identified by Harrison as a composite of the earth mother and maid-magician figures. She descends from the goddess Themis, supreme even above Zeus, who presided over sacred commu- nal feasts and the *Agora*, the marketplace used for public assembly. Har- rison calls Themis "The Mother, the supreme social fact and focus" of matrilineal Greek life; she is the spirit of community itself. The origi- nal outsider, Artemis was excluded from Homer's Olympus, and indeed Harrison claims that the values which she embodies would find no comfortable home there. In contrast to what Harrison calls "Homeric patriarchal Olympus," which exalts the heroic individual and reflects "war-like and migratory conditions," matriarchal ritual "emphasizes the

2. Woolf's diverse reading in this period of her life reflects her interest in commu- nity and communal art. It includes Freud's *Group Psychology and the Analysis of the Ego*, E. K. Chambers' *The Medieval Stage*, and Ruth Benedict's *Patterns of Culture*. Benedict's in- sistence that non-conformity, eccentricity, and even psychopathology have a place in communal life may have influenced Woolf's characterizations in her last two novels, which explore a more diverse collection of people than usual, including foreigners, homosexuals, and eccentrics such as Sara Pargiter; see especially Benedict's final chap- ter, "The Individual and the Pattern of Culture," *Patterns of Culture* (1943; rpr. Boston, 1959).

3. Graves, *The Greek Myths*, I, 83; Harrison, *Mythology*, 116. For explorations of Woolf's interest in matriarchal ritual, see Jane Marcus, "Some Sources of *Between the Acts*," *Virginia Woolf Miscellany*, VI (1977), 1–3; and Judy Little, "Festive Comedy in *Between the Acts*," *Women in Literature*, V (1977), 26–37.

group, the race and its continuance." As a ritual goddess, the focus of an impulse both social and aesthetic, she is a lost ancestress for hostess and artist alike, Woolf's two figures of female creativity.[4]

The woman in yellow is also associated with a more recent and (to Woolf) indigenous form of communal art, the pageant of Medieval and Renaissance England. Woolf traced this tradition in her essay "Anon," which posits an artist, homeless and free, serving society but not quite a part of it—both anonymous and an outsider, like the woman in the portrait, whose name and identity are unknown and who has no official place in the family.[5] This sort of unegotistical, uncompromised artist always appealed to Woolf, especially because she associates these qualities with femininity. "Anon . . . was a woman," she asserts in *A Room of One's Own* (p. 51), and she establishes the Outsiders' Society for women in *Three Guineas* (p. 28).[6] It is not surprising, then, that she represents this tradition with the portrait of a woman in explicit contrast to that of a man, the assertive, philistine insider. In "Anon," Woolf envisages an art which has not yet broken free from its communal function and character, which is still closely interwoven with the fabric of society, staged in houses and courtyards and providing festive occasions for the community. The artist "is not separate from them [the audience]. A common life unites them" (p. 398). In the present day, Woolf notes with regret, this relationship has broken down: "No audience. No echo. That's part of one's death . . . this disparition of an echo" (*Diary* V, 293). The issues implied by these comments—issues of separation, fusion, and echoing, an auditory reflection—indicate that, in Woolf's imagination, the communal pageant might fulfill a culture's need for

4. Harrison, *Mythology*, 127; Jane Harrison, *Themis: A Study of the Social Origins of Greek Religion* (1912; rpr. Gloucester, Mass., 1974), 494, 62–63. Other scholars have noted the influence of Egyptian myth, particularly that of Isis and Osiris, on *Between the Acts*, although Greek mythology fits more closely with Woolf's stated interests; see Evelyn Haller, "Isis Unveiled: Virginia Woolf's Use of Egyptian Myth," in Jane Marcus (ed.), *Virginia Woolf: A Feminist Slant* (Lincoln, Neb., 1983), 109–31; and Madeline Moore, *The Short Season Between Two Silences: The Mystical and the Political in the Novels of Virginia Woolf* (Boston, 1984), 156.

5. "Anon," ed. Brenda R. Silver, *Twentieth Century Literature*, XXV (1979), 358–441. Silver associates "Anon" with Miss La Trobe in her introductory remarks (380) and develops this theme of communal art in an article to which I am much indebted, "Virginia Woolf and the Concept of Community: The Elizabethan Playhouse," *Women's Studies*, IV (1977), 291–98.

6. See also *Diary* V, 189, 245.

wholeness and security, just as the mother provides these qualities for a child.

"Anon is dead," Woolf writes in "Anon," but she attempts a resurrection in *Between the Acts*. A diary entry describing the Gala Opera, apparently the germ of the novel's conception, implicitly touches on the concerns of that essay: "I got the feeling of this traditional English life; its garden like quality; flowers all in beds & rows; & the ceremony that has been in being so many years. Between the acts we all stood in the street; a dry brilliant night, with women all opening their cloaks" (*Diary* IV, 31). The communal "we" of the audience, which experiences the opera as both art and social occasion, is also made aware of the origin of art in the surrounding society, as the gap "between the acts" reveals the relationship between the text and its context of "traditional English life." Almost a decade later, this experience evolves into Woolf's conception of *Between the Acts*: "'I' rejected: 'We' substituted: to whom at the end there shall be an invocation? 'We' . . . composed of many different things . . . we all life, all art" (*Diary* V, 135). Structuring *Between the Acts* around the pageant, Woolf exploits her conception of drama as a unifying, unegotistical genre. In "Congreve's Comedy," she notes that, in requiring the author to speak only through characters, it enforces self-effacement (*CE* I, 82), while in "The Reader," she envies drama its engaged and intimate audience, unlike the detached, isolated readers of the printed page. As one of Miss La Trobe's spectators observes of the pageant, "It brings people together" (*BTA*, 160).

Improbably enough, the communal artist finds its living incarnation in Miss La Trobe, whose characterization is derived in part from "Anon" and in part from the portrait. She stands behind the "pillar" of a tree, as Artemis leans on a pillar, while her identity as "Miss Whatshername" is the comic counterpart to Lucy's question about the portrait, "Who was she?" An outsider like the woman in the portrait, she has no official place in the Olivers' British county life. She is a foreigner from the Channel Islands, remnants of the pre-historic link between England and Europe, suggestive of an older, more unifying tradition. The French sound of her name may also connect her to a matrilineal tradition, for Woolf notes her own mother's French heritage in "A Sketch of the Past" (*MB*, 85) and in *To the Lighthouse* gives Mrs. Ramsay a French ancestress, the grandmother who provides the unifying Boeuf en Daube. Miss La Trobe is at odds with the society she works in, imagining herself breaking "—which of the village laws? Sobriety? Chastity?

118

Or tak[ing] something that did not properly belong to her?" (p. 211). In fact, she does all three as an artist. She makes her audience feel "intoxicated" (p. 94), feels herself "fertile" (p. 212) in creating, and constructs a pageant from materials which "did not properly belong to her"—not only the dish towels and mirrors which neighbors lend her but the history of English literature itself.

Miss La Trobe's rather bathetic congruence with the values of the portrait—"Miss Whatshername"—suggests that the tradition is somewhat tarnished in the hands of its inheritor, and indeed this is so. She and her art remain imperfect versions of an ideal tradition, unmistakably flawed and impossible to idealize. Her pageant never achieves the wholeness which Woolf postulates as art's achievement. Nevertheless, it at least attempts to restore the tradition and enjoys moments of success which testify to its intention if not its ultimate achievement. The pageant does, literally, embed art in society: it is enclosed by the social context of the neighborhood audience, which is treated not only to culture but to refreshments, proffered in the barn which, had it rained, would have served as the theater as well. Illuminated by a yellow shaft of light (p. 99) and decorated with "canary festoons" (p. 104) the color of Artemis' robe, reminding some people of a Greek temple and some of a medieval structure (pp. 26, 99), the barn is clearly a space appropriate to this communal art. The pageant automatically creates one source of community: the audience as a unified entity. Before the play begins, before the audience takes shape as such through its function, the individual spectators exist in uneasy relation to one another: "Their minds and bodies were too close, yet not close enough. We aren't free, each one of them felt separately, to feel or think separately, nor yet to fall asleep. We're too close; but not close enough. So they fidgeted" (p. 65). Woolf solves this problem of spatial relations by a gesture toward closeness; the pageant instills in its spectators a sense of formal if not psychological unity through their communal role. They must be instructed to "disperse" at intermission.

The pageant itself attempts—imperfectly—to complete the resurrection of its distant precursor which the audience has begun. We are continually reminded that the tradition is lost and awaits restoration by the recurring "empty centre" of the stage, which recapitulates the emptiness of the portrait and the empty room in which it stands: "For the stage was empty" (p. 76), "Yet the stage was empty . . . Nothing whatsoever appeared on the stage" (p. 82), "The stage was empty" (p. 120),

"Nothing whatever appeared on the stage" (p. 176). Dispersing itself throughout the performance, the empty, silent center appears as a series of awkward gaps and breakdowns, missed cues and inaudible speeches. The pageant must fill these spaces—literally, by mounting a spectacle, and metaphorically, by renewing the tradition of communal art.

Paradoxically, the spaces and silences help the pageant achieve its sporadic moments of unity. For Miss La Trobe, these gaps occasion intense, even histrionic despair, akin to Clarissa's awareness of death in the midst of her party and Lily Briscoe's sense of loss in *To the Lighthouse*: "Illusion had failed. 'This is death,' she murmured, 'Death'" (p. 140); "This is death, death, death . . . when illusion fails" (p. 180). But, luckily, context rushes in to fill the vacuum of the text. When the wind blows the words away and "illusion petered out" (*BTA*, 140), the cows in the surrounding fields begin, obligingly, to low, creating a "primeval voice sounding loud in the ear of the present moment" (p. 140) and taking over the chorus' description of the historical past through Rome to Ancient Greece (pp. 139–40).[7] This comic recovery of art's origin, both the sense of community which Woolf associates with Greek ritual and the primitive instinct which transcends history, salvages the play: "The cows annihilated the gap; bridged the distance; filled the emptiness and continued the emotion" (p. 141). The second moment of "death" through the failure of illusion has an even more restorative aftermath when nature provides a shower to fill the awkward silence of "present time" (pp. 179–80). Dripping down the faces of the audience, the raindrops seem transmuted into human tears, creating the image of catharsis, the release of emotion which a work of art should engender, and fulfilling Miss La Trobe's specific intention "to douche them, with present-time reality" (p. 179).

Thus, the moments of "death" are filled by collapsing the discrete categories of theatrical performance, including the physical context. When the song celebrating English country life is enacted by the view and the cows in their own odd ways, the unusual cooperation actually wins over the audience: "Folded in this triple melody [the chorus' song, the cows, and the view], the audience sat gazing; and beheld gently and approvingly without interrogation, for it seemed inevitable, a box tree in a green tub take the place of the ladies' dressing room" (pp. 134–35).

---

7. This passage probably derives from Woolf's speculation about a primitive "song-making instinct" which inspires all art, in "Anon," 382.

It is as if the "triple melody" has not only affirmed a sense of common purpose and experience but has also revealed some essential if subtle continuity between the natural world and the pageant which validates Miss La Trobe's conception. The setting, not simply nature but the grounds of the manor house which focused Elizabethan pageantry, has literally given its support to the play as it did in the past, when, perhaps less magically, it provided a physical environment and, implicitly, a sustaining culture.

Finally, of course, the audience itself becomes the text as Miss La Trobe holds up her collection of makeshift mirrors to represent "Ourselves" in her most concerted attempt to bridge the "vast vacancy" between audience and pageant (p. 78). The device interweaves art and experience, culture and the individual; private moments of self-reflection—Isa brushing her hair (pp. 13–16), Lucy "reflected in the glass" in the room where she was born (p. 70), even Mrs. Manresa's preening—become part of the public domain and the collective experience. The boundary between art and life blurs in the play's unstructured denouement; no one is sure that the play has ended, but all are somehow captivated with the actors, still in costume but out of character, one foot on either side of the footlights, as it were. "Beauty was on them. Beauty revealed them," thinks the audience. For the actors, who were scattered in different skits in the play proper, this appreciation creates a moment of unity: "The actors joined hands and bowed" (p. 196).

Like *A Midsummer Night's Dream*, *Between the Acts* puts forth a species of drama which, in calling attention to its own artifice, disrupts the conventional distinctions between life and art. The very ineptitude of the pageant works to this end, as it does in "Pyramus and Thisbe" within Shakespeare's comedy. Even as the pageant is unfolding, the audience is as aware of the real identities of the actors as they are at the denouement: they always perceive a double image of, for example, Queen Elizabeth and Eliza Clarke, waving her distinctly unregal arms, "swarthy" and "muscular" (p. 84). Shattering the dramatic illusion has the concomitant effect of emphasizing the human reality from which art is made, the process which transforms ordinary individuals into donkeys and queens, and towels into turbans. Whereas *A Midsummer Night's Dream* exploits self-conscious drama to prompt metaphysical speculation about the relationship between illusion and reality, *Between the Acts* offers a social investigation of the relationship between text and context, considering how art is constructed from the materials of society—including its individual members, the Eliza Clarkes and village idiots—and takes a place in the ongoing life of that society.

Of course, it would be a mistake to idealize Miss La Trobe's pageant as the perfect re-creation of communal art. Miss La Trobe struggles with the burden of her inheritance, more often than not fracturing the tradition she is supposed to carry on, revealing comically imperfect human efforts as well as a communal human past behind the portrait's ideal. We catch a glimpse of her as "Anon," the self-effacing author, for instance, only to see her frenzied behind-the-scenes attempts to continue the pageant:

> As for the play, he [the reporter] would collar Miss Whatshername for a synopsis. But Miss La Trobe had vanished.
> Down among the bushes she worked like a nigger. Flavinda was in her petticoats, Reason had thrown her mantle on a holly hedge. Sir Spaniel was tugging at his jack boots. Miss La Trobe was scattering and foraging. (p. 150)

The iconic mother again frustrates her daughter by inaccessibility, but instead of emotional distance she presents an unrealizable ideal. Like Lily, Miss La Trobe is an inadequate daughter who both reveres and resents what the mother represents, but the comedy of Miss La Trobe's frustration mitigates, to some extent, charges of tragic failure. Her exasperation enlists our sympathies: "Do you think it's easy to be an anonymous artist?" the narrator seems to ask, "to exert constant, invisible control over your work, to create the perfect, seamless surface of dramatic illusion?" "Blast 'em," Miss La Trobe says of her obtuse, restive audience, whose care and feeding she has inherited from Anon. I have said that the pageant resembles "Pyramus and Thisbe" in emphasizing the human actors beneath the dramatic roles; another point of resemblance lies in the way in which the humor of ineptitude dilutes our criticism with amusement.

In fact, Miss La Trobe's inadequacy, like Lily's, forms the ground of a distinct if untranscendent achievement. In place of her foremother's perfection, she supplies parody which, in its double attitude of irreverence and nostalgia, embodies the daughter's simultaneous needs to recover and separate from the mother. Parody generally signifies that a convention or genre has become empty or ossified; it comes into being with the death of its original. But, if Miss La Trobe's pageant mourns a lost tradition, it is often an Irish wake, making a party of a tragic occasion. Its touch is deft and amusing—Woolf evidently revised the pageant to sharpen its wit and eliminate any suggestion of crudeness or tedium[8]—with a number of perfect moments: Lady Harridan bewailing her abandonment "sans niece, sans lover; and sans maid" (p. 148) as if the last were the final, unkindest, most crushing blow of all. The humor which hovers around the pageant grows sometimes from Miss La Trobe's intention, as in the above example; sometimes it devolves on her from the narrator, as when she "forages" behind the bushes for costumes. Wherever it originates, its effect on the reader is to cast a new light on Miss La Trobe's departure from the tradition of the portrait, who, like all iconic incarnations of the mother in Woolf's work, is beautiful but inaccessible, perfect but remote. The irreverence of Miss La Trobe's comic embodiment of tradition, whether she intends it or not, offers to distract us from the more somber implications of the contrast between past and present. The narrator implicitly endorses her irreverence by rejecting the decorous advice of another mother, Lucy Swithin's, who admonishes her daughter not to play on people's names; the narrator responds by inventing a sandwich-making cook named Sands, a newspaper reporter named Page, and a religious woman named Lucy Swithin, "the light within."

Through humor, parody, and irreverence, Miss La Trobe's pageant achieves at least one revelation (although, characteristically in *Between the Acts*, it passes without recognition by any of the characters): it offers Isa the possibility of escaping her paralysis by debunking her romantic self-image as a tragically torn heroine. Isa's character is structured by warring opposites. She wishes to regard herself as a descendant of Sappho, yet recognizes herself as "Sir Richard's daughter" (p. 16); she is torn between being "in love" with a local gentleman farmer and remaining faithful to "the father of my children," a dilemma made concrete by the contrast between her reflection in the mirror—"in love"—and her actual self in front of the mirror—"the father of my children." Her "abortive" poetry, which never finds what DiBattista calls the "superogatory rhyme,"[9] reflects the self-cancelling nature of her desires—she will not commit herself to either of her selves, as her poetry will not commit itself to form and meaning but tends toward dissolution, like Rachel's Orphic music in *The Voyage Out*. It is Isa who remembers the tale of "the donkey who couldn't make up its mind between hay and turnips

8. Susan M. Kenney, "Two Endings: Virginia Woolf's Suicide and *Between the Acts*," *University of Toronto Quarterly*, XLIV (1975), 272.
9. DiBattista, *Fables of Anon*, 215–17.

and so starved" (p. 59) and who urges herself back to the pageant, which is about to lampoon the Victorian Age, by saying, "O little donkey, patiently stumble" (p. 156).

When she arrives at the pageant, she finds a parodic version of this self-image, a donkey composed of two villagers (one of them Albert the idiot), carrying the stout Mrs. Hardcastle. The specific symbolism of the scene—that Isa bears a burden of outmoded feminine expectations?—seems less important, and a good deal more ambiguous, than the general effect: Isa's self-styled tragic pose of emotional conflict is rendered comical by the unauthorized gambol of the donkey's hindquarters (p. 171) and by the final divorce of head and tail at the end of the pageant, when "the Age of Reason hobnobbed with the foreparts of the donkey" (p. 195). This parody of conflict undermines Isa's stalemate as the donkey subverts the tragic, deterministic implications of its role as beast of burden. When the donkey rejects its perfectly minor function in the Victorian scene, breaking out of its subservient passive role in the "old," intended plot, finding new opportunities for comic self-expression in the midst of cliché, it also implies the possibility of the "new plot" which Isa desires, in which what is now the foreground recedes, and what is minor, peripheral, or hidden steps to the center of the stage, as the daughter's comic art steps into the empty center of the lost tradition. None of these insights reaches Isa in any apparent way, but the juxtaposition of two such different versions of the same image—characteristic of the inharmonious, jagged, inclusive texture of the novel, of the daughter's irreverent humor—raises the possibility to the reader.

Nevertheless, while the daughter's art suggests the possibility of new forms, it does not achieve them. Unlike Lily's transformations of a sentimental Victorian stereotype into abstract art, a re-casting of the mother's values into her own idiom, Miss La Trobe's idiosyncratic achievement appears to make do as best it can with a bad lot. If her pageant were enclosed in A Midsummer Night's Dream, we could find it an unmitigated delight, but as its context is more serious than that of "Pyramus and Thisbe," our amusement is balanced by the darker shades which lie outside of the pageant's province and compromised by the recognition that the pageant provides no real solutions to the disjointed society which surrounds it. Whereas the pageant imitates the *form* of communal art in the penetration of context into text, the participants do not experience any strong sense of communion. As a source of communal *feeling*, a social correlate to the psychological state of wholeness and security which the mother represents, the pageant fails. Individual moments of success do not add up to a coherent experience; the audience leaves still feeling the need for a "centre" (p. 198). Miss La Trobe's pageant, like Clarissa's parties, is inspired by an ethic of giving, but with a difference: "She could say to the world, You have taken my gift! Glory possessed her—for one moment. But what had she given? A cloud that melted into the other clouds on the horizon. It was in the giving that the triumph was. And the triumph faded. Her gift meant nothing. If they had understood her meaning; if they had known their parts" (p. 209). The gift has been given, but the giver is no longer certain it has been received. The pageant is a one-way transaction, failing to provide its author with the self-confirming "echo" from the audience which Woolf considered in her diary.

Nor does Miss La Trobe provide her audience with a unifying presence. Like Lily Briscoe, she lacks the woman's gift for smoothing out human relationships, for sympathizing, for nurturing. Twice her audience "locates" her with the familiar announcement of the mother's presence—"There she is, Miss La Trobe" (p. 122) and "There she is, behind the tree" (p. 179)—but, as in the analogy to Clarissa's giving, the resemblance emphasizes the gap between mother and daughter more than their likeness. The last quotation points to Miss La Trobe's incapacity to diffuse herself into an "atmosphere" or "panoply": she draws the comment because of her absence, not her unifying presence, as her audience attempts to seek her out only to catch her in the act of evading them. In short, many points of contact between past and present leave a double image: Miss La Trobe standing behind the pillar of the tree both evokes her ideal ancestress and reveals her own failure to fulfill the tradition. As with the pageant as a whole, the form of the tradition has been preserved, but the emotion has not survived.

The pageant's failure implies not only that the daughter-inheritor lacks the maternal magic to revivify the maternal values but also that the values themselves no longer compel belief. This implication emerges most fully in the figure of Lucy Swithin, who is in many ways a more appropriate descendant of the woman in yellow than Miss La Trobe. It is Lucy who calls attention to the portrait and claims her as an ancestress, and Lucy who fulfills many of the conditions of the maternal role as it has evolved in Woolf's writing. She participates in the diffuse states of consciousness which characterize these heroines, experiencing intimacy as a "mist" between herself and her brother (p. 26) and "increasing the bounds of the moment by flights into past or future" (p. 9) as Clarissa does. One of the "unifiers" by nature (p. 118), she acts as hostess to the pageant.

Moreover, Lucy participates in the clearest incident of renewal of any of the characters. Climbing to the room of her birth under the watchful eye of the portrait, Lucy finds that "the room was empty," mirroring the emptiness and silence of the portrait's surrounding space. As her voice "die[s] away" (p. 70) and her concentration wavers from the exhaustion of the climb, she seems to undergo a momentary ritual death, to have been sucked into the empty center in a return to her origin. Artemis, the woman in yellow, saves her, however, making a symbolic appearance in the billowing of the room's draperies—a recurring signal in Woolf's work that individual isolation is breaking down and the party is about to succeed: "And then a breeze blew and all the muslin blinds fluttered out, as if some majestic goddess, rising from her throne among her peers, had tossed her amber-coloured raiment" (p. 72).[10] Roused by the movement of the blinds, William Dodge, her companion, asks her to call him by his first name, and the two share a moment of rejuvenating intimacy: "At that she smiled a ravishing girl's smile, as if the wind had warmed the wintry blue in her eyes to amber" (pp. 72–73), the amber of her eyes reflecting the amber robe of the goddess under whose auspices the moment occurs.

Despite the loveliness of this moment, however, Lucy is not an effectual figure of renewal; indeed, by the end of the pageant she has forgotten William's name again (p. 206). The combination of her luminous old age, her religion, and her recurring concerns with earlier modes of life—both her own childhood and the childhood of evolutionary time—give her an air of floating above the present-day, ongoing human experience. There is something child-like and even ridiculous about her sense of wholeness and unity, her "circular tour of the imagination—one-making," in which "sheeps, cows, grass, trees, ourselves—all are one" and God appears as "a gigantic ear attached to a gigantic head" (p. 175). Her vision is entirely unconvincing to her companions who, when they see her "beaming seraphically" in contemplation of this divine unity, think indulgently, "Well if the thought gave

10. See *The Voyage Out,* 152; *Mrs. Dalloway,* 258.

her comfort . . . let her think it" (p. 175). Hers is a purely private vision and consolation.

Woolf's treatment of Lucy Swithin is one of the clearest indications that the states of consciousness which have been most compelling in the novels—"the moment," the sense of merging with the natural world and with other people—no longer occupy the center of her imagination. By attributing them to Lucy, she relegates them to the past. The only other character who experiences the moment of transcendent unity is a very young child, Isa's son George, watching a flower: "The flower blazed between the angles of the roots. Membrane after membrane was torn. It blazed a soft yellow, a lambent light under a film of velvet; it filled the caverns behind the eyes with light. All that inner darkness became a hall, leaf smelling, earth smelling, of yellow light. And the tree was beyond the flower; the grass, the flower and the tree were entire" (p. 11). The penetration of the outer world into inner consciousness, filling "inner darkness" with the smells of nature, and the unity of flower and earth recapitulate Woolf's epiphany of wholeness while looking at a flower in "A Sketch of the Past" (MB, 71). Woolf may be suggesting that these experiences have become archaic, available only to the very young or to those with a child-like faith in order.

Thus, psychological ambivalence about the mother evolves into a complex attitude toward the past represented by the mother. On one hand, she suggests a haven of harmonious unity, of order and peace. On the other hand, her order no longer obtains; she belongs to an era which has ended. It is perhaps significant that Miss La Trobe finds it impossible to fully imagine a play with an idyllic, nostalgic flavor: "The butterflies circling; the light changing; the children leaping; the mother laughing—'No, I don't get it,' she muttered, and resumed her pacing" (p. 63). Miss La Trobe's failure to "get" this childhood Eden reflects both her own departure from the maternal ideal and the failure of that ideal to sustain its potency and relevance.

There is still more to be said about the dislocations of Between the Acts and their bearings on the mother-daughter relationship. I have suggested that the "empty center" left by the mother is a space into which the daughter can step, that it offers possibilities of both renewal and change, or at least departure, as it did in To the Lighthouse. Yet for every gap filled by context or comedy, there is another one left unbridged:

words blow away without being recovered, the gramophone persists in its "chuff, chuff, chuff" as if to accentuate the delay, "scraps and fragments" (p. 12) waft to and fro, isolated and disunified. Hartman rightly observes that Woolf covers for Miss La Trobe, repeatedly saving her illusion from disintegration, but the opposite is also true—with the power to correct every flaw, Woolf nonetheless refrains.[11] Woolf's narrative technique likewise seems a deliberate rejection of the perfect whole: gone are the telepathic communications among characters, the overlapping of voices between narrator and character, the blending effect of the "wet brush" which she characteristically passed over her prose; gone is the tightly woven verbal texture, the net so dense that no detail could slip through into isolation or idiosyncrasy. The quality which Woolf praises in Henry James and which could serve equally well as a description of her own aims—"The commonest object, such as a telephone, loses its simplicity, its solidity, and becomes part of life and transparent" ("Phases of Fiction," CE II, 82)—no longer applies. In the last phase of her work, in which I include The Years and Between the Acts, Woolf seems deliberately to have eschewed her trademark style and the comfort of its lyric beauty and coherence. One can only speculate about her reasons, which must in any case have been diverse. The more heterogenous form of Between the Acts represented to her the latest of the technical experiments which inspired all her novels (she also planned it for The Years, although it is much less evident there; see Diary IV, 152, 157). In that sense, it is a happy change from tradition, the breaking of the mold which Woolf sees as characteristic of artists and of herself in particular (Diary IV, 157). The change in style has also been attributed to her increasing pessimism about the future of civilization (the precariousness of culture already mentioned) and to the disruption of her private world with the deaths of Roger Fry, Lytton Strachey, Carrington, Francis Birrell, and Julian Bell.

Each of these explanations speaks to the novelty of Between the Acts, but there is another one as well, a psychological understanding which Woolf evidently brought to the novel. In the last several years of her life, Woolf seems to have taken a strong interest in the motivations of the writer, speculating in explicitly psychological terms on the forces of rebellion and repression which drive the "Leaning Towers" poets, for

11. Hartman, "Virginia's Web," in Vogler (ed.), Twentieth Century Interpretations of "To the Lighthouse," 81.

instance: "I think there's something in the psychoanalysis idea: that the L. Tower writer couldn't describe society [because of his ambivalent relationship to it, see *n*3]: had therefore to describe himself, as the product or victim: a necessary step toward freeing the next generation of repressions" (*Diary* V, 267).

She considered her own motives as well. Part of that exploration is contained in "A Sketch of the Past," her 1939 memoir, where she describes the "rapture" of making whole (*MB*, 72). She pursues the same insight while writing *The Years*, another book of "scraps, orts and fragments": faced with brutality and loss, she says, the artist compensates by creating a perfect whole: "Is that the origin of art . . . making yourself immune by making an image!" (*TY/H*, IV, 104). Her concentration on the act of "pargeting" in *The Years*— that is, of plastering over cracks and hiding fissures—must have been bound up in this understanding of motives. The act gives its name to the central family, the Pargiters, whose story begins with the death of the mother. Her children's lives can be read as a series of attempts to fill that gap, to find the image which confers immunity, to answer the question which the dying mother asks in her delirium—"Where am I?" (*TY*, 23)—and which recurs throughout the novel (pp. 43, 213, 239, 243, 267), a symptom of the dislocation which grows from her loss. The mother's portrait, the reminder of her unifying influence in life, can neither substitute for her presence nor compensate for her absence; having assumed "the immunity of a work of art"—the unruffled surface of perfect order—the mother has become remote, unreachable and detached, "indifferent to our right and wrong" (p. 327). Her transformation into an immortal image no longer consoles, as it did in *To the Lighthouse*; the hope that art can bridge the gap between life and death becomes a delusion.

In *Between the Acts*, Woolf examines her own pargeting through art. Given her understanding of the creative impulse, her fracturing of the coherent whole of an art work is courageous, for it leaves her confronting again and again the empty center, untransformed and untransforming. A case study reported by Winnicott captures the meaning of this act. He describes a woman patient who has just begun to understand that her present unhappiness is due to her mother's absence and unreliability during her infancy and childhood. Winnicott invites the woman to fetch a rug from his waiting room in order to act out her desire for regression, as she has done before, but the woman refuses, saying, "You know, don't you, that the rug might be very comfortable, but reality is more important than comfort, *and no rug can therefore be more important than a rug*" (italics in original).[12] The gaps in *Between the Acts* uncover the loss behind the image which has been erected to hide it. The sense of immunity conferred by the perfect compensatory image is sacrificed to reveal the reality beneath, what Rhoda calls "that grey cadaverous space which is yet the truth" (*TW/H* II, 468).

Some of the ineptitude of Miss La Trobe's pageant, especially in the early scenes, works toward this end: we see the recognition scene of the Renaissance skit without the plot which leads up to it, whereas the opposite is true for the Restoration: we see development and denouement, but lack of time prevents Miss La Trobe from representing the actual climax. The splitting of action, consequence, and resolution is a particularly apt way of undermining the ability of art to substitute for coherent and satisfying experience in life. In contrast, Reverend Streatfield's explanation of the pageant insists on finding order where there is clearly confusion; it reveals itself as a false comfort by "the smooth way in which the tale is made to unfold into full blown success like some profuse peony," as Woolf says of another too-inspirational clergyman, the Reverend Canon (*Diary* I, 256). Reverend Streatfield draws all the phenomena of the pageant into the secure realm of clear meaning and intended effect; no problem, no breakdown, is permitted to disturb or perplex: "Then again, as the play or pageant proceeded, my attention was distracted. Perhaps that too was part of the producer's intention? I thought I perceived that nature takes her part. Dare we, I ask myself, limit life to ourselves? May we not hold that there is a spirit that inspires, pervades" (*BTA*, 192). In ignoring all anomalous moments, selecting only those features about which he can construct an affirmative explanation, Reverend Streatfield reveals more than his tact; he reveals the falsification of systems which promise immunity—among them, religion and, ironically, a perfect artistic whole.

The narrator, too, participates in the destruction of the image by exposing the tricks with which artistic illusion is achieved. "The weather looked a little unsettled," the narrator tells us, and an instant later "someone" remarks, "'Looks a little unsettled'" (p. 150); such an obvious attempt to perfect the illusion—that there is real and consistent weather within the novel—only undermines it. The correspondence is too neat, the corroboration too transparent. Even more telling is the

12. Winnicott, *Playing and Reality*, 25.

moment of catharsis provided by the convenient shower. Although the effect on Miss La Trobe and her audience seems genuine, we cannot help feeling that, in rescuing the characters, the narrator has compromised her own art. She gestures in the direction of convention, the obligatory renewal-by-water scene, playing the expected trump card and taking, perhaps wearily, the expected trick. Again, we feel a loss of faith in the artistic illusion—and, with particular explicitness here, in its ability to serve an emotional function. In "On Re-reading Novels," Woolf writes, "The 'book itself' is not form which you see, but emotion which you feel" (CE II, 126), but surely this cathartic moment is precisely the opposite. It is a form which we see rather than emotion which we feel—in short, a fraudulent imitation. The artistic illusion has failed to satisfy emotionally because it has not adequately addressed the gap—which it covers, indeed, too neatly.

In calling attention to her own sleights of hand, Woolf calls the coherence of the image into question, implicitly raising the spectre of loss beneath it. The narrator's pro forma catharsis and the narrative dislocations of Miss La Trobe's pageant—climaxes with no plot, plots with no climax—are mirror images of each other. Although they work in the opposite way, their effect is the same: to undermine the immunity of the image. And, just as the specific failure of Miss La Trobe's pageant, offering the form of a communal whole without the concomitant feeling of communion, reveals the tradition as unrenewed in an essential element, the failure of the narrator's catharsis encodes the loss of the mother, for the communal emotional experience stands at the center of the ritual art which she represents. Miss La Trobe's disappointment with her own accomplishment reflects this larger disillusionment with the artistic image. Before the pageant begins she insists "that a dish cloth wound round a head in the open looked much richer than real silk" (p. 64); when the pageant ends, she thinks, "If the pearls had been real and the funds illimitable—it would have been a better gift" (p. 209). It is as if the course of the pageant has revealed the materials of art as imperfect substitutes, devices for making do, pitiful and unconvincing shams.

In place of a coherent rounding-off of emotion, Woolf closes *Between the Acts* with an open and ambiguous silence. In doing so, she departs unmistakably from the summarizing statements of *Mrs. Dalloway* and *To the Lighthouse*, which offer perfect verbal images of the heroine's achievement: "For there she was," celebrating the mother-hostess in *Mrs. Dalloway*, and

"I have had my vision," celebrating the daughter-artist in *To the Light-house*. An early version of the novel deliberately rejects such a conclu-sion: lumping together artists and maiden aunts as champions of con-vention and superficial decorum (*PH*, 46–47), the narrator refuses to "write as novelists do The end with a flourish" (p. 62), preferring in-stead to preserve the irresolution, absence, and silence evaded by pat novelistic endings.

Nor does the conclusion achieve any communal form or feeling. Al-though it is, in a sense, a collaboration between Miss La Trobe, the artist, and Isa, the audience, neither one recognizes the other's part in the vision, which is imagined and realized only after the play is over. The coherence exists for the reader only, who sees Isa's wish for a "new plot" coming to fruition when Miss La Trobe begins to imagine a new play: "'I should group them,' she murmured, 'here.' It would be mid-night; there would be two figures, half concealed by a rock. The cur-tain would rise. What would the first words be? The words escaped her" (p. 210). Isa steps into the new plot to close the novel:

> Isa let her sewing drop. The great hooded chairs had become enor-mous, and Giles too. And Isa too against the window. The window was all sky without color. The house had lost its shelter. It was night before the roads were made, or houses. It was the night that dwellers in caves had watched from some high place among the rocks.
> Then the curtain rose. They spoke. (p. 213)

The ending is less a conclusion than a starting over in the light of the knowledge of loss, both cultural and psychological, which has been achieved in the course of the novel. After the daughter's parodic art has acknowledged its lost original, after the narrator's jaded resolutions have exposed the banality of the artistic image, at this point the woman in yellow, the ancient ancestress, reasserts her purifying silence through which new words might emerge.

"Reading at Random," another late, unpublished essay in which Woolf explores the superiority of earlier art, describes this uncontami-nated language as "words without associations";[13] Miss La Trobe calls it "words without meaning—wonderful words" (p. 212). What optimism resides in the ending is seriously qualified by the failure of the expected forms, the pageant and the narrative as a whole, to carry forward the

---

13. "Notes for Reading at Random," edited, with an introduction, by Brenda R. Silver, *Twentieth Century Literature*, XXV (1979), 373–79 (quotation, p. 377).

communal art of the mother, although the possibility of a new plot and a renewed language is at least implied, and the lack of resolution is at least potentially a regenerative empty center. But whether or not Rhoda's squares and oblongs will domesticate this space remains unknown. *Between the Acts* reaches only the point of departure. It stops halfway through Lily's painting: the brushstrokes have outlined the space, but have not filled it. Woolf's writing ends, and the new forms begin, in silence.

7

Female Literary History

FOR VIRGINIA WOOLF, literary history was a family affair. She was related to Thackeray through her father's first marriage, James Russell Lowell was her godfather, Henry James and George Meredith were frequent visitors at her parents' home. Her father, of course, was a noted essayist and critic. She often describes literary history as a series of family relationships, speaking of Victorian "grandparents," Edwardian "parents," and Georgian "children" ("On Re-reading Novels," *CE* II, 122), or announcing that "books are descended from books as families are descended from families. . . . They resemble their parents; yet they differ as children differ, and revolt as children revolt" ("The Leaning Tower," *CE* II, 163). With this vocabulary, Woolf suggests not only her own literary background but also the psychological and emotional issues which weave themselves into literary inheritance.

In Woolf's case, these issues are especially tangled, complicated not only by her special intimacy with the tradition but also by her identity as a woman. In spite of fathers and godfathers, Woolf often felt excluded from the literary establishment, past and present, because it was male. The gates of the great universities were closed to her, a situation which she dramatizes in *A Room of One's Own* when she is repeatedly chased from "Oxbridge's" property. She feels as much a stepchild as a privileged offspring. Abandoned by the dominant male tradition and critical of its egotistical ways, Woolf seeks an alternative female heritage, symbolically joining the Outsiders' Society in *Three Guineas*, composed by definition only of women, rather than a more prestigious male organization. This is not to say that Woolf repudiates or ignores male writers; she continually and often enthusiastically assesses their achievements. Nevertheless, she takes a special interest in women, turning to them for a heritage distinct from the male tradition. "[A] woman writing thinks back through her mothers," Woolf asserts (*AROOO*, 101). Her reviews of women writers and her feminist essays embark on this consciously chosen program of thinking back through the maternal line. As a critic, Woolf constructs a female literary history; as a writer, she seeks a place in it.

Woolf's idealized memories of Julia Stephen, her own mother, shape these efforts. When Woolf calls Judith Shakespeare, the original female predecessor of her own invention, a "continuing presence"—like Julia's "invisible presence"—she implies the psychological needs and expectations which she brings to this intellectual task. I have suggested that Woolf tries to recapture her relationship with her mother through creative experiences such as viewing a painting and, of course, writing; the same desire informs her interest in female literary history as she seeks connections with other women writers. Woolf does not simply name writers who might contribute to a tradition but traces the dynamics of literary inheritance between women, raising issues and values which define, for her, the mother-daughter relationship and the figure of the mother.

"A Women's College from the Outside," for instance, seems pure regressive fantasy (*Books and Portraits*, 6–9). The women's college is an important symbol of a female intellectual tradition just as the party symbolizes a female social tradition; it takes a central place in both *A Room of One's Own* and *Three Guineas*. Yet in this essay it is the site of almost stifling female bonding rather than self-assertion or accomplishment. Woolf does not imagine studying, reading, or writing—surprising omissions, given her life-long resentment at having been denied a formal education. Instead, she pictures a dreamy nighttime camaraderie among female students. Although she remarks in passing on the necessity of taking examinations, Woolf focuses more on the embodiment of the feminine in the institution, calling it a "dairy or nunnery" (we recall Mrs. Ramsay's obsession with the quality of milk in *To the Lighthouse* and Clarissa's nun-like aspect in *Mrs. Dalloway*). Angela, the main character, experiences perfect female nurturance there, including the enrapturing kiss from another woman (again, we remember Sally kissing Clarissa in *Mrs. Dalloway* and Julia Craye kissing Fanny Wilmont in "Moment of Being: 'Slater's Pins Have No Points'"). This kiss bestows on Angela the sense of wholeness which Woolf associates with her own mother: "After the dark, churning, myriad ages here was light at the end of the tunnel;

life; the world. Beneath her it lay—all good; all lovable . . . She lay in this good world, this new world, this world at the end of the tunnel" (*Books and Portraits*, 8–9). Woolf completes this regressive fantasy—tunneling back to the womb after "dark ages" of separation—as Angela falls asleep sucking her thumb. In this essay, the female tradition is primarily a way of repairing the psychological separation of mother and daughter.

But, although such personal issues inform Woolf's writing about women, they do not overwhelm it. "A Women's College from the Outside" is a rare instance of pure regression. In contrast, most of her essays transform the private materials of her biography into intellectual values: the nurturance and sense of wholeness which she associates with her mother become resemblance and continuity among women writers. When Woolf writes female literary history, she has in mind not only her own emotional needs but the more general needs of the female artist.

One might argue that resemblance and continuity define any tradition as such, male or female. Nevertheless, a writer within a tradition may try to deny these values and emphasize revolt rather than resemblance, to adopt Woolf's own vocabulary. This is the version of literary inheritance which Harold Bloom advances in *The Anxiety of Influence*, a work especially valuable in clarifying Woolf's ideas by contrast, because it is both psychologically oriented and specifically male. Bloom bases his theory on the Freudian Oedipal struggle: "Battles between strong equals, father and son as mighty opposites, Laius and Oedipus at the crossroads; only this is my subject here."[1] According to Bloom, "strong poets" must challenge and even distort their predecessors "to clear an imaginative space for themselves" in a well-stocked tradition. Just as the son in the Oedipal phase of development wishes to kill his father and marry his mother, Bloom's strong poet must wrest the female muse from his predecessor. He must win her with some sense of definitiveness in order to assert not only his power but his "priority," his status as the first man to chart this poetic territory and not that of a mere latecomer. Bloom stresses the poet's self-definition *against* his predecessor, with metaphors of battling and wrestling, emphasizing both antagonism and masculinity.[2]

1. Harold Bloom, *The Anxiety of Influence: A Theory of Poetry* (New York, 1973), 11.
2. *Ibid.*, 9–10, 11, 88.

In Freudian theory, the son in the Oedipal phase establishes a sense of individuality, abandoning his pre-Oedipal ties to the mother and seeing her as an object to be possessed. Similarly, Bloom's strong poet strives to construct "the ego to meet the whole world of the Not-me." The poet's desired state is one of "solitude" and even "estrangement"; the process of achieving poetic identity is the process of separation. Finally, the poet wishes to deny any relation at all to precursors, even denying the existence of precursors: "How can they [strong poets] receive the deepest pleasure, the ecstasy of priority, of self-begetting, of an assured autonomy, if their way to the True Subject and their own True Selves lies through the precursor's subject and his self?" Bloom quotes Wallace Stevens' assertions, "I know of no one who has been particularly important to me" and "I am not conscious of having been influenced by anybody."[3]

The problems presented by this model for the woman writer are immediately apparent. Most obviously, how can we reassign the roles to accommodate a principal actor of the opposite sex? Gilbert and Gubar ask: "Where, then, does the female poet fit in? Does she want to annihilate a 'forefather' or a 'foremother'? What if she can find no models, no precursors? Does she have a muse, and what is its sex?"[4] Bloom's model may be compelling for a man writing within a male tradition, but the situation of a woman writer is far different, as Woolf was intensely aware. To begin with, the assumption of a weighty and intimidating tradition simply does not obtain for a woman. "The history of England is the history of the male line, not the female," Woolf observes, and she bemoans the lack of even an intermittent female tradition between Sappho and Jane Austen ("Women and Fiction," CE II, 141, 142–43). Women writers have no need to "clear an imaginative space for themselves"; their aesthetic terrain is underpopulated, if not deserted. Women who do write may find Bloom's "priority" turned into freakishness or even monstrosity.[5] The assumption that "Women can't paint, women can't write" (TTL, 75) turns a would-be author into a deviant. Even with her friend Desmond MacCarthy, Woolf found herself defending women against charges of natural incapacity (Diary II, Appendix III, 339–42) and the implication that women who were not sat-

---

3. Ibid., 84, 115, 105, 116, 7.
4. Gilbert and Gubar, The Madwoman in the Attic, 47.
5. Ibid., 30–36.

isfied with "courageously acknowledging the limitations of their sex" would make fools of themselves (*Diary* III, 195–96 n5; this remark was doubly galling to Woolf as MacCarthy was praising her for just such courage in maintaining a "butterfly lightness" in her writing; p. 197).

Woolf's replies to MacCarthy, published in the *New Statesman* over a series of several weeks, are interesting because they demonstrate how well Woolf understood the value of a literary tradition. She offers Sappho as a woman poet of unquestionable greatness and uses her knowledge of female literary history to refute MacCarthy's claim that education has not, and hence cannot, change women's abilities. Woolf argues: "When I compare the Duchess of Newcastle with Jane Austen, the matchless Orinda with Emily Brontë, Mrs. Haywood with George Eliot, Aphra Behn with Charlotte Brontë, Jane Grey with Jane Harrison, the advance in intellectual power seems to me not only sensible but immense" (*Diary* II, 339). Even as she asserts a general advance in female achievement, Woolf corrects MacCarthy's assertion that women do not write, simply by naming names. Moreover, for Woolf these writers are more than immediate ammunition. She claims among the "indisputable . . . conditions" which allow a great writer to exist "that he shall have had predecessors in his art . . . that you will not get a big [Sir Isaac] Newton until you have produced a considerable number of lesser Newtons" to break the early ground (p. 341). Conversely, the apparent lack of female authors is not simply a lack of support but an active impediment, for it fuels the argument that "women can't write," as MacCarthy's column amply demonstrated.

For Woolf, then, estrangement means inferiority and exclusion, not achievement; separation is a problem to be solved, not a condition to be cultivated. It is not surprising, then, that Woolf wishes to see the female artist as "an inheritor as well as an originator" (*AROOO*, 113) and stresses what predecessors she can find. This sense of self as inheritor differs significantly from Bloom's self-begetting strong poet. It is not the struggle for separation but the need for attachment which defines Woolf's identity as a woman writer and critic. For an artist like Woolf, object-relations theory, which insists on the self as relational, offers a better model of literary descent than Bloom's Freudian explanation.[6]

6. One must immediately note that Bloom is writing about a male tradition and that his paradigm is descriptive rather than prescriptive, in Gilbert and Gubar's words (*The Madwoman in the Attic*, 48).

The female precursor, acting as mother and mirror, affirms the daughter's identity as an artist.

Just as the myth of Oedipus and Laius enacts Bloom's Freudian model, so the myth of Demeter and Kore enacts the object-relations model. Kore, we recall, was raped by Pluto and abducted to Hades. When Demeter, her mother, found her there, she bargained for Kore to live aboveground for nine months of the year. To celebrate Kore's return, Demeter renewed her own creativity, which she had suppressed while grieving for her lost daughter, by fructifying the earth. Like Kore, the woman who is a potential writer is driven underground, stigmatized as deviant by male disapprobation. But the existence of mother-predecessors rescues the daughter, legitimating her ambition. At the same time, the daughter-writer reveals the mother-predecessor's creativity by following her example and writing about her. A forgotten figure—a novelist or even a letter-writer—is renewed when her inheritor emerges. Thus, literary influence becomes an act of mutual creation between mother and daughter just as Demeter and Kore collaborate in each other's creativity.[7] For the daughter, the "True Self" does "lie through the precursor's . . . self," the situation deemed by Bloom to be intolerable to the male artist. Woolf, the daughter, begins the rescue mission by "thinking back through her mothers"; when she constructs her precursors, they return the favor by giving her an identity as an artist within a tradition.[8]

Far from repudiating female precursors, then, Woolf searches them out, reviewing not only novels and poems but also obscure private letters and diaries, like the narrator of *Jacob's Room*, who takes a particular interest in "the unpublished works of women" (p. 91). One of Woolf's earliest fictional efforts, "The Journal of Mistress Joan Martyn," written in 1906, is a case study in this process of female literary history. A female historian, who feels a "maternal passion" for the manuscripts she discovers, stumbles upon the diary of an unknown Englishwoman of the sixteenth century, Joan Martyn. She brings Joan's life to light, and the diary becomes the young scholar's material. When the story of the scholar's discovery is supplanted by the journal itself, that document

7. Neumann, *The Great Mother*, 305–11; Graves, *The Greek Myths*, I, 89–96.
8. See also Sara R. Throne, "Virginia Woolf's Feminist Identity and the Parthenogenesis of Female Culture," *University of Michigan Papers in Women's Studies*, II (1975), 146–61.

becomes both Joan's story and the scholar's research, the point at which the mother and daughter's common interests fuse.[9] Although Woolf remains a discriminating critic (rejecting Eliza Haywood as an utterly worthless writer in "A Scribbling Dame," *Books and Portraits*, 126–29), she views these women in a sympathetic light, re-evaluating their divergence from dominant (that is, male) artistic conventions as a source of strength rather than weakness, and occasionally bending even her own standards to admit women into the fold. Unlike Bloom's strong poet, who misreads predecessors to distance himself from them, Woolf is more inclined in the opposite direction, re-interpreting women writers so that they resemble her.

One must balance this model with the recognition that Woolf is susceptible to Bloom's "anxiety of influence." She experiences this threat mainly in relation to her contemporaries, however, and it is qualified when the contemporary is a woman. Her reviews of Dorothy Richardson, for instance, praise the distinctly female aspects of her art while criticizing Richardson's limitations in precisely that area which she and Woolf have in common, experiments with narrative technique and point of view ("The Tunnel" and "Romance and the Heart," *Contemporary Writers*, 120–25). Assessing similar experiments in Joyce, Woolf herself attributes her criticism to jealousy (*Diary* II, 69). The salient point in these criticisms—that is, of distinguishing her own narrative experiments from those of Richardson and Joyce—seems to be contemporaneousness, not inheritance.

In fact, Woolf's ambivalence toward Richardson may reflect conflicting desires to identify with her as a woman but reject her as a modernist. In her attempts to define what is "feminine" in Richardson, Woolf seems to change her mind in order to accommodate these desires. She begins: "She has invented, or, if she has not invented, developed and applied to her own uses, a sentence which we might call the psychological sentence of the feminine gender. It is of a more elastic fiber than the old, capable of stretching to the extreme, of suspending the frailest particles, of enveloping the vaguest shapes." So far, we are reading about a feminine form. Yet Woolf continues immediately: "Other writers of the opposite sex have used sentences of this description and stretched them to the extreme. But there is a difference. Miss Richardson has fashioned her sentence consciously, in order that it may de-

9. Woolf, "The Journal of Mistress Joan Martyn," 240–68.

scend to the depths and investigate the crannies of Miriam Henderson's consciousness. It is a woman's sentence, but only in the sense that it is used to describe a woman's mind" (*Contemporary Writers*, 124–25). Woolf criticizes Richardson's technical experiments because they leave us "distressingly near the surface" of experience despite the vivid impression they create; she suggests that "the old method [of realistic narrative] seems sometimes the more profound and economical" (p. 122). Yet she retains Richardson as an important figure in the female tradition by finally defining Richardson's female perspective as a choice of subject matter. Although Woolf begins by locating Richardson's femininity in the form of her sentences, their elasticity and inclusiveness, she quickly changes her mind and identifies the femininity of the sentence exclusively in its content—"only in the sense that it is used to describe a woman's mind." Richardson the modern novelist can then be chided for triviality and extreme subjectivity while Richardson the woman novelist is praised for investigating "the psychology of her sex" (p. 125) and for demonstrating that "the accent upon the emotions has shifted" from a male point of view (p. 125).

With other contemporaries, Woolf stresses resemblance as a source of support. Although, according to the common wisdom, Woolf's professional regret about Katherine Mansfield's death centered on the loss of a worthy adversary who could spur her own efforts by competition, Woolf's description of that relationship suggests that she lost a source of affirmation as well, of reassurance that a woman writer could find a companion as well as a rival. (In criticizing Mansfield's "Terribly Sensitive Mind," however, she seems to be distancing herself from a sensibility which resembles her own perhaps too closely; *CE* I, 256–58.) Woolf notes "a common certain understanding between us—a queer sense of being 'like'" (*Diary* II, 45) and "the queerest sense of echo coming back to me from her the second after I've spoke" (p. 61), the self-confirming reflection from another woman artist. When the novelist Stella Benson dies, Woolf calculates the loss to her own sensibility by insisting on creativity as a shared property: "My effusion—less porous & radiant—as if the thinking stuff were a web that were fertilised by other peoples (her that is) thinking it too; now lacks life" (*Diary* IV, 193). The metaphor of the unifying web, one of Woolf's common female symbols, and the emphasis on relationship and mutuality distinguish Woolf's stance from that of Bloom's "strong poet" by emphasizing continuities of thought among female artists.

Thus, despite certain caveats, the impulse to find connections with other writers dominates Woolf's approach to female literary history. In particular, she channels her energies into establishing a female Great Tradition of writers who reveal the nature of women and the female consciousness without falling too far into special interest and personal grievance. The nineteenth-century novel marks the female Renaissance, dominated by the Brontës, George Eliot, and, of course, Jane Austen, the tradition's most perfect representative and Woolf's touchstone. When Woolf considers these writers, she searches for a common ground to secure her identity as an inheritor. In light of her notion of female literary history, it is not surprising that at least two, Emily Brontë and Jane Austen, bear remarkable similarity to Virginia Woolf.

In "*Jane Eyre* and *Wuthering Heights*," Woolf praises Emily Brontë's poetic gift for submerging human idiosyncrasy in "some more general conception" (*CE* I, 189)—a gift which Woolf obviously shares. Brontë "could free life from its dependence on facts, with a few touches indicate the spirit of a face that needs no body" (p. 190). These comments recall the consciousness which defines so many of Woolf's heroines, especially Rachel Vinrace, Mrs. Dalloway, and Mrs. Ramsay, as well as her criticism of the novel of "facts" in "Mr. Bennett and Mrs. Brown" (pp. 319–37). Woolf's assessment that in Emily Brontë's work "there is love, but it is not the love of men and women" (p. 189) echoes a similar pronouncement in *The Voyage Out*, published the year before this review: "It might be love, but it was not the love of man for woman" (*TVO*, 315). In this early stage of her career, after the intense seven-year anxiety of writing *The Voyage Out*, Woolf must have been particularly eager for the reassurance of a direct foremother. Woolf finds her own image in Emily Brontë: the tendency to generalize, abstract, and disembody rather than individuate, especially in the portrayal of sexual love. When Catherine Earnshaw carefully distinguishes physical attraction from spiritual communion to explain her love for Heathcliff, she speaks in terms which recall the merging and telepathy of Woolf's own characters: "There is, or should be, an existence of yours beyond you. What were the use of my creation if I were entirely contained here? . . . Nelly, I am Heathcliff—he's always, always in my mind—not as a pleasure, any more than I am always a pleasure to myself—but as my own being."[10] Indeed, probably only a genuine kindred spirit

10. Emily Brontë, *Wuthering Heights* (New York, 1972), 72–74.

(and kindred, significantly, in characterization and representation of consciousness) could find the willful, difficult, and frequently sullen Catherines "the most lovable women in English fiction" (*CE* I, 190). They are by their own admission intractable and egotistical—especially the first Catherine, who flies into rages and shams fits to manipulate her pallid husband, and who torments Heathcliff from her deathbed with the accusation that he has killed her by breaking her heart. She is hardly a lovable figure in any conventional sense, although she is undeniably a compelling one, but she attracts Woolf's imagination by participating in other selves, escaping the boundaries of body and ego.

However strong her attraction to Emily Brontë, Woolf reserves her highest praise for Jane Austen, the Shakespeare of women writers. Like Shakespeare, Austen achieved the perfect incandescence which burns away any trace of impure personal interest; she wisely lets time "disinfect" her experience before she writes about it ("Jane Austen," *CE* I, 153). One aspect of her genius lies here, in eschewing the anger and resentment bred by the oppression of women ("Women and Fiction," *CE* II, 144). The second aspect lies in the apparently opposite direction: Austen never compromises her female sensibility and values but, incredibly, refashions a male sentence to express a female consciousness (*AROOO*, 77, 80). Not forcing her sexual identity on the reader, but remaining unmistakably female, Austen writes "as a woman, but as a woman who has forgotten that she is a woman, so that her pages were full of that curious sexual quality which comes only when sex is unconscious of itself" (*AROOO*, 96). Neither a strident complainer nor a male impersonator, Austen is the ideal woman writer. It is not surprising that Woolf should seek such a precursor, both respectable and distinctly female in her subject matter, in 1923, while writing *Mrs. Dalloway*. Woolf praises Austen for treating those aspects of experience which she pursues in her own fiction, the female social world of parties and everyday human interaction. Austen's "insight into [the] profundity" of these apparent "trivialities" raises her work to the highest level of art (*CE* I, 151); Woolf's own concern about the "tinselly" character of Clarissa Dalloway and her self-conscious attempt to reevaluate apparently minor social activities against the male world of politics and public life must certainly have influenced her assessment of Austen's achievement. Like Emily Brontë, Austen offers the reassurance of a kindred spirit, a woman writer attempting the same unusual project as Woolf herself.

And, as with Emily Brontë, when Woolf attempts to describe the essence of Austen's art, she seems to recreate Austen in her own image. She praises Austen for capturing epiphanies which sound much like Woolf's own in "A Sketch of the Past," especially the awareness of the "panoply of life" which her mother guarded: "It [the "moment" in Austen's writing] fills itself; it shines; it glows; it hangs before us, deep, trembling, serene for a second; next, the housemaid passes, and this drop, in which all the happiness of life has collected, gently subsides again to become part of the ebb and flow of ordinary experience" (CE I, 151). Woolf predicts what Austen would have written if she had lived longer in words that could easily describe Woolf's own writing: "She would have devised a method, clear and composed as ever, but deeper and more suggestive, for conveying not only what people say, but what they leave unsaid; not only what they are, but what life is. She would have stood further away from her characters, and seen them more as a group, less as individuals" (p. 153). The telepathic communications of Mrs. Dalloway and the communal "they" which Naremore points out in The Voyage Out could easily fit this description; it echoes as well Terence Hewet's desire to write "a novel about Silence . . . the things people don't say" (TVO, 216).[11] In fact, this description applies more easily to Woolf's writing than to Persuasion, Austen's final novel on which Woolf bases her prediction. If anything, the social conventions which separate rather than unite are stronger than ever here. Far from enjoying a sense of communal life and easy access to each other's consciousness, Anne Elliot and Captain Wentworth are frustrated by society and misunderstood by each other at every turn. To reach her lover, Anne finally engages in an obliquely significant conversation with the third party, arranging for Wentworth to overhear. The prisons of ego, along with social decorum, make "what people say"— that is, straightforward face-to-face communication—a major triumph, and the end to which the novel aspires. A relationship dependent on "what they leave unsaid" is scarcely to be imagined, let alone desired.

Despite similar subject matter, Austen's realistic social satire and her periodic Augustan sentences do not, to me, make her a perfect foremother for Woolf, but Woolf certainly wishes to claim her as such. She sees Austen as the female version of those male writers with whom she feels strong affinity, James and Proust (CE I, 153). Proust especially captures Woolf's imagination, evidently supplying the metaphor of the "envelope of consciousness" which she uses to describe both an abstract

11. Naremore, World Without a Self, 24.

vision of life in her novels and criticism and her sense of maternal protection in childhood. Proust's putative descent from Austen confirms the
essentially feminine quality of this state of consciousness, for he is "perhaps too much of a woman" according to Woolf's yardstick of androgyny
in *A Room of One's Own* (p. 107). Nevertheless, Woolf's desire to find a
female predecessor, rather than merely feminine ones like Proust, reflects her self-consciousness as a woman writer and the seriousness with
which she regards the issue of sexual identity in literary history. Thus,
through imaginative identification with Emily Brontë and Jane Austen,
Woolf encourages herself to pursue her own vision. The degree to
which her writing actually resembles theirs is beside the point, for she
does not set out to imitate them in a kind of apprenticeship as Bernard
imitates Byron in *The Waves*. In fact, her efforts are the opposite of imitation; rather than submerge her own voice in someone else's, she re-
constructs these foremothers so that they confirm the validity of her
own conception of fiction. Her identification with them enables her to
be more herself, giving her the confidence and authority of one who is
the inheritor of a tradition rather than an outcast. As Ellen Hawkes says
of Woolf's friendships with women who affected her vocation, "This is
the story not of the 'anxiety of influence' but of its reassurance."[12]

Woolf has a more difficult time reconstructing George Eliot and
Charlotte Brontë, for both obviously violate her ethic of detachment
and artistic integrity, the incandescence for which she praised Austen.
Woolf returns to these virtues again and again, singling out Tolstoi and
Shakespeare, among others, as representing the highest possible reaches
of art because of their impersonality (*AROOO*, 75). Yet one senses that,
given the meager female tradition, Woolf is reluctant to sacrifice a
major figure even to this central doctrine. Woolf cannot ignore Eliot's
sense of personal grievance, but she excuses her, precisely on the
grounds that her intensely aggrieved heroines—thinly disguised versions of George Eliot who "say what she herself would have said"—
form an invaluable contribution to female psychology: "Those who fall
foul of George Eliot do so, we incline to think, on account of her heroines; and with good reason; for there is no doubt that they bring out
the worst in her, lead her into difficult places, make her self-conscious,
didactic, and occasionally vulgar. Yet if you could delete the whole sis-

12. Hawkes, "Woolf's 'Magical Garden of Women,'" in Marcus (ed.), *New Feminist
Essays*, 32.

terhood, you would have a much smaller and much inferior world, albeit a world of greater artistic perfection" ("George Eliot," *CE* I, 202). Woolf accepts a violation of "artistic perfection" caused by Eliot's sense of personal grievance as a woman because the result is an accurate representation of women. Thus, Eliot's contribution to female psychology grants her partial immunity from charges of self-consciousness and didacticism, affronts to the doctrine of impersonality.

The case of Charlotte Brontë is even more interesting. Woolf clearly finds her a fascinating and maddening figure in light of the conflict between impersonality and personal grievance. Although Woolf considers Emily Brontë the better artist, she devotes most of her essay on Haworth to Charlotte, a figure more to be reckoned with in literary history if only because of her greater productivity ("Haworth, November 1904," *Books and Portraits*, 66–69). Woolf sees her as a powerful writer but flawed in a familiar way. Her works are "deformed and twisted" because she is distracted by personal grievance (*AROOO*, 76). Yet, despite the intensity of this language, Woolf describes these deformities as local flaws in otherwise sound novels; she convicts Brontë of the lesser charge of occasional technical incompetence to acquit her of a greater one, the fundamentally angry vision implied by the title of her most famous novel, *Jane Eyre* ("ire").[13]

In Woolf's aesthetic, such a judgment would disqualify Brontë a place in the Great Tradition. Instead, Woolf treads a fine line in assessing Brontë's achievement: she praises her characters for destroying the image of female "servility" ("Men and Women," *Books and Portraits*, 29) but attributes their most outspoken moments of rebellion to lapses in technique. The distinction between self-assertion and disfiguring anger can be a subtle one, and I do not mean to insist that Woolf has erred in her judgment. I only suggest that, given alternative views of Brontë which were not only plausible but widespread, Woolf's evaluation seems at least partially conditioned by her need for a respectable female tradition. That tradition could better withstand local flaws in craftsmanship than a chronic infection of personal grievance.

These four novelists—Charlotte and Emily Brontë, George Eliot, and especially Jane Austen—form Woolf's female Great Tradition. But Woolf is also interested in less famous, less public names. She con-

---

13. For a full description of female rage and the connection between Jane Eyre and Bertha Rochester, see Gilbert and Gubar, *The Madwoman in the Attic*, 336–71.

structs her tradition from the "lives of the obscure" as well as the great (*AROOO*, 80), fleshing out the slim record of major achievement with minor talent, tracing the origin of great accomplishment in ordinary activities. Woolf's assertion that "the extraordinary woman depends on the ordinary woman" ("Women and Fiction," *CE* II, 142) informs her criticism in practice as in theory. She reads and reviews the works of admittedly second-rank female writers and the letters and diaries of women with no professional aspirations as well.

Resurrecting these women, Woolf encounters the extremes of female stereotypes, the singing thrush and the silent Madonna, impulsiveness and self-effacement. These qualities distort and inhibit women's writing, assisted by social disapprobation which judges "writing . . . slightly ridiculous in a girl; rather unseemly in a woman" ("Dr. Burney's Evening Party," *CE* III, 132). A brief vignette from *A Room of One's Own* illustrates the dynamics of these inhibitions. The Duchess of Newcastle, naturally impetuous as a person and a writer, publishes copious, ambitious treatises and earns for herself both contempt and neglect. Without constructive criticism, her work becomes wilder; stung by ridicule, she isolates herself further, and her isolation drives her deeper into social and literary eccentricity. Thus confirming the imputed freakishness of women writers, she becomes "a bogey to frighten clever girls with" (*AROOO*, 65). A girl with "a great turn for writing," Dorothy Osborne, concludes from the Duchess' example that "no woman of sense and modesty could write books" and so "wrote nothing"—that is, nothing but letters to her fiancé (p. 66). An effective monitory tale, the Duchess' sad career encourages the self-effacement of women, sending them to the safety of male pseudonyms (p. 52); to marginal, private forms such as letters and diaries; or to silence, as Osborne ceases to write altogether when she marries. "We do not know that silent lady," Woolf remarks when she reports Jonathan Swift's portrait of Osborne (Swift served as her husband's secretary; "Dorothy Osborne's Letters," *CE* III, 65); the potential author is silenced into a stereotype, the object of a great man's writing rather than a writer herself.

In light of these issues, Woolf's essay "'I Am Christina Rossetti'" is especially interesting. It not only addresses the conflict between self-effacement and artistic self-assertion but obliquely explores the implications of this conflict in the formation of a literary tradition. Woolf begins by calling Rossetti "one of the shyest of women" (*CE* IV, 54) in a roundabout, heavily qualified opening sentence which seems to respect Rossetti's reserve. The essay proceeds carefully, not grasping for presumptuous intimacy with its shy subject, until it reaches the moment when Rossetti reveals another, more assertive self. Having sat silently at a tea party for some time, Rossetti suddenly rises to her feet, states "I am Christina Rossetti," and sits down again. At this moment, Woolf says, "the glass was broken. Yes [she seemed to say] I am a poet" (p. 58). By speaking out so abruptly and calling attention to herself, Rossetti breaks the social decorum of the party, just as her self-expression as a poet rejects the more general social insistence on women's self-effacement.

Rossetti's example has a potent effect on the author. She honors Rossetti's self-assertion by addressing her directly, as if she were present. "She" becomes "you" after the moment of the party, a shift which Woolf emphasizes by repeating certain observations: "in her case, [she served] a dark God, a harsh God" (CE IV, 55) becomes "your God was a harsh God" (p. 58). Moreover, in the course of the essay, Woolf is inspired by Rossetti to assert her own opinions. Rejecting other critics, she decides "better perhaps to read for oneself" and continues with a series of sentences beginning with "I," modeled on the announcement "I am Christina Rossetti." Woolf reinforces her debt to Rossetti's example in the final paragraph, employing again the motif of breakage to emphasize their shared assertiveness: "Had I been present when Mrs. Virtue Tibbs gave her party, and had a short, elderly woman in black risen to her feet and advanced to the middle of the room, I should have committed some indiscretion—have broken a paper knife or smashed a teacup in the awkward ardor of my admiration when she said 'I am Christina Rossetti'" (p. 60). The essay also points out the value of tradition: Woolf's discovery of Rossetti sets the example for her own self-assertion. At the same time, Woolf the inheritor has reaffirmed Rossetti by praising her works and telling her story. The motif of mirroring, the closeness of subject and object, the mutual affirmation of precursor and inheritor—in fact, the central patterns and values of female literary history—underlie this essay.

Despite the efficacity of Rossetti's model, Woolf often finds self-expression as problematic as self-effacement. Women's emotional impulsiveness, a version of the biological immanence which de Beauvoir discusses in *The Second Sex*, mars their writing: "impetuosity of thought" hurts the Duchess of Newcastle ("The Duchess of Newcastle," CE III, 52) as "rambling verbosity . . . [and] impetuosity" hurt Harriette Wilson

("Harriette Wilson," CE III, 229). Mme. de Sévigné is guilty of "writing down what came into her head as if she were talking" ("Mme. de Sévigné," CE III, 66); Sara Coleridge is "diffuse and unable to conclude" ("Sara Coleridge," CE III, 225). Frequently, this impulsiveness expresses itself in the anger of personal grievance, as it did with Charlotte Brontë and George Eliot, a failing which Woolf charges almost exclusively to women. Women's writing tends to be "the dumping-ground of personal emotion" ("Women and Fiction," CE II, 148), a repository of spontaneous feeling untamed by artistic control.

The letters and diaries which form a large part of the female tradition offer particularly strong temptations in this direction. By nature, they are essentially mongrel documents, partly art and partly life, answering to and determined by real people and events rather than the imperatives of reason or the imagination. While men write theological treatises, women arrange visits, report gossip, heal quarrels. Lady Augusta Stanley's letters, "personal and emotional," represent the dominant form of female self-expression ("Two Women," CE IV, 65). Woolf finds these tendencies in her own informal writing as well. Although she prizes the "looseness" which diary-writing lends her style, she adds, "But the looseness quickly becomes slovenly. . . . I confess that the rough and random style of it, often ungrammatical and crying for a word altered, afflicts me somewhat. . . . No one can let the pen write without guidance, for fear of becoming slack and untidy" (Diary I, 266). She assures Pernel Strachey, "I'm breaking the habit of profuse and indiscriminate letter writing. I can only write, letters that is, if I don't read them: once think and I destroy" (Letters III, 63).[14]

Thus, female literary history remains problematic, however much Woolf desires to reconstruct it and draw on it. She resurrects as many women writers as she can, dignifying their efforts with her reviews. Yet she shows her ambivalence about their legacy in the recurring hypothetical loss of Jane Austen, her touchstone, threatened by the opposing tendencies toward self-effacement and aggrieved outcry. Had Austen written a hundred years earlier, Woolf speculates, she might have writ-

14. When Woolf considers letters written by men—Coleridge, Walpole, and De Quincey, for example—she observes impulsiveness there as well, but decides that it is actually an elaborate fiction designed to create the effect of spontaneity ("The Man at the Gate," CE IV, 220; "Horace Walpole," CE III, 106; "De Quincey's Autobiography," CE IV, 5). Thus, the same effect marks different relationships to a literary tradition: for women, the crude, untutored beginnings; for men, a self-conscious artistic stance.

ten nothing but private letters ("A Scribbling Dame," *Books and Portraits,* 128); had she lived Mary Wollstonecraft's life, "all her novels might have been consumed in one cry for justice" ("Mary Wollstonecraft" in "Four Figures," *CE* III, 194). Of course, it is too simple to say that Austen is threatened by inherent female weakness, as Woolf often explains women's failures as resulting from social oppression. But the female tradition which Woolf constructs, tending on one hand toward self-effacement and on the other to impulsive self-expression, seems to work against Austen's achievement as well as toward it.

Nevertheless, Woolf does not discard that tradition. It charts an authentic record of female experience, and its failures reveal at least as much about the characteristic nature of that experience as do its successes. Woolf criticizes, but she also re-evaluates the very qualities which have impeded women, often finding these "liabilities" a source of strength. Seen in light of male conventions, women may indeed appear flawed, "weak, or trivial, or sentimental," but in fact they may simply differ, "for the values of a woman are not the values of a man" ("Women in Fiction," *CE* II, 146). Woolf's general insistence on the difference between men and women and her desire for continuity with her female precursors result in a strategy of revision—of retelling women's history, re-interpreting their stories, redefining their style. In doing so, she becomes their legitimate heir. For Woolf, female experience grows out of and creates a distinctively female sensibility which naturally requires new forms of expression. Thus, female literary history must be made to yield positive values, for male models are unsuitable: "It is useless to go to the great men writers for help . . . the weight, the pace, the stride of a man's mind are too unlike her own for her to lift anything substantial from him successfully" (*AROOO,* 79). The form of books themselves must be adapted to women, Woolf says; even the sentence, a male instrument, will not serve (pp. 81, 80). It is a "clumsy weapon" in women's hands (p. 80), "pompous" and "heavy" ("Women and Fiction," *CE* II, 145). When Fanny Burney models herself on Dr. Johnson, "enlarged and swollen sentences formed on her pen" ("Dr. Burney's Evening Party," *CE* III, 133). Woolf turns to female precursors, then, not only for validation but for a necessary artistic model. In reconstructing female literary history, she also constructs a female aesthetic, built in part from the inescapable inheritance of self-effacement and impulsiveness.

For example, Woolf finds in women's writing a narrative stance which is looser and more inclusive—"suggestive" is her word—than masculine authority. Where a purely masculine sensibility might enforce a single meaning or point of view on the reader, a woman's more self-effacing nature would not be so dogmatic, so assertive. Not presuming infallible authority, lacking the egotism which makes men wish to make an Englishwoman from "a very fine Negress" (AROOO, 52) and to leave an indelible, individual stamp on their material, women writers automatically admit many different shades of meaning and possibility. Woolf advances Kipling to illustrate the masculine sensibility in subject matter and style: "his Sower who sows the Seed; and his Men who are alone with their Work; and the Flag" (p. 106). Kipling exalts the traditionally masculine spheres of profession and patriotism. Stylistically, Woolf points in particular to the capital letters, which simultaneously aggrandize and reduce. They label rather than evoke, fixing Men and Sowers in a single emblematic function, assuming that the Flag must have a single public meaning which it will invoke in every right-thinking reader. Woolf's use of Kipling, the reference to the flag, and the notion of transforming a Negress into an Englishwoman all reinforce this description of stylistic imperialism. She finds that Kipling's "crude and immature" style needs to be leavened by female "suggestive power" (p. 106). The egotism which Woolf considers masculine is a temptation of authorship; unaccustomed to such self-assertion, women can resist this aesthetic temptation just as their political disenfranchisement makes them indifferent to the charms of public honors and official uniforms in *Three Guineas*.

In implying that an artist needs to subjugate his subject matter, Bloom speaks clearly from a model in which the separation of the ego from its environment is highly desirable, but, as we have seen, other models exist which may better serve a female consciousness. The inclusiveness of Woolf's "suggestive power" recalls the diffuse ego of pre-Oedipal experience. It defines as well the achievement of Woolf's would-be novelist Dorothy Osborne. Woolf may regret Osborne's lack of professional ambition, but she praises its counterpart, an unegotistical style: "By being herself without effort or emphasis, she envelops all these odds and ends in the flow of her own personality" ("Dorothy Osborne's Letters," CE III, 62). The word "envelops" and the idea of a presence which unifies a fragmentary world suggest Woolf's memory of her mother as well. The metaphors of enveloping and flowing describe an artist who is part of her material, not one who subjugates it.

This sort of relationship can exist between writer and reader as well.

I have suggested that, in Woolf's mind, letters are too close to life to achieve the perfection of art, too tied to specific individuals and pragmatic ends to find transcendent impersonality. But, at the same time, the closeness of the relationships between human beings distinguishes Dorothy Osborne's letters; her gift for writing makes her fiancé come alive: "A good letter-writer so takes the color of the reader at the other end, that from reading the one we can imagine the other" ("Dorothy Osborne's Letters," CE III, 63). This language recalls Woolf's description of symbiotic relationships in aesthetic experiences, particularly those from "Walter Sickert" in which insects drink color from flowers. Woolf defines Osborne's talent as a writer as her ability to merge with both subject matter and audience, suggesting that feminine self-effacement can develop into an aesthetic value.

Mme. de Sévigné offers a particularly clear example of such values. She is perhaps a special case: her desperate attachment to her daughter fascinated Woolf, who describes her in words which recall idealized memories of Julia Stephen—"We sink down into her . . . We live in her presence. We are very little conscious of a disturbing medium between us" ("Mme. de Sévigné," CE III, 67–68). Woolf explicitly attributes Mme. de Sévigné's appeal to her lack of pretension and egotism. Woolf's closing celebration of the letters depends on their being embedded in experience and ongoing human relationships as Dorothy Osborne's were; they are part of a personal and emotional context rather than a public one, communal rather than individualistic in their genesis:

> So she takes her way through the world, and sends her letters, radiant and glowing with all this various traffic from one end of France to the other, twice weekly. As the fourteen volumes so spaciously unfold their story of twenty years it seems that this world is large enough to enclose everything. Here is the garden that Europe has been digging for many centuries; into which so many generations have poured their blood; here it is at last fertilised, bearing flowers. And the flowers are not those rare and solitary blossoms—great men, with their poems, and their conquests. The flowers in this garden are a whole society of full-grown men and women from whom want and struggle have been removed; growing together in harmony, each contributing something that the other lacks. By way of proving it the letters of Madame de Sévigné are often shared by other pens; now her son takes up the pen; the Abbé adds his paragraph; even the simple girl—la petite personne—is not afraid to pipe up on the same page. (p. 70)

The scene is almost entirely feminized, defined by flowers, the garden, and the party. It specifically excludes the transcendent art and public works of men—"their poems, and their conquests"—in favor of the immanent worlds of nature and human relationships which, under Mme. de Sévigné's influence, flower into a kind of panoply of life, "radiant" and "enclos[ing]." In this feminine atmosphere, authorship has become so flexible as to admit many individuals so that the letters mirror their setting. The text grows out of and reflects the inclusive social harmony of the party. Art and life interpenetrate to produce letters of special charm, possible only because Mme. de Sévigné does not fancy herself a Promethean artist writing for posterity. Woolf's final sentence—"But what was happening outside?"—suggests that she recognizes the element of fantasy in the scene, but this does not undermine her appreciation of it.

This loosening of a single author's authority resembles Woolf's own distinctive narrative stance in which the novel slips imperceptibly from third-person narration to the thoughts of a character.[15] This characteristic owes a debt to the experiments of modernism, but I believe it grows from Woolf's notion of femininity as well. Without entering into the debate about which terminology best describes Woolf's particular experiments, we may note that Woolf rejected Joyce's stream of consciousness for its egotism (*Diary* II, 14). In other words, she is preoccupied not only with the inner workings of a consciousness, as "Mr. Bennett and Mrs. Brown" might suggest, but also with the interpenetrations of several consciousnesses, an inclusive arrangement in which narrative privileges of authority or priority are marginal at best.[16]

As these discussions of Dorothy Osborne and Mme. de Sévigné suggest, impulsiveness also takes a role in a feminine aesthetic. Most obviously, Woolf praises women writers for their "flow and abundance," "instinctive and natural understanding," and "impressive fire" even as she chides their untempered emotion ("Mme. de Sévigné," *CE* III, 66, 68; "The Duchess of Newcastle," *CE* III, 57). This is certainly the most conventional of Woolf's revisions; she simply finds the occasional effective

15. Erich Auerbach, "The Brown Stocking," *Mimesis*, trans. W. R. Trask (Princeton, 1953); Miller, "Virginia Woolf's All Soul's Day," in Friedman and Vickery (eds.), *The Shaken Realist*; Naremore, *World Without a Self*.

16. For a full and exciting account of anonymity and feminism in Woolf's novels, see DiBattista, *Fables of Anon.*

expression of tendencies which are more often extreme and uncontrolled. More interesting is her reassessment of the role of emotion in women's writing, especially in light of the emotional differences between men and women which she insists on. Considering the case of Kipling, the quintessential male author, Woolf observes: "Do what she will a woman cannot find in them that fountain of perpetual life which the critics assure her is there. It is not only that they celebrate male virtues, enforce male values and describe the world of men; it is that the emotion with which these books are permeated is to a woman incomprehensible . . . the emotion which is so deep, so subtle, so symbolical to a man moves a woman to wonder" (AROOO, 106). If women are perplexed by male emotions, men may be equally perplexed by women's, and the forms which are designed to express one may not be congenial to the other. With her remarks about Kipling, Woolf raises the possibility that, in some cases, women's writing is not marred by emotion itself but by emotion twisted into male conventions which have the effect of "crushing and distorting" what they are supposed to shape ("Women and Fiction," CE II, 145). Quoting Bathsheba in Far from the Madding Crowd—"I have the feelings of a woman, but I have only the language of men"—Woolf insists that women must find new means of expression to complete their political and economic emancipation: "From that dilemma arise infinite confusions and complications. Energy has been liberated, but into what forms is it to flow? To try the accepted forms, to discard the unfit, to create others which are more fitting, is a task that must be accomplished before there is freedom or achievement" ("Men and Women," Books and Portraits, 30).

Woolf takes up this task in "Memories of a Working Women's Guild," in which she assesses a collection of essays—often memoirs, we are not surprised to see—by working women. Like so many of their precursors, they write in the midst of obstacles and distractions, lacking as a result the appropriate artistic impersonality. Woolf begins her review with the characteristic judgment that "the writing lacks detachment and literary breadth. . . . [It is] an impure art, much infected by life" (CE IV, 146–47). Nevertheless, Woolf wonders whether detachment would be possible when she confronts the case of a working girl seduced by her employer. She notes that this author has chosen to suppress rather than give rein to her emotions, but even in this form her feelings distract from the aesthetic impression. She has not "disinfected" them into art, but this failure does not lie so clearly with female weakness as it has in other of Woolf's essays. We sense an experience too powerful for detachment, not a sensibility too weak or unskilled to control common human emotions, in Woolf's observation that "an extra weight of the world's grievances seemed to press upon her shoulders" (p. 139).

From this recognition, Woolf re-evaluates the awkwardness of the woman's narrative as a source of insight, not simply as a technical flaw: "The stiff words, which conceal all emotion conventionally enough, are yet illuminating" (CE IV, 147), for the repression which they imply tells the story of woman's vexed place in the world. In a male society, women's experience cannot be expressed; whatever anger or passion the woman may feel she has chosen to twist into stiff words and a severe appearance. The memoir neatly merges two central difficulties which women confront, social conventions of female propriety and literary conventions of aesthetic propriety, in an unwed mother's story, stiffly told in conventional prose. The flaws of the memoir are as much the fault of inadequate forms, which repress rather than express emotion, as of the woman's lack of training or skill. Woolf has prepared the way for this revisionist reading by an earlier comment about the suppressed passion of the women's speeches, "which even the weight of a public meeting could not flatten out entirely." She looks forward to the day when this energy, now trapped in the proprieties of public occasions, will be liberated: "This force of theirs, this smouldering heat which broke the crust now and then and licked the surface with a hot and fearless flame, is about to break through and melt us together so that life will be richer and books more complex" (pp. 141–42). The original contrast between the infection of emotion and the purity of artistic conventions is here transformed by the imagery of fire and crust, which suggests a vital force destroying a dead and obsolete surface. Woolf hopes that the conflict between male forms and female emotions may yet resolve itself in a new language, for "these [women's] voices are beginning only now to emerge from silence into half-articulate speech" (p. 148).

As Woolf revises her evaluation of these women authors, she revises her own stance as a writer as well. When she criticizes lack of artistic detachment, she speaks explicitly as a member of the upper-class literary establishment with a set of preordained standards: "What ideas does it suggest? What old arguments and memories does it arouse in me?" (CE IV, 134). Because of this identity, she is an "outcast" from the

155

group of working-class women she addresses, "benevolent" perhaps, but estranged (p. 141). As she continues, however, she closes the gap between them, calling attention to her own identity as a writer; her writing takes the shape of a letter, an appropriate female form to match their memoirs, and she interrupts herself as they are interrupted by domestic responsibilities. Finally, in the midst of a conventional encomium for the director of the guild—"you have given your best years"—she stops abruptly, saying, "With the old messages of friendship and admiration, I will make an end" (p. 148). The "old messages of friendship," of emotion and personal relationship, replace the "old arguments" of the intellectual, mainly male tradition.

The last sentence, "With the old messages of friendship and admiration, I will make an end," may carry a more radical implication as well: that Woolf will discard "old messages" of any sort, whether arguments or encomiums, having recognized how much they conceal of her audience's experience. "[You] will not let me finish that sentence," she says to the working women, as if the authenticity of their emotions and even their unpolished writing have shaken her out of her superior glibness. The pull of the female tradition has overcome class differences. As Woolf underscores the difficulties of the female writer by acting them out herself, she changes from a detached critic to an awkward female writer. Yet, although she ends abruptly, she has at least succeeded in rejecting inappropriate conventions. The deliberate anticlimax of the essay's conclusion signals Woolf's interest in creating a new, female form by making use of female experience, even if it begins in half-articulate speech or silence.

Like "'I am Christina Rossetti,'" this essay serves an important purpose for the author by bringing her in touch with the female tradition in its broad outlines. In doing so, both essays lead her to a closer relationship with her subject matter; no longer an impersonal critic detached from her material, she mirrors it, acting out its own tendencies, drawing an identity from its distinctive character. She both creates the female tradition by writing about it and is created by it as she redefines herself in its image. Like the women's college, the Working Women's Guild offers the possibility of female community, but this time Woolf turns a potentially regressive fantasy into a serious exploration of female experience and literary form. Yet despite the optimism implicit in this mutual female creating, "Memories of a Working Women's Guild" marks only a provisional achievement. The old forms are destroyed, but the new ones have yet to be created. The great triumph of "'I am Christina Rossetti'" is an act of self-assertion—"I am"—but here Woolf suggests that a more complex female narrative must complete that beginning. She seems struck—and struck dumb—by the enormous task of charting a woman's place in a man's world.

The difficulties of this position are great, but Woolf resists the temptation to evade them because they stand at the center of a woman writer's point of view. Woolf insists on recognizing women's place outside of the mainstream of society and even cultivating that place as a source of shared and potentially fruitful experience among women: "Different we are, as facts have proved, both in sex and in education," she writes in *Three Guineas* (p. 103). In that work, an explicit attack on what she perceives as a masculine, warmongering culture, Woolf recommends "an attitude of complete indifference" among women (p. 107)— meaning not only the refusal to cheer or wring hands over male escapades, which she names explicitly, but also the careful guarding of feminine qualities from masculine encroachment, the formulating of the relationship of the sexes "in difference" so that women are neither marginalized nor absorbed. This assertion, made in the political context of *Three Guineas*, also serves for Woolf's view of literary history. Although both masculine oppression and feminine reaction, in the form of either self-effacement or emotional outcry, have cramped female achievement, Woolf nevertheless finds a strong source of support in women's writing, where exclusion breeds a different, feminine aesthetic and even silence holds the promise of a distinctively feminine voice.

It is certainly fitting that *A Room of One's Own*, Woolf's fullest exploration of female literary history, should act out the tendencies of the female tradition. It does so most obviously in the movement of the story, beginning with the narrator's expulsion from Oxbridge, as the isolated woman writer is denied access to the male tradition and its intellectual resources. The narrator constructs a female tradition—one in which a contemporary woman might find a legitimate place—and simultaneously makes her way through a series of alien rooms—the British Museum, an inn, and the "common sitting room" which reflects woman's enslavement in domesticity—to a room of her own.

A Room of One's Own is also modeled on the Demeter-Kore myth.

Both Mary Beton and Judith Shakespeare are resurrected in the narrative and leave a permanent, life-giving legacy: Mary Beton passes on her name and the inheritance which will last "forever" (p. 37); Judith Shakespeare leaves her "spirit," which "lives in you and me" (p. 118). The narrator is the most obvious beneficiary of these legacies, both as Mary Beton's niece and as a writer. A woman writer writing about women and fiction, she is both the author and subject matter of the essay. The room where she arrives is not simply material independence; it is a role in the tradition which she herself has created in the essay and which creates her as a writer. At the end of her investigations, in her own room, she writes the first sentence of an essay entitled "Women and Fiction" (p. 108). This series of reflections, in which the writer finds herself in her subject matter, and mother-precursor and daughter-inheritor create one another, is only one way in which A Room of One's Own acts out the motifs of resurrection and mutual creativity.

Equally interesting is the way in which the warring impulses of self-effacement and the desire to express personal grievance govern the narrative structure. Woolf's narrator faces contradictory sets of rules for women and authors, complicated still further by her subject matter. She must not assert herself, but she must write. She must write about women and writing, but she must not be angry. Certainly, she must not degenerate into personal grievance, no matter what her difficulties. Above all, she must not offend men, even though, as a woman writer, she experiences them as the chief impediment to women's writing and, as the writer of this essay, she must explain the subject "Women and Fiction." And so on. The narrator resembles Laetitia Pilkington in "The Lives of the Obscure": "It is her wish to entertain, her unhappy fate to sob. . . . It is her duty to entertain; it is her instinct to conceal." Caught squarely between two opposite impulses, personal grievance and self-effacement, both of which threaten the aesthetic imperative to entertain, "Laetitia is in the great tradition of English women of letters" (CE IV, 129–30). Like Laetitia, the narrator finds herself in a series of double binds—a predicament which, if it does not induce schizophrenia, can inspire creativity.[17] And A Room of One's Own is creative. The narrator spins a sophisticated, ironic narrative from apparently self-defeating materials; she invents a cover story which reveals when it

17. Gregory Bateson, Steps Toward an Ecology of Mind (London, 1972), 276–78.

conceals, and conceals most when it is apparently most direct. *A Room of One's Own* may ultimately be one version of the new female form which Woolf anticipated in "Memories of a Working Women's Guild," subverting conventional narrative expectations and fashioning new strategies from old stereotypes.

Yet, on the few occasions when the essay's formal aspects have been considered, it has been praised for the most innocuous of virtues, "lightness of touch" and "playfulness." It is called "delicately whimsical," avoiding, above all, "any taint of shrillness."[18] Woolf, however, was concerned about its "shrill feminine tone" (*Diary* III, 262). How can we explain this discrepancy of opinion? An answer is suggested by a passage in *A Room of One's Own* itself, in which the narrator considers the contrast between dinners at women's and men's colleges, the one plain and frugal, the other sumptuous: "If I had said anything of the kind [at the women's college] I should have been prying and searching into the secret economies of a house which to the stranger wears so fine a front of gaiety and courage" (p. 18). *A Room of One's Own* has its own "secret economies" for allowing a front of gaiety, lightness, and whimsy—not thriftiness, but hidden mechanisms of repression, irony, and encoding which maintain the equilibrium of the narrative, barely preventing it from splintering into angry incoherence or resigned silence. Its roundabout argument does not result from undisciplined "fancy" or from "following its own impulses wherever they lead."[19] Quite the contrary, it reflects the inhibitions of its narrator, afraid to assert herself by stating her own opinions and voicing her own emotions, returning again and again to the same unfinished business and veering away at the last moment from the obvious conclusion.

The difficulties and conflicts of a woman writer express themselves at the outset. Woolf (for she apparently is still Woolf at this point) promises, "I am going to develop in your presence as fully and freely as I can the train of thought [that a woman needs money and a room of her own to write, and to] . . . lay bare the ideas and prejudices that lie behind

18. J. B. Batchelor, "Feminism in Virginia Woolf," in Claire Sprague (ed.), *Virginia Woolf: A Collection of Critical Essays* (Englewood Cliffs, 1971), 169; Showalter, *A Literature of Their Own*, 282.

19. Arnold Bennett, *Evening Standard*, November, 1929, in Robin Majumdar and Allen McLaurin (eds.), *Virginia Woolf: The Critical Heritage* (London, 1975), 259; Rosenthal, *Virginia Woolf*, 230.

this statement" (p. 4). With this assurance, the obfuscation begins. Woolf immediately drops the veil of fiction with elaborate, conspiratorial subterfuge—"I need not say that what I am about to describe has no existence" (p. 4). She advances thinly disguised versions of Oxford/Cambridge ("Oxbridge") and Newnham, the women's college at which she is delivering this very lecture ("Fernham") as "inventions," or, less politely, "lies" (p. 4). She is already covering her tracks. Retreating still further, she adopts the unreal narrative persona "I"—"only a convenient term for someone who has no existence" (p. 4). In the context of this essay, this statement is at least odd: Woolf has been asked to speak about women and fiction, presumably being something of an authority as "the finest living critic" in English (*Diary* III, 16; see also p. 22), as well as the author of *Mrs. Dalloway* and *To the Lighthouse*, both critically acclaimed (*Orlando*, a great popular success, was just beginning to receive notice when Woolf delivered the first of these talks). Why would she choose to stand behind this unreal "I"? Who is this persona whom Woolf has chosen to adopt?

She tells her readers to call her "any name you please—it is not a matter of any importance" (p. 5) in a typical gesture of feminine self-effacement. Yet the names she suggests, "Mary Beton, Mary Seton, Mary Carmichael," are indeed important. They are taken from an old English ballad in which the fourth Mary, Mary Hamilton, anticipates her death for having borne the king's illegitimate son:

> Last night there were four Mary's
> Tonight there'll be but three,
> There was Mary Beton, and Mary Seton,
> and Mary Carmichael, and me.[20]

We recall the theme of seduction and silence in "Memories of a Working Women's Guild," and the general dangers of immanence to creativity; we look ahead to the story of Judith Shakespeare, whose suicide stills a potentially great literary voice. Thus, in denying a "real" existence, the narrator associates herself with anonymity, immanence, and silence—all, apparently, the enemies of literary tradition.

If we turn this statement around, however, asserting that "someone who has no real being" is Everywoman, we begin to see the possibilities

---

20. Patricia Meyer Spacks, *The Female Imagination* (New York, 1975), 12.

of a cover story. If "Anon, who wrote so many poems without signing them, was often a woman" (p. 51), then this unreal "I" who might be any of several women is the perfect architect of female literary history. In denying that she has an identity or experience, the narrator covertly describes both; Judith Shakespeare is not a "lie" but a version of herself.

In finding a common experience with other women, even if that experience is anonymity, she further defines the female consciousness and aesthetic. The casual suggestion of multiple narrators recalls Mme. de Sévigné's inclusive letters. The equally casual deployment of these personas as objects of the narrator's attention—Mary Beton becomes, at one point, the aunt who leaves the narrator £500 a year; Mary Carmichael becomes a contemporary novelist whom the narrator is reading—loosens the rigid separation of narrator and subject matter, a strategy which Woolf uses in "'I am Christina Rossetti'" and "Memories of a Working Women's Guild." These examples are doubly significant: the narrator resurrects her dead aunt in the story; the aunt makes it possible for her niece to write by leaving her an income. Similarly, the narrator brings the novelist Mary Carmichael to life by writing about her, while Mary Carmichael serves as subject matter for the narrator, making her writing possible. Each pair of Marys shares a name. We see again mutuality and reflection which define the female tradition. Paradoxically, it is revealed here by an act of self-effacement, the one by which the narrator disclaimed identity.

The structure of the narrative—that is, the narrator's story of her inquiry into the subject "women and fiction"—proceeds by the same paradox of revealing concealment. Head bowed submissively in the face of her task, the narrator seems to strike a genuine insight when she begins her musings, recounted in the imagery of the darting fish (pp. 3–4). But once she lands the fish, the narrator blushes at its insignificance. Having just promised to "develop in your presence as fully and freely as I can . . . [my] train of thought . . . [to] lay bare [my] ideas" (p. 4), she demurs: "I will not trouble you with that thought now" (p. 5).

Nevertheless, she is still excited by the idea which she hesitates to express; preoccupied, she wanders onto the grounds of a male college, whence she is chased by a beadle, an incident which "sent my little fish into hiding" (p. 6). She observes, "What idea it had been that had sent me so audaciously trespassing I could not now remember" (p. 6). Repression has replaced reticence as the controlling force of the narrative:

she first refrained from mentioning the idea and now has forgotten it. In the words which she uses to describe other women, she is both "locked out" and "locked in" (p. 24)—the narrator means both excluded and imprisoned, but the latter term implies the repression which she has just experienced.

These incidents apparently frustrate the narrator's inquiry and the audience's enlightenment. But when she withholds her thought, the narrator coyly remarks, "If you look carefully you may find it for yourselves in the course of what I am going to say" (p. 5). Her thought is this: a woman is afraid to think her own thoughts because she thinks they are not good enough; excluded from male centers of learning, she finds her self-doubt confirmed and so refuses to acknowledge her own ideas. After the beadle's assault, the woman writer whose subject is fiction turns, not to herself or to her sisters, but to Charles Lamb, the male essayist, writing about Milton, the "bogey" who inhibits women's writing (pp. 6–7). This passage apparently develops by free association, but the "chance" which brings Lamb to mind is "some stray memory of some old essay about revisiting Oxbridge" (p. 6). In other words, the narrator bows to the authority of a man with access to the authorized intellectual tradition, access which she lacks.

The narrator routinely denies her own authority in this way, preferring to consult male historians and excuse the ideas which she does advance as mysterious apparitions which intrude on the narrative without her conscious thought: "I only take what chance has floated to my feet," she protests (p. 78). A pair of pictures contrasting male privilege with female poverty comes to her mind unbidden; like "a current setting in of its own accord . . . [they] had me entirely at their mercy." Despite the obvious significance of the two pictures as a pair, she evades their implications and insists that they are "disjointed and disconnected and nonsensical"; she reports them "shamefacedly" (p. 19). She even evades her own evasions: although she calls for an investigation of male psychology by women with £500 a year, she does not undertake one herself (p. 37). This oversight is certainly meaningful, because, immediately after the narrator makes her recommendation, she describes how she came to inherit her own £500—an apparent *non sequitur* which she herself calls an "interruption." But, of course, a narrator who calls attention to her own *non sequiturs* must have some strategy in mind, and "interruption" is a loaded word in this narrative of repression.

Her conspicuous reticence calls attention to itself, reminding us of all the women of the past who, she says, "altered their values in deference to the opinion of others" (p. 77), "so terribly accustomed to conceal- ment and suppression" (p. 88). Covertly, she tells their story by acting it out. Her own silences mirror the absence of books by women on the library shelves, and both "blank spaces" (p. 54) ask us to remark on them. Her comment "if I were rewriting history" (p. 68) carries a simi- lar double message: she does not take credit for doing so but she is rewriting history by uncovering her female predecessors, and she does so with the female strategy of self-effacement, revising history's meth- ods as well as its content.

One aspect of this self-effacement is the fiction—"invention" or "lies," according to one's taste—with which she cloaks her identity. In fact, the explicitly fictitious parts of A Room of One's Own are the only pas- sages for which the narrator asserts authorship. Twice she refers to "the story of Judith Shakespeare as I made it" (pp. 51, 56), and admits that she has "made up" Lady Wilchisea's biography (p. 64): "She must have shut herself up in a room in the country to write, and been torn asunder by bitterness and scruples perhaps, though her husband was of the kindest, their married life perfection. She 'must have,' I say, because when one comes to seek out the facts about Lady Wilchisea, one finds, as usual, that almost nothing is known about her" (p. 63). Lady Wilchisea and her struggles to write inevitably slip through the net of male his- tory. In the absence of facts, the narrator's guess is as good as any.

But the narrator's achievement is more substantial than that. Her revi- sionist strategy of history does not simply add new faces to the pageant but implicitly challenges the authoritative structure of objective, unas- sailable, factual history which is the prerogative of Oxbridge-educated men. At the British Museum, she expects "unprejudiced" conclusions, rigorously drawn, from male authors (p. 25). She discovers that they possess "no apparent qualification save that they are not women" (p. 27) —a condition which quickly reveals itself as an aid to misunderstand- ing, not disinterestedness. Her research uncovers centuries of prejudice and insults, including the recurring remark that a woman's acting/ preaching/composing music is like a dog's walking on its hind legs: "It is not done well, but you are surprised to find it done at all." Drily she remarks, "So accurately does history repeat itself" (p. 56)—by telling the same misogynist joke over and over again. By deferring to male authority, the narrator reveals its inadequacy. Her own mirroring fiction of self-effacement records more accurately the nature of women and their place in a male-dominated society.

The narrator's self-effacement covers (and reveals) more than a lack of intellectual confidence and a fear of male reprisal, although it certainly responds to these pressures. It defends her against intense emotions within herself. At the British Museum she discovers the "submerged truth" of her investigations in her own doodling (again, insight comes unbidden): not the contradictory opinions of the men she has read, but her own anger. The narrator could hardly discover more clearly the importance of her own emotions, or the "authority of experience," as the Wife of Bath says, to the subject "women and fiction." Nevertheless—or perhaps consequently—she immediately sets out to explain the insight away. Having begun the passage with surprise— "But what was anger doing there?"—she begins to defuse it. She denies both its justification—it is "foolish," a term she uses twice—and its unexpectedness—"There was nothing specially remarkable" in the anger. By the end of the passage, the "submerged truth" becomes "foolish vanities." The narrator fails to confront the power of her anger, especially apparent in her surprise at it—that is, it threatens her enough to warrant repression. She concludes complacently, "Soon my own anger was explained and done with" (p. 302), switching her inquiry to a more distant and hence safer subject, the anger of men against women. She describes this anger in words which could easily define her own, suggesting that she has simply projected her emotions onto the opposite sex rather than "explained" them: "But it was anger that had gone underground and mixed itself with all kinds of other emotions. To judge from its odd effects, it was anger disguised and complex, not anger simple and open" (p. 32). As she hides herself behind her enemy, the Professor, men have again become the focus of this inquiry about women.

Nevertheless, she keeps the subject of female anger before us by examining and quoting the works of authors such as Lady Wilchisea and Charlotte Brontë. While we cannot deny that Woolf really does object to Brontë's bald expression of personal grievance, the accusation of "jerks" and interruptions in the narrative of *Jane Eyre* calls attention to the same characteristics in *A Room of One's Own*. That one book jerks because of overt anger and the other because of repressed anger dramatizes the double binds in which women writers find themselves. We should remember, too, that Woolf has constructed an unreal "I" who discovered her anger in a doodle. The many-layered cover story of the narrative by which anger is expressed—Woolf standing behind "I" standing behind Charlotte Brontë—reveals the stubborn knot of art, emotion, and repression at least as much as it recommends a detached, impersonal artistry.[21]

This ironic subtext, which conceals the narrator's authority in general and her anger in particular, reveals itself most clearly when she suggests that women might contribute to literature by writing about men. We are cautioned to look for concealed messages by the circumspection with which she approaches the subject, "very warily, on the very tips of my toes (so cowardly am I, so afraid of the lash that was once almost laid on my own shoulders)" (p. 94). Fear of reprisal guides the progress of the argument, particularly likely to draw attack, as it concerns critiques of men by women. The narrator hopes to sidestep the attack by suggesting gently, in a "murmur," that the woman novelist "should learn to laugh, without bitterness, at the vanities—say rather at the peculiarities, for it is a less offensive word—of the other sex" (p. 94). The parenthetical expression emphasizes fear of offending men as a primary consideration governing even the narrator's choice of words. The choice itself is striking, considering that the narrator judged "vanities" (in fact, "foolish vanities") an appropriate enough term for her own self-respect. The deliberate comic exaggeration of the narrator's caution calls attention to it as dramatic artifice, as part of a rhetorical strategy.

Carefully, the narrator encodes her real message beneath the surface of politeness. She recommends revealing to men the "spot the size of a shilling at the back of the head" which they cannot see themselves, and the coin imagery raises the issue of economic oppression around which the whole book revolves (p. 96). The narrator's program is not simply the dispassionate quest for truth but carries an undertone of malice. This hint, that women might expose oppression and hypocrisy as well as harmless peculiarities, undercuts her recommendation against bitterness. Her choice of male models in the ostensibly genial truthtelling confirms this subtext: "Think how much women have profited

21. For a discussion of Jane Eyre's anger and its odd role in *A Room of One's Own*, see Mary Jacobus, "The Difference of View," in Mary Jacobus (ed.), *Women Writing and Writing About Women* (London, 1979), 10–21.

by the comments of Juvenal, by the criticism of Strindberg. Think with what humanity and brilliancy men, from the earliest ages, have pointed out to women that dark place at the back of the head! . . . Not of course that anyone in their senses would counsel her to hold up to scorn and ridicule of set purpose—literature shows the futility of what is written in that spirit" (p. 94).

The passage is deeply and bitterly ironic. The bulk of the narrative consists of the incessant and frequently insulting catalogue of male views of women: "Lord Birkenhead's opinion of, Dean Inge's opinion of, La Bruyère's opinion of, Dr. Johnson's opinion of, Mr. Oscar Browning's opinion of" (p. 29). When the narrator discovers the anger and inconsistency of these men, she belies the humanity and brilliancy of at least a few critics. And her insistence on the "futility" of scorn and ridicule is made a laughingstock by the reference to Juvenal, our most ancient and vitriolic misogynist. The passage does not counsel good taste and moderation in women's writing. It first of all points out the hostility which permeates male writing about women, mocks the "for your own good" rhetoric used to justify such attacks, and acts out the pressures of gentility which, in contrast, restrict women's writing and force their true feelings "underground."

This veil of concealment lifts away when "Mary Beton ceases to speak" (p. 109) and is replaced by another "I" whom I will call Virginia Woolf. In this final section, Woolf recapitulates Mary Beton's argument as if participating in a ceremony of investiture, summarizing Mary Beton's general points and affirming a personal connection with her. Woolf notes that she has "not been educated at a university" (p. 113), reminding us of the narrator's expulsion from the grounds, and insists "I often like women," echoing Mary Carmichael's astonishing proposition that "Chloe likes Olivia," the basis of her new female novel (p. 86). The narrator's fictions appear here as facts—"Oxbridge" translates, without fanfare, into Cambridge—although, given the revisionist role of fiction within the narrative and Woolf's closing passage exalting the fictional Judith Shakespeare, we cannot read this shift as a triumph of objective fact over subjective fiction. Rather, Woolf bridges the gap between these two apparent opposites by claiming these fictions as her own experience. Significantly, although she maintains the fiction of Mary Beton's authorship for a few paragraphs, she quickly identifies herself as the true author. "She has told you" (p. 109), Woolf begins, but soon assumes responsibility: "when I look back through these notes and criticize my train of thought as I had made them" (p. 113). Woolf adopts authority and authorship hesitantly, as Mary Beton did, revealing her resemblance to the unreal "I."

The final section insists on the special characteristics of women—ostensibly liabilities but fruitful enough to produce *A Room of One's Own*—and the forms and traditions which can be created from them. When Woolf begins her "peroration," she quickly discovers that this rhetorical convention, male in its assertiveness, is as clumsy a weapon as the male sentence. The first idea which comes to her mind is to remind women of their responsibilities, "but these exhortations can safely, I think, be left to the other sex, who will put them, and indeed have put them, with far greater eloquence than I can compass" (pp. 114–15). Then, on the authority of male sources, she remembers that women dislike women and so decides to end with "something particularly disagreeable" (p. 115). But, again, the male conventions do not suit her: "But how does it go? What can I think of? The truth is, I often like women" (p. 115). And she likes them for all the qualities which the male peroration could not encompass or express but which the narrative has just enacted: "I like their unconventionality. I like their subtlety. I like their anonymity" (p. 115).

Woolf closes *A Room of One's Own* with a tribute to Judith Shakespeare, describing the process of reciprocal literary history which she has sought as a woman writer, novelist, and critic.[22] She experiences her relationship with Judith Shakespeare as a continuity, even an identification: "She lives in you and me, and in many other women" (p. 117). As Woolf continues, she describes a mutual, circular process of giving birth to the poet; Judith Shakespeare, precursor of contemporary women writers, is born both from her own precursors—more ancient and anonymous than she—and from contemporary writers, her inheritors:

> The opportunity will come and the dead poet who was Shakespeare's sister will put on the body which she has so often laid down. Drawing her life from the lives of the unknown who were her forerunners . . . she will be born. As for her coming without that preparation [self-assertion by contemporary writers, including the repudiation of "Milton's bogey" and

22. See also Alice Fox, "Literary Allusion as Feminist Criticism in *A Room of One's Own*," *Philological Quarterly*, LXIII (1984), 155–56.

another patriarchal oppressions], without that effort on our part, without that determination that when she is born again she will find it possible to live and write her poetry, that we cannot expect, for that would be impossible. (p. 118)

As mothers validate their daughters' ambitions, those daughters recreate their mothers. With their achievements, daughters invite the revision of literary history which reveals not only particular precursors but the sense of female creativity which is continuity itself, the "continuing presence" which inhabits the body of every woman artist.

Bibliography

Abel, Elizabeth. "(E)merging Identities: The Dynamics of Female Friendship in Contemporary Fiction by Women." *Signs*, VI (1981), 413–35.
———. "Reply to Gardiner." *Signs*, VI (1981), 442–44.
Abel, Elizabeth, Marianne Hirsch, and Elizabeth Langland, eds. *The Voyage In: Fictions of Female Development.* Hanover, N.H., 1983.
Albright, Daniel. *Personality and Impersonality: Lawrence, Woolf, Mann.* Chicago, 1978.
Ames, Kenneth J. "Elements of Mock-Heroic in Virginia Woolf's *Mrs. Dalloway.*" *Modern Fiction Studies*, XVII (1972), 363–74.
Annan, Noel. *Leslie Stephen: His Thought and Character in Relation to His Time.* London, 1951.
Auden, W. H. *The Dyer's Hand.* New York, 1962.
Auerbach, Erich. *Mimesis.* Translated by W. R. Trask. Princeton, 1953.
Baldanza, Frank. "*To the Lighthouse* Again." *Publications of the Modern Language Association*, LXX (1955), 548–52.
———. "Clarissa Dalloway's Party Consciousness." *Modern Fiction Studies*, II (1956), 24–30.
[Banks], Joanne Trautmann. *The Jessamy Brides: The Friendship Between Virginia Woolf and Vita Sackville-West.* University Park, Pa., 1973.
———, ed. "Some New Woolf Letters." *Modern Fiction Studies*, XXX (1984), 175–202.
Bateson, Gregory. *Steps Toward an Ecology of Mind.* London, 1972.
Bazin, Nancy Topping. *Virginia Woolf and the Androgynous Vision.* New Brunswick, N.J., 1973.
Beja, Morris. "*To the Lighthouse*": A Casebook. London, 1970.
Bell, Barbara Currier, and Carol Ohmann. "Virginia Woolf's Criticism: A Polemical Preface." *Critical Inquiry*, I (1974), 361–71.
Bell, Clive. *Art.* London, 1913.
Bell, Quentin. *The Biography of Virginia Woolf.* 2 vols. London, 1972.
Benedict, Ruth. *Patterns of Culture.* 1943; rpr. Boston, 1959.
Bloom, Alan, trans. *The Republic of Plato.* New York, 1968.

Bloom, Harold. *The Anxiety of Influence: A Theory of Poetry.* New York, 1973.

Boone, Joseph Allen. "The Meaning of Elvedon in *The Waves*: A Key to Bernard's Experience and Woolf's Vision." *Modern Fiction Studies,* XXVII (1981–82), 629–37.

Bowlby, John. *Attachment.* New York, 1969.

Boyd, Elizabeth French. *Bloomsbury Heritage: Their Mothers and Their Aunts.* New York, 1976.

Broner, E. M., and Cathy N. Davidson, eds. *The Lost Tradition: Mothers and Daughters in Literature.* New York, 1980.

Brontë, Emily. *Wuthering Heights.* New York, 1972.

Campbell, Joseph. *The Hero with a Thousand Faces.* Princeton, 1949.

Chodorow, Nancy. *The Reproduction of Mothering: The Sociology of Gender.* Berkeley, 1978.

————. "Gender, Relation, and Difference in Psychoanalytic Perspective." In *The Future of Difference,* edited by Hester Eisenstein and Alice Jardine. Boston, 1980.

Chodorow, Nancy, and Susan Contratto. "The Fantasy of the Perfect Mother." In *Rethinking the Family: Some Feminist Questions,* edited by Barrie Thorne and Marilyn Yalom. New York, 1982.

Chopin, Kate. *The Awakening.* 1899; rpr. New York, 1976.

Cixous, Hélène. "The Laugh of Medusa." Translated by Keith Cohen and Paula Cohen. *Signs,* I (1976), 875–93.

————. "Poetry is/and (the) political." Thirty Years After: Feminism Since *The Second Sex.* Conference, New York University, October, 1977.

————. "Castration or Decapitation." Translated by Annette Kuhn. *Signs,* VII (1981), 41–55.

Cook, Blanche Wiesen. "'Women Alone Stir My Imagination': Lesbianism and the Cultural Tradition." *Signs,* IV (1979), 718–39.

Corsa, Helen Storm. "*To the Lighthouse*: Death, Mourning and Transfiguration." *Literature and Psychology,* XXI (1971), 115–31.

de Beauvoir, Simone. *The Second Sex.* Edited and translated by H. M. Parshley. New York, 1952.

de Courtivron, Isabelle, and Elaine Marks, eds. *New French Feminisms: An Anthology.* Amherst, 1980.

DeSalvo, Louise. "Sorting, Sequencing and Dating the Drafts of Virginia Woolf's *The Voyage Out.*" *Bulletin of Research in the Humanities,* LXXXII (1979), 271–93.

————. "Lighting the Cave: The Relationship between Vita Sackville-West and Virginia Woolf." *Signs,* VIII (1982), 195–214.

DiBattista, Maria. *Virginia Woolf's Major Novels: The Fables of Anon.* New Haven, 1980.

Diehl, Joanne Feit. "'Come Slowly—Eden': An Exploration of the Women Poets and Their Muse." *Signs,* III (1978), 572–87.

Dinnerstein, Dorothy. *The Mermaid and the Minotaur: Sexual Arrangements and Human Malaise*. New York, 1976.

Edwards, Lee R. "War and Roses: The Politics of *Mrs. Dalloway*." In *The Authority of Experience*, edited by Arlyn Diamond and Lee R. Edwards. Amherst, 1977.

Faderman, Lillian. *Surpassing the Love of Men: Romantic Friendship and Love Between Women from the Renaissance to the Present*. New York, 1981.

Flax, Jane. "The Conflict Between Nurturance and Autonomy in Mother-Daughter Relationships and Within Feminism." *Feminist Studies*, IV (1978), 171–89.

Fleishman, Avrom. *Virginia Woolf: A Critical Reading*. Baltimore, 1975.

Fox, Alice. "Literary Allusion as Feminist Criticism in *A Room of One's Own*." *Philological Quarterly*, LXIII (1984), 145–61.

Freedman, Ralph, ed. *Virginia Woolf, Revaluation and Continuity: A Collection of Essays*. Berkeley, 1980.

Freud, Sigmund. "Three Essays on the Theory of Sexuality." *The Standard Edition of the Complete Psychological Works*, Vol. 7 of 24 vols. Translated by James Strachey. London, 1962.

——. "Introductory Lectures on Psychoanalysis." Vols. 15–16.

——. "Beyond the Pleasure Principle." Vol. 18.

——. "The Ego and the Id." Vol. 19.

——. "Some Psychical Consequences of the Anatomical Distinction Between the Sexes." Vol. 19.

——. "The Dissolution of the Oedipus Complex." Vol. 19.

——. "Civilization and Its Discontents." Vol. 21.

——. "Female Sexuality." Vol. 21.

——. "Femininity." Vol. 22.

——. "New Introductory Lectures on Psychoanalysis." Vol. 22.

Fry, Roger. *Vision and Design*. New York, 1956.

Frye, JoAnn S. "*The Voyage Out*: Thematic Tensions and Narrative Techniques." *Twentieth Century Literature*, XXVI (1980), 402–23.

Gardiner, Judith Kegan. "The (US)ses of (I)dentity: A Response to Abel on '(E)merging Identities.'" *Signs*, VI (1981), 436–42.

Gibson, Susan Monteith. "'Our Part Is to Be the Audience': Virginia Woolf's *Between the Acts*." *Gypsy Scholar*, II (1974), 5–12.

Gilbert, Sandra, and Susan Gubar. *The Madwoman in the Attic: The Woman Writer and the Nineteenth-Century Literary Imagination*. New Haven, 1979.

Gordon, Lyndall. *Virginia Woolf: A Writer's Life*. London, 1984.

Gorsky, Susan. "'The Central Shadow': Characterization in *The Waves*." *Modern Fiction Studies*, XVIII (1972), 449–66.

Graves, Robert. *The Greek Myths*. 2 vols. 1955; rpr. New York, 1980.

Guiguet, Jean. *Virginia Woolf and Her Works*. Translated by Jean Stewart. New York, 1966.

Hafley, James. *The Glass Roof: Virginia Woolf as Novelist*. New York, 1963.

Hardwick, Elizabeth. *Seduction and Betrayal: Women and Literature*. New York, 1970.

Harrison, Jane. *Prolegomena to the Study of Greek Religion*. 1903; rpr. New York, 1966.

―――. *Themis: A Study of the Social Origins of Greek Religion*. 1912; rpr. Gloucester, Mass., 1974.

―――. *Mythology*. 1924; rpr. Ann Arbor, 1979.

Hawthorne, Jeremy. *Virginia Woolf's Mrs. Dalloway: A Study in Alienation*. Sussex, 1975.

Heine, Elizabeth. "The Earlier *The Voyage Out*: Virginia Woolf's First Novel." *Bulletin of the Humanities*, LXXXII (1979), 294–316.

Homans, Margaret. *Women Writers and Poetic Identity: Dorothy Wordsworth, Emily Brontë, Emily Dickinson*. Princeton, 1980.

Irigaray, Luce. "When Our Lips Speak Together." Translated by Carolyn Burke. *Signs*, VI (1980), 69–79.

―――. "And the One Doesn't Stir Without the Other." Translated by Helene Vivienne Wenzel. *Signs*, VII (1981), 60–67.

Jacobus, Mary, ed. *Women Writing and Writing About Women*. London, 1979.

Janeway, Elizabeth. "On the Power of the Weak." *Signs*, I (1975), 103–109.

Jardine, Alice. "Theories of the Feminine: Kristeva." *Enclitics*, IV (1980), 5–15.

Kahane, Claire. "The Nuptials of Metaphor: Self and Other in Virginia Woolf." *Literature and Psychology*, XXX (1980), 72–82.

Kaplan, Sidney Janet. *Feminine Consciousness in the Modern British Novel*. Chicago, 1975.

Kenney, Susan M. "Two Endings: Virginia Woolf's Suicide and *Between the Acts*." *University of Toronto Quarterly*, XLIV (1975), 265–89.

Kenney, Susan M., and Edwin J. Kenney, Jr. "Virginia Woolf and the Art of Madness." *Massachusetts Review*, XXIII (1982), 161–85.

Kristeva, Julia. *Desire in Language*. Edited by Leon S. Roudiez. Translated by Thomas Gora and Alice Jardine. New York, 1980.

Lacan, Jacques. "The Mirror Stage as Formative of the Function of the I as Revealed in Psychoanalytic Experience." In *Ecrits*, translated by Alan Sheridan. New York, 1977.

Langer, Suzanne. *Philosophy in a New Key*. Cambridge, Mass., 1942.

Leaska, Mitchell A. *Virginia Woolf's "To the Lighthouse": A Study in Critical Method*. New York, 1970.

―――. "Virginia Woolf's *The Voyage Out*: Character Deduction and the Functions of Ambiguity." *Virginia Woolf Quarterly*, I (1973), 18–41.

―――. "Virginia Woolf, the Pargeter: A Reading of *The Years*." *Bulletin of the New York Public Library*, LXXX (1976–77), 172–210.

Lilienfeld, Jane. "The Necessary Journey: Virginia Woolf's Voyage to the Lighthouse." Ph.D. dissertation, Brandeis University, 1975.

————. "'The Deceptiveness of Beauty': Mother Love and Mother Hate in *To the Lighthouse*." *Twentieth Century Literature*, XXIII (1977), 345–76.

Lipking, Joanna. "Looking at Monuments: Woolf's Satiric Eye." *Bulletin of the New York Public Library*, LXXX (1977), 141–45.

Little, Judy. "Festive Comedy in *Between the Acts*." *Women in Literature*, V (1977), 26–37.

Love, Jean. *Virginia Woolf: Sources of Madness and Art*. Vol. 1. Berkeley, 1977. 2 vols. projected.

Majumdar, Robin, and Allen McLaurin, eds. *Virginia Woolf: The Critical Heritage*. London, 1975.

Marcus, Jane. "Art and Anger." *Feminist Studies*, IV (1977), 69–98.

————. "Some Sources of *Between the Acts*." *Virginia Woolf Miscellany*, VI (1977), 1–3.

————. "Pargeting 'The Pargeters': Notes of an Apprentice Plasterer." *Bulletin of the New York Public Library*, LXXX (1976–77), 416–36.

————. "Liberty, Sorority, Misogyny." In *The Representation of Women in Fiction*, edited by Carolyn G. Heilbrun and Margaret R. Higgonet. Baltimore, 1983.

————, ed. *New Feminist Essays on Virginia Woolf*. Lincoln, Neb., 1981.

————, ed. *Virginia Woolf: A Feminist Slant*. Lincoln, Neb., 1983.

Marder, Herbert. *Feminism and Art: A Study of Virginia Woolf*. Chicago, 1968.

McLaurin, Allen. *Virginia Woolf: The Echoes Enslaved*. Cambridge, England, 1973.

Meisel, Perry. *The Absent Father: Virginia Woolf and Walter Pater*. New Haven, 1980.

Mendez, Charlotte Walker. "Virginia Woolf and the Voices of Silence." *Language and Style*, XIII (1974), 94–112.

Miles, Rosalind. *The Fiction of Sex: Themes and Functions of Sex Differences in the Modern Novel*. London, 1974.

Miller, J. Hillis. "Virginia Woolf's All Soul's Day: The Omniscient Narrator in *Mrs. Dalloway*." In *The Shaken Realist: Essays in Honor of Frederick J. Hoffman*, edited by Melvin Friedman and John B. Vickery. Baton Rouge, 1970.

Moers, Ellen. *Literary Women*. New York, 1977.

Moore, Harry T., ed. *The Collected Letters of D. H. Lawrence*. 2 vols. New York, 1962.

Moore, Madeline. *The Short Season Between Two Silences: The Mystical and the Political in the Novels of Virginia Woolf*. Boston, 1984.

Naremore, James. *The World Without a Self*. New Haven, 1973.

Neumann, Erich. *The Great Mother: An Analysis of the Archetype*. Translated by Ralph Manheim. New York, 1955.

Nicolson, Nigel. *Portrait of a Marriage*. New York, 1973.

Nobel, Joan Russell, ed. *Recollections of Virginia Woolf*. New York, 1972.

Ohmann, Carol. "Culture and Anarchy in *Jacob's Room*." *Contemporary Literature*, XVII (1977), 160–72.

Partridge, Frances. *Love in Bloomsbury: Memories*. Boston, 1981.

Patmore, Coventry. *Poems*. London, 1928.

Plath, Sylvia. *The Bell Jar*. New York, 1972.

Poole, Roger. *The Unknown Virginia Woolf*. Cambridge, 1978.

Poresky, Louise A. *The Elusive Self: Psyche and Spirit in Virginia Woolf's Novels*. Newark, Del., 1981.

Pratt, Annis. "Sexual Imagery in *To the Lighthouse*: A New Feminist Approach." *Modern Fiction Studies*, XVIII (1972), 417–31.

————. *Archetypal Patterns in Women's Fiction*. Bloomington, 1981.

Proudfit, Sharon. "Lily Briscoe's Painting: A Key to Personal Relationships in *To the Lighthouse*." *Criticism*, XIII (1971), 26–38.

Rachman, Shalom. "Clarissa's Attic: Virginia Woolf's *Mrs. Dalloway* Reconsidered." *Twentieth Century Literature*, XVIII (1972), 3–18.

Rich, Adrienne. *Of Woman Born: Motherhood as Experience and Institution*. New York, 1976.

Richter, Harvena. *Virginia Woolf: The Inward Voyage*. Princeton, 1970.

Rigney, Barbara Hill. *Madness and Sexual Politics in the Feminist Novel*. Madison, 1978.

Rose, Phyllis. *Woman of Letters: A Life of Virginia Woolf*. New York, 1978.

Rosenthal, Michael. *Virginia Woolf*. New York, 1979.

Saunders, Judith P. "Mortal Stain: Literary Allusion and Female Sexuality in 'Mrs. Dalloway in Bond Street.'" *Studies in Short Fiction*, XV (1978), 139–44.

Schaefer, Josephine O'Brien. *The Three-fold Nature of Reality in the Novels of Virginia Woolf*. London, 1965.

Schlack, Beverly. *Continuing Presences: Virginia Woolf's Use of Literary Allusion*. University Park, Pa., 1979.

Showalter, Elaine. *A Literature of Their Own: British Women Novelists from Brontë to Lessing*. Princeton, 1977.

Silver, Brenda R. "Virginia Woolf and the Concept of Community: The Elizabethan Playhouse." *Women's Studies*, IV (1977), 291–98.

————, ed. *Virginia Woolf's Reading Notebooks*. Princeton, 1983.

Smith-Rosenberg, Carol. "The Female World of Love and Ritual: Relations Between Women in Mid-Nineteenth Century America." *Signs*, I (1975), 1–21.

Spacks, Patricia Meyer. *The Female Imagination*. New York, 1975.

Spalding, Francis. *Vanessa Bell*. New York, 1983.

Spelman, Elizabeth V. "Woman as Body: Ancient and Contemporary Views." *Feminist Studies*, VIII (1982), 109–31.

Spilka, Mark. *Virginia Woolf's Quarrel with Grieving*. Lincoln, Neb., 1980.

Spivak, Gayatri C. "Making and Unmaking in *To the Lighthouse*." In *Women and Language in Literature and Society*, edited by Sally McConnell-Ginet, Ruth Borker, and Nelly Furman. New York, 1980.

Sprague, Claire, ed. *Virginia Woolf: A Collection of Critical Essays*. Englewood Cliffs, 1971.

Storr, Anthony. *The Dynamics of Creation*. New York, 1972.

Throne, Sara R. "Virginia Woolf's Feminist Identity and the Parthenogenesis of Female Culture." *University of Michigan Papers in Women's Studies*, II (1975), 146–61.

Trombley, Stephen. *"All That Summer She Was Mad": Virginia Woolf and Her Doctors.* London, 1981.

Twentieth Century Literature, XXV (1979). Special issue of previously unpublished Woolf essays.

Vogler, Thomas, ed. *Twentieth Century Interpretations of "To the Lighthouse."* Englewood Cliffs, 1970.

Watson, Barbara Bellow. "On Power and the Literary Text." *Signs*, I (1975), 111–18.

Winnicott, D. W. *The Maturational Processes and the Facilitating Environment.* New York, 1965.

———. *Playing and Reality.* London, 1971.

Woolf, Leonard. *Growing: An Autobiography of the Years 1904–11.* New York, 1961.

———. *Beginning Again: An Autobiography of the Years 1911–18.* New York, 1963.

———. *Downhill All the Way: An Autobiography of the Years 1919–39.* New York, 1967.

———. *The Journey Not the Arrival Matters: An Autobiography of the Years 1939–69.* New York, 1969.

Wyatt, Jean M. "*Mrs. Dalloway*: Literary Allusion as Structural Metaphor." *Publications of the Modern Language Association*, LXXXVIII (1973), 440–51.

Zwerdling, Alex. "*Mrs. Dalloway* and the Social System." *Publications of the Modern Language Association*, XCII (1977), 69–82.

Index

Aesthetics, female, 39, 140–41, 150–
54, 157–68; in *Between the Acts*, 114,
117; in *Mrs. Dalloway*, 75, 84, 87–
88, 91–92; in *To the Lighthouse*, 93,
100–101
Angel in the House, the, 66–67, 69, 96,
97, 99, 100, 112. *See also* Patmore,
Coventry
Anger, in women's writing, 146, 164–66
"Anon," 117–18
Anonymity, 115, 117, 160–61, 167
Artemis, 116–17, 119, 126
Austen, Jane, 3, 137, 138, 142, 143–45,
146, 149–50

Bell, Clive, 30, 62–63
Bell, Vanessa, x, 10–11, 13, 18, 57, 107;
and *The Voyage Out*, 30
Benson, Stella, 141
Between the Acts, 17, 39, 71, 106, 114–33
Bloom, Harold, 136–40, 151
Brontë, Charlotte, 3, 138, 142, 145,
146; 149, 164–65
Brontë, Emily, 3, 142–43, 144, 146

Characterization, 20–21, 22, 23, 39–
40, 143
Chodorow, Nancy, viii, 12–13, 39–40
Common Reader, First Series, The, 39, 92
"Congreve's Comedy," 118
Creativity: compensation for maternal
loss, 15–19; source of wholeness,
36–39; relationship to motherhood,

x, 56, 57–59; shared among women
writers, 141; in *Between the Acts*, 117–
25, 129–31; in *Mrs. Dalloway*, 75, 87,
91–92, 93–94; in *To the Lighthouse*,
93–94, 95–96, 97, 99–102, 106–
13; in *The Voyage Out*, 40–41; in *The
Waves*, 41–44

Daughter: in psychological theory,
12–16; ambivalence of, ix, 14, 35,
93, 104, 127; dependence of, 14,
31–33, 34–35, 60, 68, 101, 104,
108; contingency of, 23–24, 47, 51,
68; devaluation of, in family, 47–48,
99, 103–104, 109
Death wish, 14; in *The Voyage Out*, 23,
28, 41, 43, 101
Demeter and Kore, 70–71, 102, 139,
157–58
de Sévigné, Mme., 149, 152–53, 161
Dickinson, Violet, 11, 13
"Dorothy Osborne's Letters," 39, 147,
151, 152
"Dr. Burney's Evening Party," 147, 150
"Duchess of Newcastle, The," 138, 147,
148. *See also* Newcastle, Duchess of
Duckworth, Stella, 10, 14, 58, 61

Eliot, George, 3, 138, 142, 145–46, 149
Eliot, T. S., 115; *The Waste Land*, 114
Empathy, as female characteristic, 13,
114; in *Mrs. Dalloway*, 76, 77, 78, 81,
84, 86, 91; in *To the Lighthouse*, 98

"Evening Over Sussex: Reflections in a Motor-car," 40

Femininity. See Angel in the House, the; Identity, female; Mother; Women
Feminism, 46, 51, 114
Freud, Sigmund, 11, 12, 15–16, 40, 116n, 136, 137, 139
Fry, Roger, 62–63, 110, 128
Fusion, 30, 31, 45, 117; in Mrs. Dalloway, 90; in To the Lighthouse, 102; in The Voyage Out, 23, 41; in The Waves, 42; in The Years, 51. See also Merging

"George Eliot," 145–46. See also Eliot, George
Great Mother, the, 26, 28, 33

"Harriette Wilson," 148–49
Harrison, Jane, 116, 138
"Haworth, November 1904," 146. See also Brontë, Charlotte; Brontë, Emily
Heterosexual love: in Night and Day, 31, 33–34; in To the Lighthouse, 95–97, 100, 109; in The Voyage Out, 23, 24–29, 142. See also Masculinity; Sexuality; Virginity
Hostess-figure: as artist, 55; in Between the Acts, 117, 126, 131; in Mrs. Dalloway, 55, 71, 75–77, 84–86, 88, 92; in To the Lighthouse, 55, 94, 98, 107, 109; in The Years, 48, 52–53. See also Parties

"I Am Christina Rossetti," 147–48, 156, 161
Identity, female: Woolf's definition of, vii; in psychological theory, viii–ix, 12–13; in Between the Acts, 125–26; in Mrs. Dalloway, 75–77, 78–79, 84–88, 92; in To the Lighthouse, 94, 95–98, 101, 105
"Indiscretions," 56
Inheritance, female, x, 45–71; in literary history, 134–57; in Between the Acts, 114, 119–20, 122–23, 124, 127; in Mrs. Dalloway, 76–77, 82, 89; in A Room of One's Own, 157–68; in To the Lighthouse, 47–48, 94, 99, 104, 107,

111–12; in Three Guineas, 46–47; in The Voyage Out, 47; in The Years, 48–55

Jacob's Room, 22, 35, 39, 64–65, 67, 81, 82, 83, 91, 139
"Jane Austen," 143–45. See also Austen, Jane
"Jane Eyre and Wuthering Heights," 142–43. See also Brontë, Charlotte; Brontë, Emily
"Journal of Mistress Joan Martyn, The," 55–56, 139–40
Joyce, James, 39, 115, 140, 144, 153; Ulysses, 115

Kipling, Rudyard, 151, 154
Kore. See Demeter and Kore

"Lady in the Looking-Glass, The," 49, 87
Language: in psychological theory, 15; of men, 154, 155; in To the Lighthouse, 101. See also Silence
Lawrence, D. H., 21, 83; The Fox, 83n
"Leaning Tower, The," 134
Leaning Tower poets, 128–29
"Lives of the Obscure, The," 158

MacCarthy, Desmond, 137–38
Mansfield, Katherine, 141
"Mary Wollstonecraft," 150
Masculinity: and writing, 150–51; in Mrs. Dalloway, 77–78; in Three Guineas, 46; in To the Lighthouse, 96. See also Heterosexual love; Sexuality
"Memories of a Working Women's Guild," 154–57, 159, 160, 161
"Men and Women," 146, 154
Menstruation, 59, 82
Merging: as element of characterization, 20, 142; in Dorothy Osborne's letters, 152; in To the Lighthouse, 94, 98, 104; in The Voyage Out, 29. See also Fusion
Mirroring: in psychological theory, 12; in female inheritance, 45; in female literary history, 148, 156; in Between the Acts, 117; in Mrs. Dalloway, 81, 85–88, 89–91; in A Room of One's

Own, 158, 163, 164; in *To the Lighthouse*, 98; in *The Voyage Out*, 23–24, 102; in *The Waves*, 23; in *The Years*, 49, 50–51. See also Mutuality
"Mme. de Sévigné," 149, 152–53
Moments of Being, viii, 3–19, 21, 24, 36, 45, 57, 67, 68, 70, 102, 103, 107, 118, 127, 129
"Moments of Being: 'Slater's Pins Have No Points,'" 112, 135
Mother: in psychological theory, 12–16; as model of femininity, 14, 45, 47, 49, 53, 57, 59, 76–77, 108; possessiveness of, 31–32, 35–36, 81, 84; as artist, 39, 55, 56, 107, 111, 114–18, 122–23, 127; remoteness of, 48, 102–103, 115–16, 122; as icon, 49–50, 71, 97–98, 99, 103–104, 105, 122–23; omnipotence of, 50, 56, 108; as object of art, 69, 97–100, 107–13; and nature, 88, 94–95, 105 —loss of, 15–19; in aesthetic theory, 37; in *Between the Acts*, 127, 131; in *To the Lighthouse*, 105–13; in *The Voyage Out*, 23–25, 40; in *The Waves*, 20; in *The Years*, 48, 52–54, 129
"Mr. Bennett and Mrs. Brown," 75, 91–92, 142, 153
Mrs. Dalloway, 13, 20, 28, 35, 39, 40, 45, 55, 71, 75–92, 93, 95, 96, 98, 101, 106, 110, 112, 114, 120, 125, 126, 131–32, 135, 142, 143, 144, 160
"Mrs. Dalloway in Bond Street," 81–82
"Mrs. Gaskell," 56
Mutuality: in psychological theory, 12; in female literary history, 138, 141, 148; in *Mrs. Dalloway*, 85, 88; in *A Room of One's Own*, 158, 161, 167; in *To the Lighthouse*, 96. See also Mirroring

Narrative technique, 39–40, 56, 128, 153
Newcastle, Duchess of, 138, 147, 148
Night and Day, 27–28, 31–35, 63–64, 67–68, 69, 88, 98
Nurturance, 4, 7, 8, 9, 10, 14; in Woolf's aesthetic theory, 37–39; in the female tradition, 135, 136; in *Between the Acts*,

125; in *Mrs. Dalloway*, 75–76; in *To the Lighthouse*, 67, 94–95, 96, 97, 102, 104, 108; in *The Voyage Out*, 24; in *The Waves*, 42; in *The Years*, 51, 53–54

Object-relations theory, 12, 70, 78, 138. See also Chodorow, Nancy; Winnicott, D. W.
Oedipal stage, viii, 106, 136, 137, 138
"On Re-reading Novels," 134
Orlando, 160
Osborne, Dorothy, 147, 151, 152, 153. See also "Dorothy Osborne's Letters"

Parody: in *Between the Acts*, 122–24; in *To the Lighthouse*, 105; in *The Years*, 53
Parties: in *Between the Acts*, 125, 126; in *Mrs. Dalloway*, 75–77, 79, 86, 88–89, 90, 92, 93; in *To the Lighthouse*, 94, 97, 104, 108. See also Hostess-figure
Patmore, Coventry, "The Angel in the House," 65–66, 69–70. See also Angel in the House, the
"Patron and the Crocus, The," 37
"Phases of Fiction," 128
"Pictures," 38
Pre-Oedipal bond, viii, 11–12, 20, 23, 30, 31, 38, 41–43, 137, 151. See also Chodorow, Nancy; Winnicott, D. W.
Procreation: analogous to writing, 55–56; antithetical to creativity, 58–61; in *Mrs. Dalloway*, 84; in *To the Lighthouse*, 104, 105; in *The Years*, 53. See also Sexuality
"Professions for Women," 66–67, 69, 111–12
Proust, Marcel, 144–45

"Reader, The," 118
"Reading at Random," 132
Regression, 14, 36, 38, 40, 44, 45–46, 129, 135–36; in *Mrs. Dalloway*, 90; in *Night and Day*, 33, 34, 35; in *To the Lighthouse*, 101, 102, 104–105, 108–109; in *The Voyage Out*, 25–30, 40–41; in *The Waves*, 23, 41–44; in *The Years*, 51, 52–53

Repression, in women's writing, 155, 159, 161–62, 164–65
Richardson, Dorothy, 39, 140–41
"Romance and the Heart," 39, 140–41
Room of One's Own, A, xi, 60–61, 107, 134, 135, 138, 143, 145, 146, 147, 150, 151, 154, 157–68
Rossetti, Christina. See "I Am Christina Rossetti"

Sackville-West, Vita, 11, 13, 43n, 59–60, 102
"Sara Coleridge," 149
"Scribbling Dame, A," 140, 150
Separation: in psychological theory, 12–16; in literary history, 136–38; in Between the Acts, 122; in Night and Day, 33–34, 35; in To the Lighthouse, 104–105, 109; in The Voyage Out, 26–27, 31; in The Waves, 20–21
Sexuality: in Mrs. Dalloway, 43n, 76, 83–84, 86–87, 95, 96; in To the Lighthouse, 43n, 95–97, 98–99; in The Voyage Out, 24–25, 28, 29, 142; in The Waves, 43. See also Heterosexual love; Procreation; Virginity
Shakespeare, William, 143, 145; A Midsummer Night's Dream, 121, 124
Significant form, theory of, 62–63, 110
Silence: and Julia Stephen, 70; and women's writing, 155–57; in Between the Acts, 115–16, 120, 126, 131, 132, 133; in Night and Day, 34; in A Room of One's Own, 160, 163; in To the Lighthouse, 101; in The Voyage Out, 27–28; in The Waves, 97. See also Language
Stephen, Julia: life of, 4–7; archetypal quality of, ix, 6; idealized by Woolf, 5, 8, 10, 103; devotion of, to husband, 7, 68; model for Burne-Jones's Annunciation, 7, 70; remoteness of, 10, 11, 70, 103; relationship with Stella, 14; as artistic precursor, 55; as the Angel in the House, 67, 68–69; as model for Mrs. Ramsay, 93; and "Moments of Being: 'Slater's Pins Have No Points,'" 112; and literary inheritance, 135; and Mme. de Sévigné, 152
Stephen, Leslie, 4, 55, 134

"Terribly Sensitive Mind, A," 141
Three Guineas, 46–47, 68, 77, 114, 134, 135, 151, 157
Tolstoi, Leo, 145
To the Lighthouse, 13, 16–17, 20, 28, 35–36, 40, 42, 47, 50, 55, 56, 60, 67, 70, 71, 83, 93–113, 118, 120, 125, 127, 129, 131–32, 135, 137, 142, 161
Transitional object, 15, 90
"Tunnel, The," 140–41. See also Richardson, Dorothy
"Two Women," 149

Virginity, 60; in Between the Acts, 116; in Mrs. Dalloway, 83, 84, 86, 88; in To the Lighthouse, 93, 109–10. See also Heterosexual love; Sexuality
Voyage Out, The, 14, 17, 20, 23–31, 35, 37, 40–41, 47, 56, 67, 68, 101, 102, 106, 108, 123, 142, 144

"Walter Sickert," 37–38, 152
Waves, The, 17, 20–23, 36, 39, 40, 41–44, 56, 59, 65, 84, 97, 101, 102, 145
Wholeness, 7, 9, 10, 13, 20, 21, 22, 45; in act of writing, 15; in Woolf's aesthetic theory, 36–40; in female tradition, 135, 136; in Between the Acts, 117–18, 119, 124–31 passim; in Mrs. Dalloway, 79; in To the Lighthouse, 111; in The Voyage Out, 25, 40; in The Waves, 20, 21–23, 42
Winnicott, D. W., 12, 15, 49, 129–30. See also Transitional object
Women: "atmosphere" of, 7, 8, 32, 37, 53, 55, 79, 84, 88, 89, 92, 97, 103, 108, 125, 153; associated with nature, 28, 58–59, 64–65, 81–83, 97; self-effacement of, 39, 58, 65–70, 71, 147–48, 149–50, 151–53, 157, 159, 160–64; "gift" for social life, 57, 76, 78–79, 81, 86, 94, 95, 110, 111, 125; associated with death, 28, 61; impulsiveness of, 61–63, 148–50, 153–57, 159
"Women and Fiction," 3–4, 63, 137, 143, 147, 149, 150, 154
"Women's College from the Outside, A," 135–36

Woolf, Leonard, x, 30, 57

Woolf, Virginia: definition of femininity, vii; madness of, ix, 10, 30, 90; compares self to Vanessa, x, 18, 57, 107; reaction to mother's death, 10, 50; aesthetic theory of, 36–40; attitude toward body, 59, 81–82; and *Between the Acts*, 128–29; and *Mrs. Dalloway*, 92; and *To the Lighthouse*, 93, 107, 111, 112–13; and *The Voyage Out*, 30

Years, The, 39, 48–55, 106, 128, 129

Yeats, William Butler, "Sailing to Byzantium," 61